COW COUNTRY CAVALCADE

COW COUNTRY CAVALCADE

Eighty Years of the Wyoming Stock
Growers Association

BY MAURICE FRINK

The Old West Publishing Co.
Fred A. Rosenstock
Denver, Colo.
1954

Copyright 1954
Wyoming Stock Growers Association
Cheyenne, Wyoming

Printed by Johnson Publishing Co.
Boulder, Colo.

In the words of the
time-honored toast:

TO THE COWMAN—
GOD BLESS HIM!

THE WAY IT WAS

"Tell it the way it was. Don't make us any better—or any worse—than we are."

When J. Elmer Brock engaged me in March of 1953 to write this book, those were almost the only instructions he gave me. I have tried to carry them out.

My assignment was to bring down to date the history of the Wyoming Stock Growers Association. This was last recounted by Agnes Wright Spring in *Seventy Years Cow Country,* published in 1942. Since then some additional information on the Association's early years has become available through assembly and reorganization of its files and records at the University of Wyoming in Laramie.

For Mr. Brock, chairman of the Association's historical committee, this book was from the start a labor of love. For me it became that as I studied the records of the Association, learned the stories of the men who made its early history, and came to know some of those who are keeping it so strongly alive today, 81 years after its birth in old Cheyenne.

One of the distinctions of the Wyoming Stock Growers Association is its awareness of historical values. It has realized the importance of preserving the record.

Some of this record is in the form of such primary material as letters and documents. Some is in the form of brochures and books which the Association has caused to be written —a by-product unique for an organization of this kind.

But there is a precedent: The earliest cowboys, trailing the Longhorns into the new grazing country to become the foundation of a great industry, sang to the cows they were herding—such songs as:

> . . . ti yi yo,
> Git along, little dogies,
> You know that Wyoming
> Will be your new home—

Thus they established a kinship with the cattle, an understanding, a comforting oneness of man and horse and cow that made them all feel good and kept them shoving along together. The cowboys made up their songs out of the things they were doing, and so the songs became a part of the historical record.

Similarly, this Association has put into words the story of what it has done and is doing. This is vital and valid—for any part of the story of the making of America belongs to the whole. And who can tell such a story better than those who have lived it—as long as they try to tell it the way it was?

Many persons in addition to Mr. Brock have helped me gather material for this book and tried to keep me from getting too far off the trail. Among these are:

Joe H. Watt, Moorcroft, Wyoming, of the historical committee.

Dean F. Krakel, University of Wyoming archivist and custodian of the Association records in the University Library at Laramie.

Miss Lola M. Homsher, director of the State Archives and Historical Department at Cheyenne, and her deputy, Miss Henryetta Berry.

Russell Thorp of Cheyenne, grand old man of the Association, for nineteen years its executive secretary.

Robert D. Hanesworth, the present secretary-treasurer; and the assistant secretary-treasurer in the Cheyenne office, Mrs. Myrna F. Agee.

Dr. G. H. Good, state veterinarian and executive officer of the Wyoming State Live Stock and Sanitary Board.

L. C. Bishop, state engineer and Oregon Trail authority.

Dr. Robert H. Burns, head, Wool Department, the University of Wyoming.

Warren Richardson, Cheyenne's oldest oldtimer.

Mrs. Fred D. Boice, Sr., who presides so graciously over the former Hi Kelly house in Cheyenne.

Mr. and Mrs. Tom Sun of the historic Hub and Spoke ranch on the Sweetwater.

Mr. and Mrs. Clarence Gammon of the TA ranch on Crazy Woman creek.

Agnes Wright Spring, executive assistant to the president of the Colorado State Historical Society, a native of Delta,

Colo., who grew up on the Laramie Plains and is an authority on Wyoming.

Mrs. Margaret Smith of Buffalo, Wyoming.

Casey Barthelmess, who, although he ranches in Montana, knows Wyoming cowboys too and shared his knowledge with me.

Fred A. Rosenstock of Denver, who has helped so many writers with so many books.

South Dakota-born Paul Friggens, of Boulder, friend of the cowman over many years; to him I am grateful for opening the door that led to my writing *Cow Country Cavalcade,* and for counsel and advice.

These and others, including my wife Edith, have all been helpful in many ways and deserve the credit for what is good in this book.

MAURICE FRINK

Boulder, Colo., March 1, 1954.

CONTENTS

ILLUSTRATIONS

Jacket drawing by Wes Pottle.

(Jacket photo, roundup crew of Beer Mug ranch, on Difficulty creek, near Medicine Bow, Wyoming, 1880s.)

Sketches and brands by Paul A. Rossi.

Black and white:

Halftones.

Following Page 16:

Edward Burnett at Texas Trail marker.
Dedication Pine Bluffs Texas Trail marker.
A lean Longhorn.
Nelson Story's mill and elevator burn.
Roping and cutting out on open range.
Cattle branding near Rawlins, 1884.
Roundup crew at chuck wagon, Medicine Bow.
Hat Creek Postoffice, 1883.
Bob Fudge and other cowboys.

Following Page 48:

Ben Morrison, stock detective.
Cowhorse, Oxford Ranch, in 1890s.
Breaking horse on JK ranch, 1902.
Hi Kelly, aged 21.
Some of the boys, Bennett's Ferry ranch, 1883.
Old Rock River, 1880s.
Rancher inspecting herd of half-breeds, 1880s.
U Cross cowboys at chuck wagon, 1898.

Following Page 96:

A. L. Brock ranch interior, 1891.
Voting in Raw Hide Buttes precinct, 1900.

xiv

FOREWORD

The Historical Committee of the Wyoming Stock Growers Association, to which was assigned the duty of getting out this publication, was most fortunate in securing the services of Mr. Maurice Frink. The committee felt that, due to Mr. Frink's ability, and the new material at his command, it was justified in publication of this extensive history.

The Committee thinks the author has done an excellent job, and extends to him our appreciation. We also thank the numerous persons who co-operated by providing information, loaning pictures and helping in other ways.

The death of Committeeman Charles A. Myers, Past President, pioneer cattleman and philosopher, deprived us of much wise counsel and advice. He was a true son of the West and a balance wheel in our organization. We miss him greatly since his departure down that long trail which we all must sometime take where the grass is always green.

The Wyoming Stock Growers Association has written many glorious pages of history. Civilization in Wyoming, as in most of the West, remote from navigable waters, was established along a cattle trail. Our industry took over in a wild land. There was no state, no civil government, no rail transportation, no churches, schools, hospitals nor courts, no law except the law of the six-shooter. Too much has been written about early lawlessness and not enough credit given those who established order out of chaos. Many times our pioneers established their own code of law, their own standards of justice, their own courts, without constitutional authority. Moreover, they made these work through fortitude and an unswerving sense of justice.

The Wyoming Stock Growers Association, and the industry it represents, established the society we enjoy today. It took over a land left by the retreating red man, and in many ways suffered his disappointments and broken promises. It established a state in name, although statehood in the fullest meaning of the word is yet to be attained. Two thirds of our minerals, our forests, our scenic wonders and more than half our surface are still ruled from Washington. We do not enjoy the political and economic independence to which we are legally entitled and which is accorded to older states. We have accomplished much, our responsibilities have increased, but we are still only a western province—a Crown Colony of the East. Our work is not finished.

The cattle business always beckons to many whom it will disappoint. In this business there exists more of potentially adverse circumstance than in almost any other human endeavor. Rewards for courage, industry, and perseverence are uncertain, but lack of these, in great abundance, assures failure. A man who has been able to stay in the cattle business for fifty years must possess outstanding qualities. For each such man a hundred contemporaries quit. Of this highly select group a pre-eminent few have done more than stay in the business, and of these it may be said as Whittier said of the faithful old seamen—

> In thy lone and long night watches,
> Sky above and wave below,
> Thou didst learn a higher wisdom
> Than the babbling schoolmen know.

These men represent America at its best. It is well to associate with and learn from them, for thus we may avoid much grief and misfortune. Their record and example with the history of our industry deserve our respectful heed. To those wise enough to profit therefrom, we dedicate this book.

In the words of General Jas. G. Harbord: "The roads you travel so briskly lead out of dim antiquity and you study the past chiefly because of its bearing on the living present and its promise of the future."

Historical Committee:
Chas. A. Myers, deceased;
Joe Watt;
J. Elmer Brock, chairman.

PART ONE

SHORT-GRASS COUNTRY
AND
THE COMING OF THE CATTLE

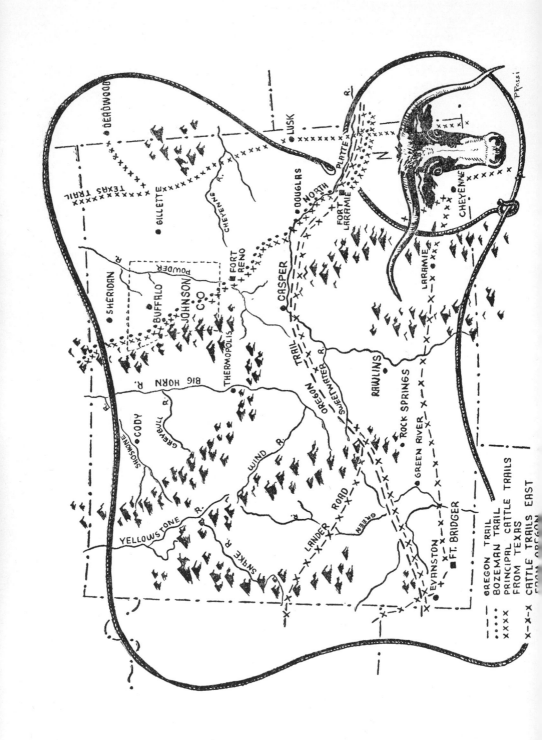

PPossi

DEADWOOD

LUSK

TEXAS TRAIL

GILLETTE

CHEYENNE R.

DOUGLAS

NORTH PLATTE R.

FORT LARRAMIE

CHEYENNE

LARRAMIE

SHERIDAN

POWDER R.

FORT RENO

CASPER

BUFFALO

JOHNSON CO.

THERMOPOLIS

BIG HORN R.

OREGON TRAIL

SWEETWATER R.

RAWLINS

ROCK SPRINGS

CODY

GREYBULL R.

SHOSHONE R.

WIND R.

GREEN RIVER

YELLOWSTONE R.

SNAKE R.

LANDER ROAD

GREEN R.

EVANSTON

FT. BRIDGER

• OREGON TRAIL
••••• BOZEMAN TRAIL
xxxx PRINCIPAL CATTLE TRAILS
       FROM TEXAS
x-x-x CATTLE TRAILS EAST
       FROM OREGON

CHAPTER ONE

CAVALCADE

Old Tom Jefferson, what do you mean,
    Buying up land that we've never seen?
All Louisiana for a whopping sum,
    From the Mississippi river to Kingdom Come?
And we only know that there's rain and snow
    And grass and Injuns and buffalo . . .

From 'Louisiana Purchase,' by Badger Clark.

It was a land of lifting hills, of fragrant sagebrush flats and white peaks shining in the sun, a land of little rivers flowing through great plains of grass—grass whose life-giving power lived on even under the snows of winter—a wild, free land: Wyoming.

There were people with a strength to match the land, to meet the quick urgency of blizzard and of cloudburst, or the slow death of drought—people with self reliance bred in their bones, with freedom lifting their hearts like the cloud shadows sliding over the plains and up the distant hills: People to fight the Indian, slay the beast, rid the range of the rustler.

In a long, slow cavalcade they came this way, riding into the short-grass country one by one as their parts in the drama came on-stage: The fur trapper and explorer; the scout showing the way for the white-topped-wagon train; the pony express rider and the stagecoach driver; the vigilante and the regulator—and last only in the sense that he alone of the cavalcade is still here:

The cowman.

Others blazed the trails but the cowman is the one who stayed—stayed first in lonely independence, later learning to work with the others who came and settled near him. Together they built a grassland commonwealth.

Helping the people of Wyoming to work together has been the job since 1872 of the organization whose story this book tells: The Wyoming Stock Growers Association. It was founded in a livery stable, by five men who thought only to form a vigilance committee but actually laid the groundwork for an organization that has represented eighty percent of the Wyoming cattlemen for more than eighty years. The Association was and is made up of human beings, with human aspirations and human weaknesses. In length of service to Wyoming it yields to but two corporate institutions—the United States Army and the Union Pacific Railroad. The value of its services is for others to appraise. In this book is the record on which an appraisal can be formed.[1]

The story of the Association—which is the story of Wyoming—begins with the coming of the people and the cattle to the land, with the first of the riders in the long, slow cavalcade. The story ends—there is no ending. Others to come will write the future chapters, and no one now can say what they will tell. But this is sure: Through the future as through the past will run the theme of men and women bold and self-reliant, yearning to be free and not afraid to fight for what they yearn for.

[1]Badger Clark, poet laureate of South Dakota, in a letter to the author in November 1953, authorizing quotation of the poem on Page 3 (which Clark wrote for his state's observance of the Louisiana Purchase Sesquicentennial), makes this observation: "I don't believe most of us fully appreciate the boldness, the sheer nerve, of the old fellows who built this Republic. Jefferson, with all his wisdom, could not foresee the steamboat nor the railroad, and he reckoned it would take a thousand years to settle Louisiana Territory, yet he went ahead and borrowed the money to close the deal. I had an uncle who settled in Wyoming so early that he rode with a carbine under his leg. The movement of the trail herds had a political significance along with its economic meaning. As Philip Ashton Rollins has pointed out, the cowboys, North and South, by fraternizing over a steer's back, wiped out the Mason and Dixon Line west of the Missouri river. The Line between North and South is still perceptible from Omaha east but the Great Plains is just West, from Canada to Mexico."

4

CHAPTER TWO

UP FROM TEXAS

Keep your eye on the North Star and drive straight ahead
until you can wet your feet in the waters of the Yellowstone.

—Directions given to Texas trail outfits.

Darkness hid the sagebrush flats from the squinting eyes
of the man trotting his horse toward the sleeping camp. A
few rods from the mess wagon, he pulled up and stepped off,
staked his horse and turned it away with a slap on the flank.
In from night guard with a herd of Longhorns coming up the
trail from Texas to Wyoming, the man was home, at the
wagon, that is, in the trail camp.

Other men were asleep on the ground by the wagon.
Quietly, so as not to disturb the others, the man awakened
those whose turn it was now to guard the herd. As they rode
away he went to his own bed—blankets, encased in a canvas
tarpaulin, spread on the ground. He wriggled down into his
sougans.

His bones ached. His chin was scratchy with whiskers.
For days he had not been out of all his clothes. That afternoon, as the herd had moved slowly ahead over the plains, he
had ridden drag, in the dust of a thousand cows. By dusk the
herd had been grazed to the location of the bedground that
the trail boss, riding ahead, had chosen for the night. The
man had eaten supper, then he had slept a little while before
being called for his time on guard with the herd. Now it
was his turn to sleep a little while again. He knew by the
morning star it was only about an hour till daylight, when the
cook would roll out, and the boss and the day wrangler, still
snoring peacefully by the wagon. In a few hours the herd
would be moving again. He would ride with the flankers, or

5

swing men, when they started. For a while he'd be out of the worst of the dust and dirt. The morning sun would warm his chill body.

The man listened to the wind; he hoped it wouldn't get any worse. So far they'd done well: No storms, no accidents, no spooked cattle. Just a month's steady march of twelve to fifteen miles a day, the herd hardly knowing it was being guided but the men making sure that every mile it moved was toward Wyoming. Weeks more of the same thing lay ahead, with sixteen to eighteen hours a day in the saddle and more if the weather turned bad. The man may have thought of the Big Red or other rivers over which he and his fellows— lean, tough, gutty and profane, like him—must safely drive their cattle, of the danger of storms and stampedes, of men thrown from falling horses beneath the hooves of a running herd. But the chances are his thoughts were on a girl in a town that lay along the trail ahead, a town where a fleeting spree might break the monotony of the long drive.

Anyway, at the moment he was at peace and all was well. His was the boon of sleep; soon it was healing his aching bones.

•

Who was the man? Any one of a legion who in the late 1860s and early '70s helped settle the Western plains in what historians have called the greatest and most spectacular pastoral movement of all time. Opening of the free grass range on the Great Plains, by speeding up the westward migration in the wake of the Civil War, had in its way as vital an impact on the American economy as did the discovery of gold in California in 1849.

Maps published in 1867 did not show a state named Wyoming.[2] There were ten towns bearing the name, from Rhode Island to Nebraska, and there were Wyoming counties in

[2]The word comes from the Delaware Indian Mache-weami-ing, "at the big flats," and first applied to a valley in northeastern Pennsylvania. James M. Ashley, Ohio congressman, proposed the name for Wyoming Territory in 1868. Opponents argued the word had a "rootless artificiality" as applied to the western area, and suggested such alternatives as Shoshone, Pawnee, Cheyenne and Platte, but Ashley had his way.

6

New York, Pennsylvania, Ohio and West Virginia, as well as a Wyoming river valley in Pennsylvania. West of Minnesota, Iowa and Nebraska lay a border area called Dakota Territory. It was roughly the shape of a reverse L, the lower part of the L being the area that in 1869 was organized as Wyoming Territory and in 1890 became the 44th state. Arid country, it was called, for it was part of what for several decades was known as the Great American Desert. Bringing this desert into bloom was the work of a long line of romantic and historic, in some cases almost legendary, figures whose names are still on the land: Colter, Sacajawea, De Smet, Bonneville, the Astorians, Frémont, Kearny, Sublette and Broken Hand Fitzpatrick with many, many others.

Most of the first white people to traverse what is now Wyoming were explorers or adventurers on their way somewhere else,—California, or Orgon. These first blazed the way for the great emigrant trails, whose ruts, if you will slow your car at the right places, may still be seen in Wyoming. The first few whites who came to stay, in the 1820s, were trappers seeking beaver pelts (three fifths of the trappers, historians say, died at the hands of the Indians). Then a few others began to set up little businesses along the trails; the businesses were trading posts, dealing in what few essentials could be carted in for sale or trade to the emigrants coming in ever-increasing numbers along the ever-widening tracks in the prairie sod. Jim Bridger's post on Black's fork of the Green river, in what today is the southwest corner of Wyoming but then was in the northeast tip of Utah Territory, was one of the first of these.

Bridger established this post in 1843, and in 1853 the Mormons took it over. It was they who built one of the first of the agricultural settlements in what is now Wyoming—an outpost called Fort Supply, a few miles south of old Fort Bridger, near the present Green river valley towns of Evanston, Lyman and Mountain View (motor road US 30S and 189 to Salt Lake City). Fort Supply was set up in 1853, and to this spot was brought probably the first cattle herd of any size in the western part of Wyoming: 193 beef and milk cows.

7

In southeastern Wyoming in 1852 several hundred work cattle were wintered on the Chugwater river by Seth E. Ward, post trader at Fort Laramie.[3]

Alexander Majors, of Pony Express and overland freight fame, wintered 300 head in 1854 on the Chugwater range where later Hiram B. Kelly had a ranch. Majors' cattle were "poor and sorefooted" when they were turned out to graze in November; in the spring they were "in the very finest working condition" and he had not lost one. He wintered cattle in the same location for the following ten years, with a loss of less than half of one percent per winter, and invariably found them in improved condition in the spring. E. S. Newman in 1864 made a similar "discovery" of the remarkable feed value of Wyoming grass, when he was snowed in on the Laramie Plains while hauling supplies by ox train to Camp Douglas.

A few at a time, cattle were brought in by others. Some began building up herds from which they sold animals to the emigrants, or traded them,—one fat steer for two that were lean and lame. As the grass along the emigrant roads grew thinner, the herders moved their cattle farther into sheltered valleys of the richer grasslands.

Down in the Southwest, where cattle had been brought in by the Spaniards in 1521, and where stock breeding had already reached the proportions of an industry, people began to hear of the new grazing lands to the north, and of the growing market there for cattle. A herd was driven overland out of Texas, through Indian Territory and the western edges of Kansas and Nebraska, into Wyoming. Soon the sky was hazy with the dust of trail herds coming north from Texas. The Longhorns were on the way.

The first sizable herds brought into Wyoming from the Southwest were those of Nelson Story, who was born in Ohio in 1838 and came West at the age of eighteen. He mined

[3]What Plymouth was to New England, Fort Laramie was to Wyoming. First a trading outpost, then a military bastion for protection of the 49ers, since 1938 a National Monument, Fort Laramie imbues even a casual visitor with a sense of history. The fur brigade, wagon trains, pony express and Sioux wars all touched here and left their marks.

$30,000 of gold dust near Virginia City in 1866, took it east and got $40,000 in greenbacks for it. Then he went to Texas, where he bought 1,000 head of cattle at $10 a head, driving them through Wyoming in 1866 into southern Montana. There, by 1886, after selling many he still had 17,000 head. Story sold out in 1890 for between $350,000 and $400,000. He died in 1926.[4]

The Union Pacific reached Cheyenne—or the spot on the plains where the "Magic City" sprang up as the railroad came—in 1867. In the fall of 1868 the first permanent range herd came into Wyoming. It belonged to W. G. Bullock and B. B. Mills of near Fort Laramie; these cattle were driven in from Kansas, Iowa and Missouri.

Cattle coming into Wyoming from the south followed trails originating in southern Texas, trails which converged at favorable river crossings, avoiding the poorer grass areas, and gradually drew together, merging into one broad concourse that entered Wyoming through Pine Bluffs, in the southeastern corner of the state. It crossed Horse creek, swimming the Platte near the mouth of Raw Hide creek, with occasional detours across the Platte near the Platte river bridge at Fort Laramie, went on up Raw Hide past JayEm to the east of Raw Hide buttes, Running Water (near Lusk), past Hat Creek station, down Old Woman and Lance creeks to the Cheyenne river, and the crossing of the Belle Fourche. There the trail spread fanlike out to the Dakotas, the Indian agencies, northern Wyoming, eastern, central and western Montana and the Canadian border,—1,700 miles from the Texas ranges.

There are five stone, cement and bronze markers in Wyoming today to mark the Texas trail. The markers, adorned with old-time cattle brands, are dedicated "to the hardy pioneer stockmen and cowboys" who brought the cattle from the Southwest into central and northern Wyoming. The first of these markers, at the crossing of the Belle Fourche, west of Moorcroft, was erected through the efforts of Edward

[4]From MS by his son, T. B. Story, dated January 24, 1938, in files of the Wyoming Stock Growers Association.

Burnett, a long-time resident of Buffalo whose two sons still live there; the Wyoming Stock Growers Association co-operated in placing the others, which are at Pine Bluffs, Torrington, Lusk and LaGrange.

In the early days of the drives, there was not a wire fence between Fort Worth, Texas, and the head of Running Water, in Wyoming.

By 1868 the great migration of men and cattle was under way. Three hundred thousand cattle a year left Texas for the northern ranges. At the peak, in 1884, the number was estimated at 800,000. From that year, as improved railroad transportation became available, and as the small settlers, who also were coming in greater numbers, built fences, plowed the ground and dug irrigating ditches, the number declined to one last through herd in 1897.[5]

Up to the coming of the Union Pacific, what few cattle Wyoming sent to market had gone to a shipping center in Colorado Territory, a town called Denver. After 1867, the railroad provided a means of shipping eastward directly from Wyoming. Grazing land could be had for the taking. A man could move in, build a cabin and corrals, and call it a ranch, stocking it with cattle that could range far and wide to fatten on free grass.

It was the grass that made cow country. The buffalo had lived on this for an untold time, and so it was and is called buffalograss (*Buchloë dactyloides*). In early days the word as generally used and understood included a physically similar grass that is now known as blue grama (agronomists today list more than two hundred other kinds of grass as growing in the state, about a fourth of which have been introduced).

No other grass has entered as extensively into the history and literature of the west as buffalograss. It is drought-resist-

[5]"I was on hand when the last herd ever trailed from Texas to Montana went through Wyoming. It passed the Raw Hide ranch and JayEm creek on June 17, 1897. The boss was Scandlous John McChesney. He died in Trinidad, Colo., several years ago. He drove three herds of XIT cattle, all in a row, to Montana. I mean 1895-6-7." Letter from John T. Coffee, dated Sept. 29, 1948, in *Cow Country* Nov. 8, 1948.

ant, suffers little from heat or cold; the close, even turf of fine leaves which it forms is effective for erosion control. It survives drying, trampling and heavy grazing. In the entire short-grass country where it grows, including more humid areas than Wyoming, its carrying capacity has been estimated by the U. S. Department of Agriculture at fifteen acres to the head of stock. In Wyoming it is now estimated—by Alan A. Beetle, associate professor, Range Management, University of Wyoming—that the average need per cow per year is forty acres, based on 3.3 acres per cow per month as determined experimentally at a field station near Cheyenne.

The pioneer cowmen had little if any scientific knowledge of grasses such as scientists make available to today's ranchers, but they were quick to learn the grazing value of the buffalograss and to take advantage of the fact that in the high, dry climate of the Great Plains it was dried and cured early in the season, making a natural winter feed containing, like hay, abundant nutrition.

So the early comers brought in all the cattle they could get, Texas Longhorns and Oregon breeding stock. Thus the great cattle-raising industry of Wyoming came into being. It sounds quick and easy. It was quick but it wasn't easy. It was hard going all the way. Marked and unmarked graves along the old trails give some idea of how difficult it was. There were those who came through and prospered; there were many who fell or failed.

CHAPTER THREE

DOWN FROM OREGON

We moved up Snake river about four miles and camped for the night. We were now in Idaho, the Snake river being the state line. My buddy and I went fishing that night; we stood on what we thought was a drift log partly out of the water. We caught about forty fish. In the morning the log proved to be a dead horse, and nobody wanted any fish.

—Frank Abbott MS describing trail drive
from Oregon to Wyoming in '82.

While the Longhorns were trailing up from Texas, another great cattle drive started down to Wyoming from Oregon. There the cattle industry had been established early. Oregon was a state 31 years before Wyoming was, and provided the foundation for Wyoming's great Shorthorn and Hereford herds.

Prior to 1837, the only cattle in Oregon belonged to the Hudson's Bay Company, which supplied milk to the settlers but refused to sell any of its live stock to them. To break up this monopoly, a group of Willamette Valley men in 1837 went to California by boat and brought 600 cattle back with them overland to Oregon. The live stock supply was increased in 1841 by another group of settlers who built a sloop, sailed her to San Francisco and traded her for cattle which they drove to Oregon over the wilderness trails. Soon thereafter long columns of emigrants from the east began to reach Willamette Valley. They brought cows with them and in two decades there were enough cattle in Oregon to help stock the new Wyoming ranges.[6]

The trail these incoming herds followed came into Wyo-

[6]From *Oregon: End of the Trail*, American Guide Series, Portland 1940.

12

ming in the Star Valley region, crossed the mountains on the Lander Cutoff, followed the Sweetwater and then branched off to various parts of the region. If shipments were to be made east via the Union Pacific, the herds usually went south to Rock Creek for loading.

Some of the cattle from Oregon traveled longer distances than did some of the herds moving up from the Southwest, and the privations and dangers suffered by the men who trailed the herds down from the Northwest were in some instances greater than those on the route from Texas. There was no Red river on the Oregon drives, but there was the Snake. And there were lava beds to cross, and long drives between water.

Among the first large herds pointed east from Oregon were two that reached Wyoming in 1876. One of these herds was trailed more than 1,600 miles, from The Dalles to Cheyenne, and then shipped eastward. The other, originating in southeastern Oregon, trailed through to Ogallala, Nebraska.

By 1877, some 50,000 head of "natives" were enroute to Wyoming from Oregon. For 1878 and 1879, the estimated numbers reaching Colorado and Wyoming from the Northwest were 100,000 each year. Ranchmen of the Little Laramie valley, especially J. H. Douglas-Willan and Lionel Sartoris, were heavy buyers of the early Oregon cattle. The Ell Seven company, owned by Henry and Will F. Swan, brought Oregon cattle into the Saratoga valley in the early 1880s. One of the largest drives from Oregon to Wyoming was that of the Searight brothers of Cheyenne, in 1879, of which W. P. Ricketts was the manager. According to a detailed account, written for the Association by Ricketts, 14,000 cattle were brought into Wyoming on this drive. It really was a series of seven drives, 2,000 cattle moving at a time.

N. R. Davis, driving into Wyoming with a herd of Oregon cattle in 1879, arrived too late for his cattle to become "seasoned" to the change in climate and the result was disastrous. The *Carbon County Journal*, Rawlins, Wyo., on March 13, 1880, reported that of his herd of 5,000 more than 800 died.

In the fall of the same year, Charles S. Bush of Washington

Territory arrived at Cheyenne with a large herd of "Westerns." Swan Brothers received 4,500 of these, and Hiram B. Kelly 4,000. They had ordered these early in the spring, and the cattle made the long delivery drive in good condition.

William (Billy) Johnson of Cheyenne, in his later years receiver of the United States Land Office, in 1882 was working for Tom Sun, whose ranch was on the Sweetwater. In March—"everybody was buying cattle up in Oregon that year," said Johnson—he went with a crew sent to Oregon for a herd of cattle. They gathered and branded 2,800 head five miles east of Baker City.

"In the bunch of cattle we had all kinds," Johnson said. "Some were Texas cattle, some Shorthorns, and one, I remember, had Mexican horns. I think it had come up from California."

Two hundred head from this herd were lost enroute from eating the bright-flowered but poisonous larkspur.

The drive started from Oregon in the middle of April. It took five days to get across one river. The route followed was via Eagle Rock, the Lander Cutoff, Green river, South Pass and the Oregon trail. The Sun ranch—which is near Independence Rock and the old Sweetwater Crossing, on state road 220 not far from Split Rock, and is still operated by a son of Tom Sun—was reached September 8. The drive had covered 725 miles—eight men and a hundred horses bringing 3,000 head of cows to the Wyoming grasslands.

Frank Abbott[7] of Worland, Wyo., has recorded his experiences trailing Oregon cattle in 1882. John MacFarlane, to start a ranch near Cheyenne, had bought 500 head of mixed cattle, paying $12 a head for yearlings and $18 for two-year-olds and cows. About forty unbranded calves came with their mothers, representing pure gain for the buyer. This drive started at a ranch twelve miles from Hepner, near

[7]Abbott, a native of Jackson, Mich., came to Wyoming in 1879. He died in Worland in 1945, aged 88, six hours before he was to have been taken by airplane to the home of relatives at Lincoln, Nebr. Abbott's story of his Oregon trail drive, with those of W. P. Ricketts and others, is told in detail in Agnes Wright Spring's *70 Years Cow Country* (1942).

Pendleton, and came via Boise, Ida., and South Pass City, Wyo.

"At times," said Abbott, "we did not see a house of any kind for weeks, although at times we could see the dust from trail herds in front of or behind us. Wheeler and Wilson were driving 12,000 head in five bunches . . . We finally came to where the ranch was going to be—a beauty spot on a small stream about twelve miles south of Laramie peak . . . The grass was knee high and the water clear and cold. This was October 15. We had been five months on the trail. We were glad to get there . . .

"These cattle that Mr. MacFarlane had bought in Oregon for $12 and $18 could have been sold as soon as we got to the ranch for $36 all around. Trail men figured the cost of driving cattle from Oregon to Cheyenne at a dollar a head, so Mr. Mac could have doubled his money."

Edward Burnett, sixty years a cowman, who died at Buffalo, Wyo., in 1944, in his memoirs has left this description of the Oregon cattle:

"The Spanish breed of cattle from the original Cortez herd spread, in time, all over California and Nevada and southern Utah, and they showed the Spanish blood. The cattle from Oregon and Washington were a different breed entirely. There you saw the Shorthorn descendants of the cattle driven over the Oregon trail by the '49ers,—big, blocky, rich in colors, reds and whites and roans. I'd been used to the southern variety and when I first saw these Oregon cattle I thought they were a different species."[8]

So the cattle—finding their feed and water along the way, furnishing their own transportation and needing only men on horseback to point, guide and guard them, and keep the stragglers going,—so the cattle came to Wyoming.

[8]J. Elmer Brock notes that early cattlemen further distinguished the breeds as "Southerns" or "Americans," as indicated in old maverick books, in which foremen described each animal that was branded with the Rolling M pending its sale to the highest bidder, in accordance with the maverick law. Cattle other than Spanish were also referred to as Pilgrim cattle.

CHAPTER FOUR

REVERENCE FOR RIVERS

If you take the skeleton of a cottonwood leaf
And call the stem the long Missouri river
And the other bones of the leaf the other rivers—
The Yellowstone, the River Tongue, the Big Horn,
The Stinking River and the Rosebud River,
The Wind, the Chugwater, the Sweetwater—
That's where they roamed . . .

'Fort Vasquez,' in 'New and Selected
Poems,' by Thomas Hornsby Ferril,
Harper and Brothers.

Like primitive men, Wyoming's first ranchers learned to
have what Herodotus called a reverence for rivers. Herodotus, writing of the early Persians, said Cyrus the Great
thought the water of the Choaspes, on which he lived, the
only water fit to drink, and so when he went marauding into
other countries he carried some of it along, in flagons of
silver.

The cowmen of our West, as they trailed the herds of
cattle into Wyoming, had no silver flagons. They drank
either from barrels lashed to their chuck wagons, or from the
streams, lying on their bellies and burying their wind-burned
chins in the water to cool their dusty throats.

And they revered their rivers not for any god-like qualities
that might be in the rushing waters, but because when they
came to one they faced the problem of getting their herds to
the other side without benefit of bridges. Sometimes it took
days to get a herd across a river. Occasionally it took men's
lives, and frequently the cost was high in drowned cattle, or
drowned horses, or both.

Bob Fudge came up from Texas with a trail herd in 1881.
He made the route many times thereafter, and finally settled

16

Trailing up from Texas to stock the northern ranges, the Longhorn herds crossed the Belle Fourche river near this point in northeastern Wyoming west of Moorcroft. Edward Burnett, pioneer Buffalo (Wyo.) cowman, points with knifeblade to old brands carved in the marble marker, which Burnett placed at this historic spot. For Burnett's reminiscences, see Pages 19 and 20. (Photo from J. Elmer Brock.)

Dedication on August 1, 1948, of Texas Trail marker at Pine Bluffs, where the trail herds entered southeastern Wyoming. Below, a lean Longhorn—a far cry from the well-fleshed, upgraded cattle of today.

White-bearded Nelson Story, a native of Ohio who trailed the first Longhorns from Texas into Wyoming in 1866 (Pages 8, 9 and 23), is shown here in a tense moment on August 27, 1901, when his mill and elevator at Great Falls, Montana, burned. Story was 63 at this time; he died in 1926, aged 88. (Photo from J. Elmer Brock.)

Wyoming cowboys of the open range days, slickers tied behind their saddles, pause to have their picture taken while roping and cutting out cows from the gather on a roundup. They are checking brands, to determine ownership. An inch to the right of the white calf in center of picture, a clowning cowpuncher forks an old cow. (Photo from files of Wyoming Stock Growers Association.)

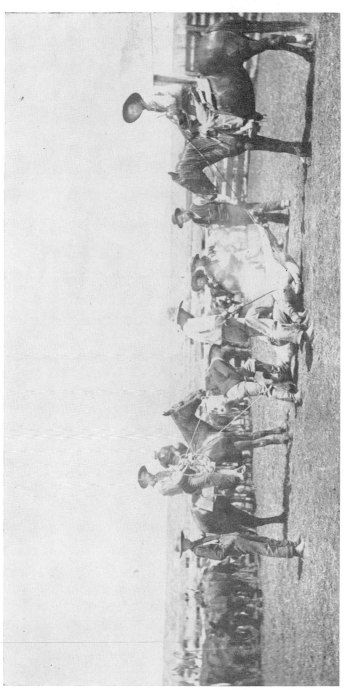

Cattle branding near Rawlins, Wyo., July, 1884, Sand Creek Land and Cattle Co., Ltd. The lad standing at the left, hands in pockets, was no drug store cowboy; as of seventy years ago, he was the McCoy. (Photo from Tom Sun.)

A roundup crew of the pre-fence era gathers for sowbelly and beans beside a stream near Medicine Bow Station. (Willing Richardson collection, from WSGA.)

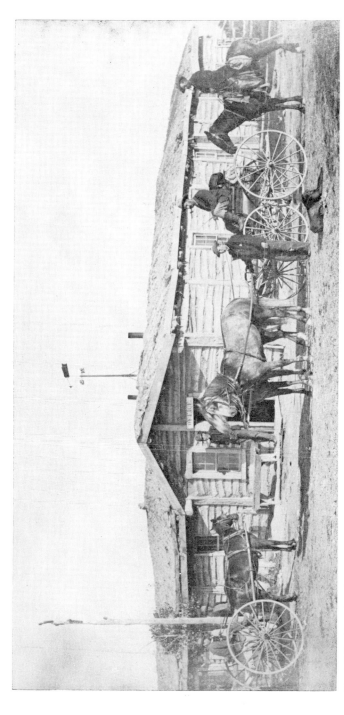

In 1883, Hat Creek Postoffice, about fifteen miles north of Lusk, along what is now U. S. Highway 85, was a log cabin with a weather vane on its sod roof. John Momos sits in the buggy on the right, with a booted heel on the wheel and a bedroll tied behind. Sol Tuckerman stands beside him, and the leather-chapped cowboy on the horse is Baldy Levies, a roundup cook. Rig at the left is unidentified. (WSGA collection, Harry E. Crain donor.)

Bob Fudge, Texas cowboy who first came up the trail to Wyoming in
1881, is third from the right in this group of cowboys relaxing in
front of an XIT cabin presumably in Montana. (For Bob Fudge's
story, see Pages 16-19, 30-31.) This photo, found when an old log
house was torn down at Missoula, Mont., in 1953, was apparently taken
in the early 1890s. On back of photo, an unknown hand had written
in faded pencil: "John Williams, Emmet Glidwell, All Denby, Si
Robenson, Louis Weisner, Bob Fudge, B. Bird, Charle Clements."

in southern Montana, dying in Gillette, Wyo., in 1937. He
was a cowman of the good old days. Here is a fragment of
the record of his experiences that he left in a manuscript
printed in the *Powder River County Examiner*, Broadus,
Mont., January 23, 1953, some twenty years after Fudge wrote
it. The cowboy crew of which he was a member was bringing a herd of 2,000 grown cattle to their purchaser, Mat Murphy, on the Little Big Horn in Montana, by way of Wyoming.
They had crossed Indian Territory (Fudge wrote) and:

" . . . then we came to the Arkansas river. This is quite
a river at all times and it was at its best now, muddy and
boiling. We had gotten used to swimming rivers, and did
not think of having trouble here. We always let our cattle
get real thirsty before swimming a river, then they would
crowd the lead cattle into swimming water before they realized it, and the point men would go in with them on the
lower side so they would not turn back or float down stream
too far. This day I caught the best swimming horse I had
in my string, for I knew there was a lot of swimming to do.
This horse, I remember well, was a big brown, branded with
a Lazy S.

"Old Fort Dodge was on the other side of the river and
we cowboys were anxious to get across. This was the Dodge
of trail herd days. (Editor's note: Dodge City was five miles
west of Fort Dodge, on the north bank of the Arkansas.)
A lot of people came out from town to see our herd swim
the Arkansas. They were about where we expected to have
our cattle come out on the opposite bank. We always put
our saddle horses into these big rivers just ahead of the cattle.
The cattle seemed to make for the other side better if they
saw our horses land safely.

"Our cattle started fine. I happened to be in the lead,
pointing them for the opposite bank. We swam within a few
feet of these lead cattle to get them pointed right. I got
within fifty feet of the bank when the cattle got scared of the
people who had come to see them swim. I kept trying to
push them to the shore but before I could get out of the way
I was surrounded with scared, mad, swimming cattle. They

became so tightly pressed together that they got my horse under them. I let the horse go, and grabbed horns, tails or necks, anything to keep the cattle from getting me under them. I don't know how long this lasted till they began to climb out on the other shore. Then the mill, as a bunch of cattle are called when they are running or swimming in a circle, broke. That freed me. I was an extra good swimmer but I will never know how I made that bank. My clothes were filled with sand and mud until I could hardly carry them on land, but I swam forty or fifty yards with them on.

"My horse was drowned. He floated down the river about a half mile and lodged on an island. The boys got a canoe and went over and got my saddle. I put it on another horse."

The West of those days as of now was a land of violent contrasts, quick changes of weather and terrain. After crossing the Arkansas, the herd with which Fudge rode in '81 moved north by a little west through Kansas, by way of Ogallala, Nebr., and Fort Laramie, into Wyoming, Then, as Fudge recorded it many years later:

"We were told at Fort Laramie that from Cheyenne to the Powder river there was likely to be no water, which we surely found out. The worst suffering I ever saw in my seventy years with cattle was on this drive from the Cheyenne to the Powder. This suffering cannot be told in words. The weather was terribly hot and at the end of the second day those cattle commenced to grind their teeth in their suffering, and when they were lying down their groans were something to make a wooden Indian's hair raise. At night those groans and the grinding of teeth were the most horrible thing I ever went through.

"We traveled at night; whenever the cattle would move a bit, we urged them on. We knew we had to get to water or lose every one of them. We did lose between one and two hundred from thirst. This was the most pitiful thing I have even seen. Every one of those cattle that died, died with its head pointed toward Texas. I suppose they thought of the last water they had drunk and maybe they thought of their native home. Anyway, they turned their heads south before kicking their last."

The Powder river was Paradise when they finally reached it. And the simple words with which Fudge ended his story of that drive are eloquent tribute to the cowman's heart and spirit:

"After leaving the Powder we came in sight of the Big Horn mountains. We went near where Sheridan, Wyo., now stands. This country had more water than any place we had gone through from Texas to the end of the trail. We crossed the Tongue and over the divide to the Little Big Horn river. Murphy's ranch was on this river, about ten miles below Custer's battlefield. When the cattle were counted to Murphy they were quite a lot short. I forget just how many . . . After the herd and our horses were counted, our work was done. Murphy bought all our horses, our wagon, and everything but our saddles. There was regret in every cowboy's heart as Mr. Murphy started with us in a mountain wagon for Miles City. We had loved those cattle and those horses and the life with them. We didn't have anything else to love, I guess."

Edward Burnett's reminiscences, like the writing of many of the oldtimers who put their recollections down on paper, also revealed imagination and a sense of humor, coupled with a strong feeling for the land and the people.

"When we got to the Red river," Burnett wrote of his first drive north, "we had already crossed so many rivers that we looked on ourselves as experienced cow navigators. Red river had a bad reputation, and it had taken its toll, as graves on the bank showed, but the river was on its good behavior with us. I couldn't help admiring it as I saw it for the first time, lots of water and some of it deep enough to swim the cattle. Most of the rivers on the trip ran in deep-cut gorges and you couldn't see them till you were right up on them, and then you had to lean over your horse's neck and peer down into the gorge to see the water. Not so the Red. The banks were low and solid, and the scattered cottonwoods showed by the driftwood what it was like when in flood. But she was kind to us, and we got across all right, with even a ferry boat for the mess wagon, so no wet, soggy beds for us boys.

19

"But we crossed some mean rivers during the next month, boggy quicksand, they were all bad. The Arkansas, about the best of them. That's an ugly river, full of business, no time or wish to be pretty. The Platte always in flood whenever I had it to cross, and dangerous. Powder river and Tongue river, good safe fords, but nothing much in the river class. If the Powder could be straightened out she'd be the longest river in the world! . . .

"The Yellowstone, she takes first prize in the beauty show of rivers; not the grandeur of the Red, nor the magnitude or mystery. These are so pronounced in the Red that they make you feel what a pigmy mortal you are. But the Yellowstone is so much smaller that a man's eye can take in all her beauties at a glance. She has a sparkle and a gleam. It wouldn't be fair to judge the Missouri from where we crossed it, at the mouth of the Big Dry, present Fort Peck dam location; that is fairly close to her start, and she has hardly had time to show what she can do; after she has run a few hundred miles, then she has nothing to be ashamed of. Milk river is mean, boggy, high banks, no crossing for thirty miles.

"Indians have signs for all the rivers, and if a man knows the natural characteristics of the rivers he can tell the one they're talking about—and they use signs even when talking with people of their own tongue. It's amusing when you recognize the river and see how truly the Indian's sign represents that particular stream: The Arkansas, crooked and swift, all shown in motions of the hands; the Laramie, which the Indians call the Goose river, sign, paddling like a goose swimming; Powder river, pick up a pinch of dust and blow on it, also sign 'very crooked'; the Yellowstone, Indian name 'Elk river,' and well named, too; the sign, spread a hand out from each ear with the little finger crooked up like an elk's horn; the Little Big Horn the Indians called the Greasy Grass, and for the sign they rubbed one hand over the other slowly. A creek called Soap creek runs into this river, and it's like soapsuds and makes the water slimy."

•

Burnett told, too, of an experience not unlike that in

which the cowboy Fudge lost his horse, except that this one had a happier ending. This was at a crossing of the Yellowstone. A man named Curry and his wife ran a ferry boat at the point of crossing. Curry would point the cattle with a skiff as the boys drove them into the water.

"Curry was an expert cowboy with that skiff," Burnett wrote. "If the steers started to mill, he'd break them up and keep the line of cattle swimming straight. It was a busy day when we crossed. Generally there was one herd a day, but this time there were two, one herd behind ours. The Texas cowboys didn't like the idea of their going across in the skiff, leading their swimming horses by the reins. They'd rather swim horseback.

"Anyway, there was an outlaw steer in the middle of the herd, and in the middle of the river he started the other steers milling. So Curry drove his skiff into the starting mill and cut out the outlaw, and let him drift downstream. A cowboy named Chapman, without being told, galloped his horse over to the river bank, saying 'I'll go get him.' The beef herd came out of the river and started for the shipping pens six miles downstream. Whenever the boys came within speaking distance of each other, the great joke was Chappie dashing off down the river bank, and when he would get back with the outlaw steer.

"We worked the herd down to the shipping pens,—and there, tied up to a gate post, was the outlaw steer. Chappie had gone on into town. The steer had swum and drifted six miles downstream to somewhere near the shipping point. How Chappie got him out I don't know as he never told it twice alike."

Such were the rivers of early-day cow country, their perils, their life-giving powers and their personalities. It was along the rivers that the ranches were established, the towns grew up. The trail drivers shoved the herds along "till they could wet their feet in the waters of the Yellowstone." They guided by the stars and by the rivers. To speak the best of a man, cowmen said: "He's a good one to ride the river with."

But they had other perils to face as they peopled the Plains —for instance, Indians.

21

CHAPTER FIVE

INDIANS

The emigrants and freighters had their choice: Bozeman trail, good grass, wood and water and fight Red Cloud; Bridger trail, poor grass, bad water, and the Shoshone Indians who were too ornry to fight. Most chose the Bozeman trail.

—Edward Burnett, manuscript.

In Wyoming soil are buried more men, women and children who were killed by Indians than in all the other mountain states combined.[9]

Wyoming was the heart of the Plains Indian country, the home or roving ground of the Sioux, Cheyennes, Arapahoes, Shoshones and Crows for so long a time that they thought it belonged to them. It did belong to them by right of occupation, though they themselves had migrated here from other regions not many generations previously. Against what they saw as invasion by the white race, the Indians fought back in the only ways they knew. It was a hopeless fight, a lost cause from the start, but they didn't know that then.

Wyoming reeks with Indian war history. Here were fought the Grattan massacre, the Platte Bridge Station affair, the Fetterman massacre at Fort Phil Kearny, the Wagon Box and Hayfield scraps, Mackenzie's battle with the fighting Cheyennes, and nobody knows how many unrecorded struggles between the Indians and wagon trains, pony express riders, soldiers—and cattlemen.

[9]W. L. Kuykendall in *Frontier Days*. One instance: June 27, 1870, six miles from where Lander, Wyo., now stands, Sioux killed three members of a wagon train, and, with a neckyoke, pounded a wagon hammer through the skull of one of the men, Harvey Morgan. In the museum of the Fremont County Pioneer Association at Lander you can see Morgan's skull with the hammer still in it.

When Nelson Story drove the first Longhorns from Texas to Montana, passing through Wyoming on the Bozeman trail,[10] in 1866, Red Cloud and Crazy Horse of the Sioux were rampant, and Story was threatened by Indians all the way. On one occasion, Sioux drove off thirty of the cattle. Story and his men followed their trail that night, found the Indians feasting on one of his cows, killed the whole band and recovered 29 of the stolen cattle. At the Bozeman crossing of Clark's fork of the Yellowstone, the Indians killed Story's game hunter. The next year, when Red Cloud burned Fort C. F. Smith, Story, then engaged in hauling wood and potatoes for the government, lost much property and equipment, although the government years later compensated him for the loss.

Captain John R. Smith, later a prominent rancher of Sweetwater and Johnson counties, had a three-day fight with Crazy Horse and his Sioux in March, 1868, at the Horseshoe Road Ranch, about forty miles west of Fort Laramie.

There were four men at the ranch when the Indians attacked.[11] The four managed to get into the ranch house, opened the port holes and held the position till night, when the Indians set fire to the house. The ranchers, in anticipation of Indian attacks, had previously constructed a small sod "fort" a little distance away; to this they escaped as the ranch house burned. That night they slipped out of the fort and made their way to Twin Springs, a nearby ranch, where they were reinforced by the two men there. These six cached

[10]John M. Bozeman of Montana laid it out in 1863, and in '65 the government established a series of forts along its line to protect emigrants. The trail began in the state of Nebraska, followed the Oregon trail into Wyoming to Fort Laramie, crossed the North Platte and ran northward to the Powder and Little Piney, thence entering Montana and running west to Bozeman and the gold fields. Red Cloud and his Sioux killed so many whites along this route (one of their victims was Bozeman himself) that in 1868 the government abandoned the forts and closed the trail.

[11]This account of the battle is taken from an article written by Captain Smith in 1893, published in *Footprints on the Frontier* (1945) by Virginia Cole Trenholm. For the Indian version of the fight, see Pages 218-221 of *Crazy Horse* by Mari Sandoz. This account says the Sioux went to the Horseshoe ranch "to visit and trade," and the white men, frightened, opened fire on them.

the Twin Springs ranch property, food and supplies, in a hole under the house, then burned the house and headed for Fort Laramie, 36 miles east. They had two horses and a mule. They encountered a French trapper searching for a lost horse, so now there were seven men.

At this point they were jumped again by sixty Sioux. A bullet penetrated Smith's shirt and grazed the skin over his heart. An arrow struck another man in the eye, and a third man was disabled by a blow on the head from a rock hurled by one of the attackers. Smith was knocked half senseless by another rock. Then an arrow passed through Smith's coat sleeve at the elbow, scraping off six inches of skin; the same arrow went through the sleeve of one of the men fighting beside Smith, pinning the two together.

The Indians fired the timber, and the white men made a dash for a defensive position in a nearby hollow. One of their little band was killed, and Smith was hit by another arrow which went through his right arm. He pulled it out with his left hand. A second member of the party fell dead. There were five men left alive, three of them wounded. One of these, unable to keep fighting, blew the top of his own head off. The four held their ground, and saw eight Indians fall beneath their fire.

The leader of the Indians, who Smith said was Crazy Horse, then signaled for a talk. Smith had only 19 rounds of ammunition left, the others a like number, so they decided to parley. The white men agreed that, in return for their lives, they would lead the Indians to where the ranch goods had been cached and turn the supplies over to the Indians. This was done, and the Indians departed.

Smith and his companions made their way to Wilson's and Bellamy's ranch, whence a courier took word of the fight to Fort Laramie. E troop, 2nd Cavalry, came out, buried the dead and hauled the wounded to the fort in an ambulance. Smith was in the hospital ten days.

"In counting our loss," wrote Capt. Smith in 1893, "we found we were out about $16,000 in ranch property, hay, goods, stock, horses, mules and work cattle, 36 head of the latter having been taken, to say nothing of $500 cash that had fallen into the hands of the Indians. I served four years and seven months in the Civil war and was in some hard battles, and I have been in several fights with the Indians, but I never had as hard a time as I experienced with Crazy Horse on Horseshoe Creek . . . It pauperized us all."

The year of the fight at Horseshoe Creek was the year the government temporarily gave in to the Sioux, ordered the Bozeman trail closed and abandoned the forts that had been built to protect it. There was an uneasy peace[12] between red man and white for a few years, during which the killing off of the buffalo went on apace,—and the destruction of the great buffalo herds meant the end of the Plains Indians' way of life.

Discovery of gold in the Black Hills brought a rush of white miners to the Indian country, negotiations for purchase of the Black Hills by the government, new clashes and finally a new war. The Sioux won some of the battles—including several fought in northern Wyoming, and the triumph over Custer in Montana—but they lost the war. Their chiefs were killed, surrendered, or fled to Canada to return in 1881 as prisoners of war, and to settle down on the small and scattered reservations that were all they had left.

Records of the WSGA show that repeatedly during the 1880s the secretary of the Association, who most of that time was Thomas Sturgis, wrote to Washington in protest at depredations by small bands of Indians from the reservations. This menace gradually diminished, as the tribes grew more complacent and slowly gave up their roving ways. One interesting and somewhat whimsical letter in the WSGA files implies doubt as to whether in 1884 the ranchers were suffering more at the hands of the Indians who were gradually withdrawing from the ranges or the Englishmen who were

[12]C. F. Coffee, writing in 1915 about his ranch on the Box Elder, 65 miles north of Cheyenne, in 1873, said: "We carried guns on our saddles all the time and never thought of going to the spring for water without a gun in one hand and a bucket in the other. When I built the ranch house, I made the windows high so no one could shoot us in the night."

invading them in ever-increasing numbers. Written from the Lazy U C Ranch, Horse Creek, Carbon county, July 13, 1884, this letter, addressed to the secretary of the WSGA, said:

"I have a letter from my foreman saying that the Indians are now in the Rattlesnake mountains and in a few days will be down on our ranges, where we are holding our beef for shipment, and as a consequence we may expect to have the beef run all over the country and the fat taken off them. I write you for advice in the matter . . . We could take our outfit and run the Indians off, but, knowing how sacred they are held by the government, would not like to attempt that only in the last extremity and then with the full support of the Association. Another evil threatens us also in the shape of a band of Englishmen who are to be here on the 20th and fit out for a hunting expedition northward. I do not know that they would wantonly run cattle but in their efforts to get at game they certainly do run them to some extent, and at any rate it is a noted fact that when a critter gets a glimpse of them it will throw up its tail and run as if it had seen the devil. If you can give us any assistance or point out any way in which we can fight these evils we will be very thankful.

"Yours truly, R. B. CONNOR."

There is a penciled memorandum at the bottom of the letter, apparently by Sturgis; it says "I appealed to Sec. Int. thro' Gov. Hale—reply was that the Arap.& Shos. had a recognized right to live, visit and hunt where they pls'd. Can see no remedy but to cause them to move back if doing damage. As regds hunters, the law forbids killing game positively. Watch them & the first break they make arrest the whole bunch and take them to Rawlins."

As recently as 1903, white men and red were still killing each other in Wyoming. In October of that year, Sheriff William H. Miller of Weston County and Louie Falkenburg, a deputy sheriff of adjoining Converse county, rode out with a dozen men to arrest a band of vagrant Sioux from a South Dakota reservation at Jake Mill's cow camp on Lightning creek, a prong of the Cheyenne river. The Indians had been killing antelope and stealing from sheep camps. When the smoke drifted away, the sheriff, his deputy and four of the Indians lay dead. The other Indians were put in jail, where they succeeded in fixing the blame for the white deaths on one of their dead tribesmen, so all the prisoners were released. The buckskin shirt of one of the Indians was later placed in the Pioneer Cabin at Douglas, Wyo. The bones of the Indian who had worn the shirt were for a while in possession of the State Pioneer Society, but, years after the shooting, were returned to the Indians, who gave them tribal interment. There is at Douglas another relic of this fight. Back of the Pioneer Cabin is a grave surmounted by an arbor of tree branches. A headstone says: "Indian, killed by John Owen, 1903." Owen was one of Miller's deputies in the fight on Lightning Creek. It was said to have been Owen's gun that killed all four Indians.

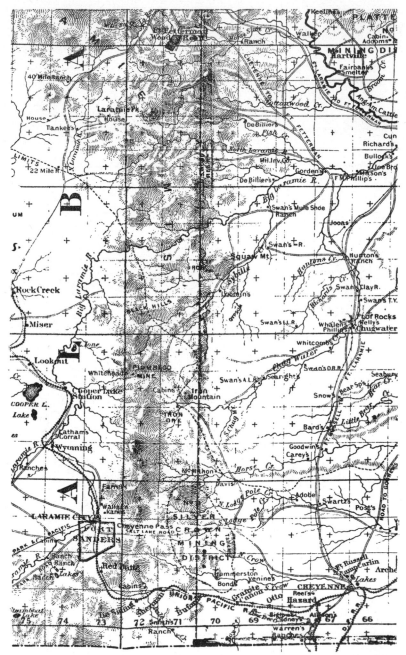

Cheyenne-Laramie area, showing ranches, from map of 1883, when Laramie mountains were known as Black Hills. (Map from Henry Swan.)

CHAPTER SIX

HORSES AND SADDLES

The West was discovered, battled over, and won by men on horseback . . . In the Old West, the phrase "left afoot" meant nothing short of being left flat on your back. "A man on foot is no man at all," the saying went. If an enemy could not take a man's life, the next best thing was to take his horse . . .

—J. Frank Dobie, in 'Guide to Life
and Literature of the Southwest.'

Old Blue, a cowpony on the F. E. Warren ranch in southern Wyoming, was probably no more of a horse than a good many others. He just seemed so to the men around him, and there was one among them articulate enough about it to rear a monument to Old Blue's memory. It has stood for many years on the state line where the road to Cheyenne from Fort Collins, Colo., enters Wyoming. A pile of stones where the horse was buried is topped by a weather-beaten headboard on which is painted—

Erected to the memory
of
Old Blue
The best old cowpony
that ever pulled on a rope
by the
Cowpunchers of the 7XL outfit.
Rest in peace.

Fred E. Warren, son of the late Senator Francis E. Warren and manager of the Wyoming ranches in Wyoming, some years ago gave to *Cow Country,* monthly publication of the Wyoming Stock Growers Association, an account of Old Blue.

He was a blue roan cowpony of average appearance but

unusual intelligence. Used in his early years for ordinary range work, Old Blue later on found his calling as an aid to the cowmen in the education of colts.

"When we had horses to break for driving, Old Blue was the horse that was harnessed with the youngster to sit on the singletree when the youngster felt like running away and to drag him ahead by main strength when the colt felt balky," Fred Warren said. "As he grew older he seemed to know what was expected of him, and became endowed with quite a sense of humor. If a new man fancied himself as a rider, Old Blue was saddled up and given to him. The rascal would look back to size up his rider and then crow-hop around to discover whether the man could really ride or not. As soon as he felt his man slipping, he would look back and almost wink an eye as he stopped dead still.

"At other times it was the custom to have the new hands lead Old Blue to water from the barn to a little stream a short distance away. He would invariably bury his nose in the stream and apparently drink with great gusto, regardless of the fact that only a few minutes before perhaps two or three of our new hands had led him at different times to the same place. In short, Old Blue was the universal pet on the ranch, and when the time came for him to cash in his chips, there was grief in the bunk house."

Bob Fudge, in his reminiscences previously quoted, tells how in the spring of 1885 he helped bring a herd of 800 horses from the Goodnight ranch in Texas to Wyoming for John Sparks and John Tinnin, on Pole creek in the Pine Bluffs area.

"This was the wildest trip I ever made up the trail," Fudge said:[13] "If a man is looking for romance, I would advise a trip up the trail from Texas to Wyoming with a horse herd. Our horses stampeded day and night. We would run with them in the daytime, but at night all we could do was hope for the best, with our hearts beating like the tramp of a regiment of soldiers.

[13]From the *Powder River County Examiner*, Broadus, Mont., January 30, 1953.

30

"When those horses would stampede, the rumble of the heaviest freight train would be quiet compared with the noise they made. I and a cowboy named Andrew Skeins broke broncs all the way with this herd. The broke horses sold for more than the stock horses so we broke as many as we could along the way. The ones we broke were good saddle stock, from four to seven years old, weighing around eleven hundred pounds. When a man ropes one of those broncs around the neck in the open as we did, the smoke, hair and fire flies and the cowboy on the horse on the other end of the rope isn't worrying about any social activities. He has more than enough to keep his mind on.

"Skeins roped a big bronc one day and somehow in letting out his rope a kink or half hitch got around his thumb, cutting the thumb off at the first joint. Blood from that thumb was everywhere, it seemed. We tied the thumb up as best we could and Skeins never did stop work. He rode and did the roping every day. We looked for the piece of thumb that had been jerked off but we never did find it. Apparently it flew a long ways, and some coyote or buzzard got it after we left camp."[14]

After two months on the trail, the horses from the Goodnight ranch were turned over to their Wyoming purchasers. Fudge said:

"Horses usually travel several times as fast as cattle, and we didn't expect to be nearly that long on the way. There were practically no stock horses in Wyoming at that time, only what the Indians had. We had about ten stallions with this herd. They were Coach, Steeldust and Morgans."

[14]There were two ways of fastening your end of the rope around the saddle horn to stop the animal on which you had dabbed your loop. One was to wrap it so it held tight; this method came from Texas, where short ropes were used in brush roping, and if you did this way you were a tie-fast man. The other method was to give the rope a turn or two around the horn and ease it gradually when the tension came. This was the dally method, and it came from the Spaniards, whose rawhide ropes would not always stand a sharp jerk. The Spanish phrase was *dar la vuelta,* which meant give it a turn, and easily became "dally" on American lips. Dally precisionists would tie a bit of tarred grass rope on the saddle horn, to facilitate holding and easing the rope without having to take too many turns around the horn. Both dally and tie-fast men lost a good many thumbs and fingers.

Arthur Chapman, Denver newspaper man who wrote the unforgettable poem "Out Where the West Begins," also wrote a piece called "The Old Timer" (printed in *The Teepee Book,* Sheridan, Wyo., September 1916), of which the first verse goes like this:

> He showed up in the springtime when
>   the geese began to honk;
> He signed up with the outfit, and we
>   fattened up his bronk;
> His chaps were old and tattered, but
>   he never seemed to mind,
> 'Cause for worryin' and frettin' he
>   had not been designed;
> He's the type of cattle puncher that
>   has vanished now, of course,
> With his hundred dollar saddle and his
>   twenty dollar horse. . .

There was a verse in the "Old Chisholm Trail," which many a cowman sang to the herd at night, that said something about "a ten-dollar hoss and a forty-dollar saddle,"—so Chapman had the ratio about right. This is also substantiated by some of the memoirs of H. V. Williams who, as he put it, "saw the tail end of the Old West, from 1878 to 1883." In his later years, when he was residing in Sidney, Nebr., Williams presented the saddle he had used in his riding days to the Wyoming Stock Growers Association with a memorandum that read in part as follows:

"Thomas Kane, an early-day cowman, had that saddle made to order by J. S. Collins of Cheyenne, Wyo., (the firm is still in business) and it cost $45. It came into my possession either late in 1881 or early in '82. It was never on a horse after 1901. The stirrups are the original 'Round House' or 'Dog House' stirrups and they were at least six inches wide. A person had to hold those stirrups by their weight on the ball of his foot. I was too light to hold them and they always got to flopping and worked off my feet. In 1885, Bill Tompett, who used to drive the stage from Rock Creek to Fetterman in 1878 and '79, sawed the stirrups down for me. The wide stirrups first came up the trail from Texas, where they were needed for protection in riding through the mesquite brush, and chaps were used for the same purpose. As there was no brush in this country, the narrow stirrup came into use, and only bull train wagon bosses used the wide ones. Tapaderos were useless and were used only by 'bronco busters.' Chaps were not needed except in wet weather or in winter, and most of the time were in the chuck wagon.

"All I can say in favor of the center-fire (single cinch) saddle is that I never knew it to make a horse's back sore, but it was a disappointment (I was never able to ride a single-rigged saddle of any make) because it never would stay on a Texas horse, it always worked forward almost to the horse's ears. Later, when the flat-withered Oregon horses came, the saddle was a Jonah for it would not stay and a rope would pull it off sideways or back over the horse's rump. As soon as we were able to get hold of double-rigged saddles, the old disappointment was laid away and now it has value only as a relic. The horn is broken across the top. A Texas horse of mine, ridden by my brother, while running struck gopher-worked ground, turned over and lit as a horse does when roped by both front feet. He lit square on the saddle horn and broke it while brother Joe landed out among the gopher nests . . . My horse was a dandy, could run all day, good for a hundred miles and ready to go the next day. I still have a picture of him, and some of his mane and tail. Got to change the subject, too sad to think about even at this late day.

"Of course, most of the early saddles were low horned. There were three styles, the common saddle, sharp cantle, low horn and double rig. Then there was the low Machere saddle. A large square cover fitted over the cantle and over the seat and laced solid up the back of the fork, no opening, and many hated them on that account, also laced on top of the fork. All the tree and cinch rigging was completely covered by the square 'Mother Hubbard.' Then there was what we called the 'half breed' saddle, very wide and a big horn, and about half covered like a Machere saddle. I never knew why but little men always rode a wide saddle (but in the early days most cowpunchers were big six-foot men). Another popular saddle was a double-rigged one made by G. H. & J. S. Collins of Cheyenne, and the price was $35. There was also the Gallatin saddle. The No. 131 Collins saddle had the front rigging crossed around the neck the same as my old saddle . . . Later, when Oregon horses were trailed through, the Quin saddle came, made by T. Quin, Walla Walla, Wash. Rather a coarse wooden farmer saddle. Later the single-cinched Visalia saddles, very deep and high horn and cantle, came from California. The sheep herder fur chaps came also. Too late, the old days were gone, the roundup over, and then someone invented the 40-gallon hat and I quit."

•

Horses and saddles, ropes and spurs, dust and smell and sweat. Brimming rivers filled with swimming cattle. Stampedes and storms, and Indian raids. Up the trail from Texas, down from Oregon, into the grassy valleys and out on the wind-swept plains the cattle came to Wyoming. Old men cherishing their memories, treasuring bits of hair from the tails and manes of their dead horses. There are markers to show where the old trails ran, there are piles of stones where horses like Old Blue were buried. Would you see the monument erected to the men who rode the horses, who herded the cattle, who tamed the wild land, the men with freedom moving through their hearts like the cloud shadows sliding over the Sweetwater hills? Look about you: Wyoming is their monument.

PART TWO

THE COWMEN THROW IN TOGETHER

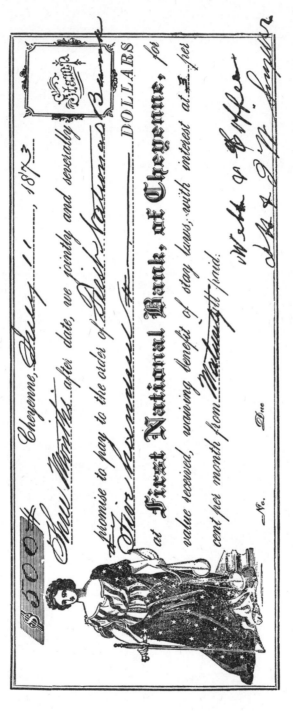

"I'd as soon make a loan on a school of codfish as on those wild plains steers running everywhere," a Boston banker told a Wyoming rancher in the open range days. When bankers did loan on cattle at that time, they had to charge high interest rates, as is indicated in the note reproduced above, from the Russell Thorp collection. The Coffee whose signature appears on the note was Charles Coffee, one of the "five men in a livery stable."

CHAPTER SEVEN

FIVE MEN IN A LIVERY STABLE

I once heard it said that the things we belong to are more important than the things that belong to us . . . The story of the Wyoming Stock Growers Association is actually an important chapter in the whole story of American life and democratic development. It parallels and descends from the pattern of the Pilgrim Fathers.

—J. L. Morrill.

In Wyoming Territory of the early 1870s, when the herds were coming in and the foundation was being laid for what would for many years be the principal industry of the area, there were only five counties, few courts and no fences.

There weren't very many people—the first census in 1869 had shown 8,014, which was about one person for every twelve square miles—but among these were a surprising number of far-seeing individuals. Perhaps there was something about the Plains, too—the far reaches of rolling land with mysterious blue peaks hiding what lay beyond the ranges—that helped stimulate their imagination and broaden their vision. At any rate, they pioneered in the empire of the mind as well as in that of the grasslands. They made history by being the first territory and state to recognize officially the economic and political equality of women. Women have voted and held office in Wyoming since 1869. Land in each township was set aside at the very beginning for school purposes. Social and educational legislation came first. Then laws were passed governing land use and stock raising.

So rapidly was the infant cattle industry growing, however, that the early legislative processes could not keep pace. At that time, it was every man for himself on the open ranges.

When a rancher thought it was time to work his cattle, he would invite his neighbors to join him and they would put on a roundup, or cow hunt as it was called in the early days. This hit-or-miss working over of the herds was hard on the cattle—it kept them "ginned up," as the cowmen put it—and detrimental to the business as a whole. Cattle drifted great distances, with nothing but natural barriers to overcome, and were identifiable as to ownership only by the brands burned into their hides—and altering of these was in many cases easy. There were no soundly established methods for dealing with questions of ownership when they arose, as they frequently did. Opportunities for enlarging one's herd by acquiring another man's calves were abundant. Unbranded calves became the property of the one who found them first,— "the longest rope gets the maverick," the cowmen said. Large investments which eastern and foreign capital was beginning to make in the grasslands were subject to many natural risks, such as weather and disease, and the added danger resulting from a lack of system in conducting the business was a threat to orderly progress.

The pioneers in the cattle business, who in most cases were risking everything they had, were quick to realize the economic necessity for improving their methods. Among these men were many who came from eastern or middle western families of prestige and integrity, with a background of business experience and frequently of good education. Leadership began to assert itself as the need for co-ordination of their separate but related activities became more and more apparent.

•

The law of self-preservation as applied to the infant industry of cattle-raising in Wyoming made itself felt in 1871. Laramie county, in which the town of Cheyenne was situated, and Albany county, which included the town of Laramie fifty miles west of Cheyenne, were then the principal cow country centers. In Albany county in 1870 there were five live stock firms with a total of 6,618 cattle valued at $98,390.[1] The

[1]Lola M. Homsher, thesis August 1949 *History of Albany County to 1880,* quoting county assessment book of 1870.

number in Laramie county was probably higher; one estimate has said there were 60,000 head of cattle within a 100-mile radius of Cheyenne in 1871, but a 100-mile radius of Cheyenne would of course take in Albany county as well as Laramie and a good chunk of Colorado and Nebraska.

By 1871 at any rate the industry was far enough along for organization, and the Laramie *Daily Sentinel* on April 13 of that year announced that a meeting for this purpose would be held at Laramie on the 15th by Albany county stock growers. At the meeting, Luther Fillmore presided and Frank Walcott was secretary. Among the other organizers were Judge J. W. Kingman, Ora Haley, George Fox, Hiram Latham, Charles Hutton and Thomas Alsop. The name adopted at the first meeting was the Wyoming Stock and Wool Growers Society, and its declared purpose was:

"To combine and work together for the attainment of certain objects, among which are to purchase in company upon a large scale, thereby buying and driving cheaper than can be done by persons singly. To form an association which will command influence in securing cheap rates of freight, and other advantages of this kind. To work together for the purpose of improving the breed in cattle, horses and sheep, by the importing of blooded stock in company, the benefit of which can be shared by all the members. To organize for the mutual protection of members against depredations upon stock. To disseminate knowledge in regard to the advantages and resources of this section for stock-raising, and to thus induce parties to invest capital in this business among us."

After a short time, the name of the organization was changed to the Wyoming Stock Graziers Association, and as such it functioned throughout 1871. Its first president was the first territorial governor of Wyoming, John A. Campbell. Vice-presidents were Thomas Alsop of Albany county, J. W. Iliff of Laramie county, E. Hunt of Carbon county, L. I. Field of Sweetwater county and W. A. Carter of Uinta county. Fillmore was treasurer, Latham secretary.

The Stock Graziers Association, short-lived though it was, obtained passage by the second territorial Legislative Assembly (Nov. 7 to Dec. 16, 1871) of the first law pertaining to the raising of live stock. This law defined the phrase "stock grower" as meaning "every person who shall keep neat[2] cattle, horses, mules, sheep or goats for their growth or increase." It also provided "protection of stock and punishment for certain offenses concerning the same."

Means of enforcing the new law, however, were inadequate. Transportation and communication were slow—"the law's a three days' ride"—and there were but few and widely scattered enforcement officers. Activities of the first and transitory organization were largely directed against depredations of cattle thieves operating out of the Black Hills. The Graziers Association passed out of the picture soon after the law of 1871 was passed, but it had served its purpose. It had shown the way.

Cattlemen of the city of Cheyenne and the nearby ranges began holding private meetings in 1872 to discuss their problems. At one such meeting, five men—Tom and John Durbin, R. S. Van Tassell, Charles Coffee and another whose name no one seems to know—decided to organize a vigilance committee to cope with rustlers who were operating in that area with ever greater daring. This meeting was held in a Cheyenne livery stable; Warren Richardson of Cheyenne, chairman of the Historic Landmarks Commission for Wyoming, said in July 1953 that this probably was the Jim Abney stable, which stood in the '70s on the northeast corner of Capitol Avenue and Sixteenth Street. This meeting was the first step in formation of the Stock Association of Laramie County, which later became the Wyoming Stock Growers Association.

The earliest written record of a meeting of the original Laramie county organization is dated November 29, 1873. It is in the handwriting of the secretary of the first meeting, W. L. Kuykendall.

Born in Missouri in 1835, Kuykendall held public office

[2]Webster gives this definition of the word "neat" in this sense: "Cattle of the ox kind, as distinguished from horses, sheep and goats; an animal of the genus *Bos*. 'The steer, the heifer and the calf are all called neat'—Shakespeare."

in that state at the age of 17, the office being that of deputy clerk for the circuit court and "deputy recorder of peace" in Platte county. In 1854 he moved with his parents to Kansas. After the Civil War, in which he became a major, he came west to Fort Collins, Colo., and 1867 found him taking part in the forming of the provisional government of the city of Cheyenne. Kuykendall was the first judge of probate in Laramie county, and after Wyoming Territory was organized, in 1869, he was a member of the lower House of the second Territorial Legislative Assembly.

The first recorded meeting of the Stock Association of Laramie County, genesis of the Wyoming Stock Growers Association, was held in Kuykendall's quarters in the county clerk's office at Cheyenne. His report of that meeting, preserved in the Association archives now at the University of Wyoming, at Laramie, reads as follows:

Minutes Stock Association.
November 29th, 1873.

At a meeting of Stock Men of Laramie County, Wyoming Territory, held at the County Clerk's office in Cheyenne on the 29th day of November 1873, M.V. Boughton was elected Chairman and W. L. Kuykendall Secretary.
On Motion of T. A. Kent, it was resolved to present a Bill for better protection of Stock and Stock interests in Laramie County.
On Motion of W. L. Kuykendall, Mess'. Orr, Kent, Coad, Durbin and Reel were appointed to draft rules and regulations for government of an Association of Stock Men hereafter to be organized also a law to present at the present session of the Legislature and that all Stock Men present sign an article for formation of Association. W. L. Kuykendall was added to said committee.
On Motion of John F. Coad, Secretary was instructed to notify Stockmen when next Meeting will be held.
On Motion of Mr. Kent meeting adjourned until Monday night at 1/2 past 7 o'clock.

W. L. Kuykendall, Secretary.

41

"This meeting was attended by nearly every cattleman in the county," Kuykendall wrote later in his autobiography, *Frontier Days*. Elsewhere the number present is given as eleven. Laramie county at that time extended from the southern to the northern border of Wyoming, and included most of the large ranches then in operation in the territory. North of the North Platte river was still Indian country, and only a few ranches were established there until after the opening of the Black Hills.

Kuykendall in his autobiography adds that "two or three" of the cattlemen refused to have anything to do with the formation of an organization for a year or two, "until they saw they might be able to use it to their own political advantage (which they did, claiming all the credit and according none to the real organizers). A permanent organization was effected at that meeting. I was made secretary and retained that position until I went to the Black Hills in the winter of 1875 to aid in wresting the country from the Indians." (He was also, in 1876, judge of the miners' court that tried Jack McCall for shooting Wild Bill Hickok at Deadwood.)

The M. V. Boughton who was first chairman of the Association served in that capacity for two years, when he too departed for the Black Hills. At one time mayor of Cheyenne, Boughton trailed the first cattle to the Custer, S. D., area,—where they were stolen by Indians. (Agnes Wright Spring in *Cow County*, issue of June 26, 1943, quoted this from the Chicago *Times* of May 2, 1876, via the Cheyenne *Leader*: "The Custer City correspondent writes to the Times: 'The first herd of beef cattle arrived yesterday, and I had the pleasure of eating steak at 20 cents a pound.' "

Twenty-five men were present at the second regular meeting of the stock men's association ("all intervening meetings being merely informal"), the record shows. It was not held until February 23, 1874. Kuykendall's minutes of this meeting show that "upon examination the following named stock men's names appear to the agreement or roll":

H. N. Orr	H. W. Devoe
M. V. Boughton	W. L. Kuykendall
Durbin Brothers	D. C. Tracy
T. A. Kent & Co.	M. A. Arnold
M. Taylor	A. H. Webb
A. H. Reel	John Sparks
G. A. Searight	J. Kelley
John F. Coad	Thomas McGee

The minutes add that the following "appeared and signed the agreement or roll as members":

D. H. Snyder, Maynard & Whitman, C. W. Wulfjen, Sturgis & Goodell, E. F. Boughton, I. H. Phillips, A. W. Haygood, Zachariah Thomasson and J. M. Carey and brother.

"Laws and regulations" were adopted. The first Monday in April, at 7 p.m., was set as the date for the annual meeting, the first Monday evening in each month for regular meetings.

"Admission fee" was fixed at $5, dues 50 cents a month.

At an adjourned session next day (February 24, 1874), the Association appointed Snyder, Carey, Maynard, Orr and Reel as a committee to draft laws for governing roundups, and instructed the secretary to ascertain the cost of printing 200 copies of the laws and regulations, then adjourned to meet the first Monday in April, in Recreation Hall, use of which had been tendered by "Mr. Arnold, secretary of the Recreation Hall Association."

This third meeting was on April 6, and thirteen members were present, twelve absent. The roundup committee reported a set of laws, which were approved section by section. Five proposed new members,—Mark M. Coad, L. A. Litton, Hiram B. Kelly, John Snodgrass and Hugh Jackson—were approved and "signed the agreement." The list of members present and absent is shown thus on the minutes:

PRESENT	ABSENT
H. N. Orr	Kent & Co.
M. V. Boughton	Taylor
John Durbin	Devoe
A. H. Reel	Arnold
G. A. Searight	J. Kelley

J. F. Coad
Kuykendall
Tracy
Webb
Sparks
Maynard
Goodell
Thomasson

McGee
Snyder
Wulfjen
E. F. Boughton
Phillips
Haygood
Judge Carey

On Monday, May 4, 1874, the Association held its fourth meeting; chief business was postponement of the roundup to June 15. There were no more meetings that year. The next was a special meeting, on February 13, 1875. Present were Boughton, Searight, Kent, Orr, Tracy and Kuykendall; absent, the "remaining members." Those present voted to assess members for payment of detectives employed by the Association, the assessments to be in proportion to the assessed valuation of the members' stock, "if such assessment or tax should become necessary in addition to the money in the treasury." This is the first reference in the minute books to action by the group on one big problem—cattle stealing—that had brought them together.

The annual meeting of 1875 was held April 5, and the following applied for membership, were voted on and accepted:

O. P. Goodwin, Thomas McShane, W. C. Moore, E. W. Whitcomb, T. M. Overfeldt, D. S. Shaw, William Lindenmeier, William Guiterman and N. J. O'Brien. O'Brien was Laramie county sheriff, and a special resolution was passed to make him a member.

The officers were re-elected, and the secretary was voted $60 as a year's salary. The Association decided to offer $200 for "apprehension and conviction of any person found killing or stealing cattle."

A meeting scheduled for Tuesday, April 6, 1875, was not held, because a quorum was lacking. The minutes show no more meetings until March 10, 1876, when "on motion by J. M. Carey a committee of three—Carey, Searight, and Swan—was appointed to consult with the county commissioners regarding employment of detectives under the new law and that no one besides said commissioners shall know detectives."

By this time, Kuykendall had pulled out to go to the South Dakota gold fields; Alexander H. Swan was secretary pro tem of the next recorded meeting, March 13, 1876. The committee on employment of detectives reported that the county commissioners had agreed to allow $150 a month for two months for this purpose. Three members—Searight, Kent and Swan—were named to procure a detective.

By the time of the next recorded meeting, April 3, 1876, the Association officers were Alexander H. Swan, president; G. A. Searight, vice president; Thomas Sturgis, secretary; and A. H. Reel, treasurer. Roundup plans occupied most of the attention at this meeting.

The annual meeting for 1877, held April 2, approved that year's roundup plan, appointed a committee to engage a detective, and adjourned to April 31, when the committee reported it had decided upon W. C. Lykins as "detective or inspector" with a recommendation to the county commissioners that they pay the inspector $150 a month. A committee of three including the president of the Association was given power to discharge the inspector "at any time, at their discretion."

The record is not clear as to identity of the detectives in 1874-5-6 and their exact time of service, but T. M. Overfelt, Henry Devoe and J. H. Ligget received pay during that time for detective-inspector work.

In 1878, Lykins was given an assistant, and the roundups were organized on a four-district basis.

•

At the 1879 meeting, numerous steps momentous in the Association's history were taken. It was then that the widening scope of the organization's influence was recognized and its name, on a resolution introduced by Thomas Sturgis the secretary, was changed to the Wyoming Stock Growers Association.

Creation of an executive committee took place at the 1879

meeting. The resolution creating it was again the handiwork of Thomas Sturgis. It provided for three members, "all residents of Cheyenne," to be elected by the Association, to serve for one year, and "to have entire control of the inspectors and all business of the Association during its adjournment, and represent the Association before the Legislature." By acclamation, Carey, Sturgis and Nagle were elected as the first executive committee.

The 1879 meeting made it impossible for a firm to be a member of the Association. Membership was in the name of individuals, and if more than one member of a firm wished to participate and vote, each had to become a member. The Association by now had cattle inspectors at Kansas City, Council Bluffs and Clinton, Ia. It adopted a resolution instructing its executive committee to seek from the territorial legislature "an enactment making it obligatory upon every man who shall hereafter turn out female neat cattle within this Territory to place with them at the time when he turned them out not less than five serviceable bulls, of the quality now provided by law, for every 100 head of female cattle two years old and upwards, and further that after the passage of such an act he shall within 12 months supply the same proportion of bulls to all female cattle of the above age that he may be the owner of." (The legislature did pass such a law.)

First discussion of the advisability of opening an Exchange Room for stock men in Cheyenne was held at this 1879 meeting. In 1881 it came into being, serving for several years as headquarters for members who did not have offices in Cheyenne, and also for representatives of commission firms, and otherwise serving cattlemen's interests during the buying season, June 1 to November 15.

The 1880 meeting was marked by a tripling of the "admission fee" and doubling of the annual dues; they now became $15 and $10.

•

The Association was not alone in its field by this time. At its 1881 meeting, it issued an invitation to stock associations elsewhere to unite with it in "one compact organization."

46

The invitation went to "the different associations of Wyoming Territory," the association of Weld county, Colorado, those at Rapid City and Deadwood, S. D., and the ones of Lincoln, Keith, Cheyenne and Sioux counties, Nebraska. The Albany County Stock Growers Association, formed at Laramie in 1877, at this time gave up its independent status and threw in with the larger Wyoming Stock Growers Association. In a few more years, the Association also included several Nebraska counties, and it was instrumental in furthering organization on a still wider scale in later years.

A change made in the wording of the stated purpose of the Association at its annual meeting in 1881 reflects the progress by the organization in its first years in obtaining legislation benefiting stock interests. As stated at the second meeting of the Association, February 23, 1874, the object of the Association had been:

"To advance the interests of stock growers and dealers in live stock of all kinds within said county and for the protection of the same against frauds and swindles and to prevent the stealing, taking and driving away of horned cattle, sheep, horses and other stock from the rightful owners thereof, and to provide means for protection of such interests."

By 1881 the Asociation had grown so that "within said county" was changed to "in said Territory," and the phrase "to provide means for the protection of such interests" was made to read "and enforce the stock laws of Wyoming." For now, thanks to the Association, there were laws to enforce.

The executive committee of three members which had been created at the annual meeting of 1879 grew to five members in 1880, and in 1881 was further enlarged to eleven, —five from Laramie county, two from Albany county, Wyoming, and two each from Cheyenne and Sioux counties, Nebraska. At this time the Sioux County Stock Association, in Nebraska, had disbanded and was taking steps to become a branch of the Wyoming association.

The executive committee as composed in 1881 was: For Laramie county, Carey, Sturgis, Davis, Swan and Searight; for Albany county, George Harper and H. G. Balch; for

Sioux county, Nebraska, Edgar Beecher Bronson (he wrote *Reminiscences of a Ranchman*) and G. L. Lawrence; for Cheyenne county, Nebraska, J. M. Adams and D. Sheedy.

The next year it was necessary to enlarge the executive committee again, as Uinta, Carbon and Johnson counties, Wyoming, were now ready to join the Association. The four officers now also were made members of the executive committee, which thus comprised a total of 19 men. (Today the executive committee consists of from two to four members from each of the 23 counties in Wyoming, a total of 70 men.)

The annual meeting of 1882 was marked by adoption of a resolution "discountenancing" the carrying of firearms "by those engaged in roundup and working of cattle, except in the immediate vicinity of Indian reservations." Toting guns, said the resolution, was "productive of great evil and frequently results in damage of person and property."

Among the powers given the executive committee in this period was the right to levy an assessment on the members, at any time but not oftener than once a year, of "not over one percent per head for all cattle, horses and mules of which each man may at that time be owner." Proceeds of any assessment were to go to the Association's general fund, and non-payment of an assessment was to be penalized by forfeiture of membership. Further, the Association had adopted a ruling by which, "after a fair and impartial hearing," a member could be expelled if he was found guilty by a majority of members present at a special meeting called for that purpose, or at an annual meeting, of anything that was "subversive of the interests generally of the Association," such as divulging proceedings of a meeting—this was the prerogative of the executive committee, which was regularly reporting to the press whatever it wished to have publicized—or committing "any act that may injure or defeat any proceedings or action of the Association or its officers."

The Association by now was an effective force in the principal matters that had brought it into being. It had got some system into the operation of the cattle industry, and it was helping the stock men to protect their herds. It had gone into

Ben Morrison, with his angora chaps and his Colt equalizer, dressed, looked and acted the part when he was running down rustlers in the late 'seventies and early 'eighties as a Wyoming Stock Growers detective-inspector. See Chapter Thirteen. (Kirkland photo.)

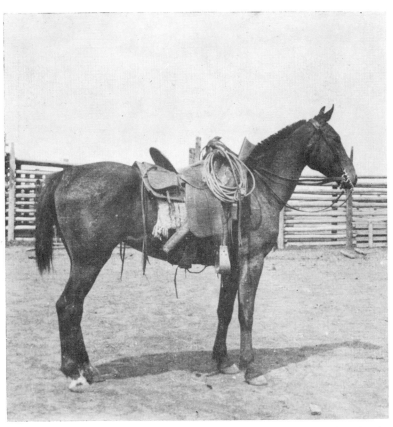

Ready to go! A cowhorse on the Oxford ranch, Laramie Plains, in the 1890s. (Photo from Robert H. Burns.) Writing in *Annals of Wyoming* January 1949, on "The Far West in the '80s," John James Fox, who came to Wyoming Territory from England in '85, said: "The good points of a cowpony were: A well-ribbed barrel with plenty of depth at the girth (behind the shoulder), denoting roomy lungs and the works to supply them. High at the withers, lean of shoulder, short in the back with muscular loins and not too short in the neck. Legs should have plenty of bone, flattish, of good quality, well set under him. Feet small and hoof dense. Fine tapering muzzle and large nostrils that will open up under stress of work. Good, full eyes with plenty of width between them, forehead slightly dished. Small jaw, small ears that are alert and move quickly, thin mane and tail."

Breaking horses on the JK ranch near Fort Washakie in 1902 was just plain work and no rodeo. In the top picture, Jake Ansell and a Shoshone Indian named Pas-se-ah-rope with the help of two other men are saddling a colt. The lower picture was taken shortly after Ansell climbed aboard. (Photos by J. K. Moore, Jr.)

Hi Kelly, who came west as a young '49er and made a fortune, which he later lost, in the cattle business on the Wyoming open range, cradled his cap-and-ball six-shooter in one arm as he posed for this picture, in 1855, when Hi was 21. His companion was unidentified in the daguerreotype. Kelly ranched on the Chugwater and shipped the first cattle east out of Wyoming by train in 1870. The story of his rise and fall is told in Chapter Seventeen. (Photo, unretouched, from his daughter, Mrs. Clara McCabe, Cheyenne.)

Some of the boys at the Bennett's Ferry ranch, Sand Creek Land and Cattle Co., Ltd., in July 1883. This was the old Pick outfit, whose former holdings are now under the Pathfinder reservoir. (Photo and data from Tom Sun.)

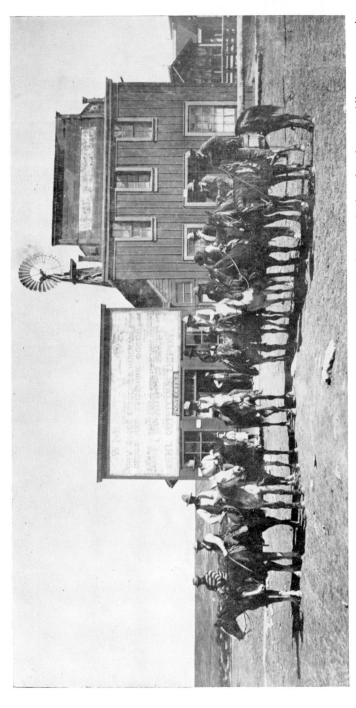

Old Rock River, early cowtown and shipping center on Rock creek, north of Laramie in what is now Albany county, in the 1880s. Rock River in the old days was known as Rock Creek. Any freight to Buffalo from the railroad was moved from here by ox teams. (Photo from Willing Richardson collection.)

This picture of a rancher inspecting his herds of half-breed cattle in the '80s was taken by C. D. Kirkland, pioneer Cheyenne photographer, and was No. 26 in his "Views of Cow-Boy Life."

Every face a story! U Cross cowboys at their chuck wagon in 1898. The brand was owned by the Pratt & Ferris Cattle Co., headquarters at the Big Red ranch, Clear creek, 30 miles southeast of Sheridan, Wyo. Left to right, standing: Fred Huston; a man known only as Tex; Bert Culivan, a bronco-buster; Bill Southers, manager; his son; and Archie Cameron, the cook. Seated: George Blake; an unidentified lad; Russell Bullock; Ed O'Connor; Ed. C. Brown, now of Huntley, Montana, who loaned this photograph; Bart Bethusem; Zeke Armington, wagon boss; and Frank Riley, day wrangler. (Photo by Mrs. Southers.)

politics in the first two years of its existence and was on its way to that dominance of legislative matters which it attained by 1882. It was logical and inevitable that it should be in politics. The men who were leaders in the cattle industry were likewise leaders in other phases of territorial life. Participation in governmental affairs was the only way by which they could attain the ends they sought for the protection and advancement of their means of making a livelihood.

•

Many years later—on June 7, 1944—when the records of the Wyoming Stock Growers Association were turned over to the Archives department of the University of Wyoming, at Laramie, for safekeeping, Dr. J. L. Morrill, then president of the University, pointed out the precedent for organization of the Association. He described how the Pilgrims, when they found themselves off the New England coast instead of farther south where they had hoped to land and where they would have held title and authority from the Virginia Company, gathered in the cabin of their little ship and drew up the Mayflower Compact.

"In that compact," said Dr. Morrill, "they agreed to constitute a 'civil body politic' to which each man pledged allegiance. This compact, though religious in its intent, became a civil covenant and the ancestor of American constitutions. This use of the religious covenant as a 'squatter' compact by Englishmen and Scotch Presbyterians in the American wilderness was to be repeated, over and over again through three centuries, from the Atlantic to the Pacific, as groups of pioneer-squatters, finding themselves beyond the reach of established law and government, proceeded to set up their own. It is a familiar pattern of the developing American democracy. The stock growers of the Western Plains repeated this same pattern. They contributed a unique chapter when again in the 1870s Americans and Englishmen and Scotchmen in a new wilderness, facing new problems—economic this time rather than religious or political—proceeded with self reliance, like the Pilgrim Fathers, to cope with them themselves."

CHAPTER EIGHT

UNCHALLENGED SOVEREIGN

The Association was fortunate during its first decade in having as leaders such men as Kuykendall, Swan and Sturgis, N. R. Davis and Judge Joseph M. Carey.

Alexander H. Swan, who was president of the Association from 1876 to 1881, came to Wyoming Territory in 1873 from Iowa, where he had been a dealer in live stock. In partnership with his brothers, Thomas (Black Tom) and Henry, and a nephew, Will F. Swan, he formed the Swan Brothers cattle company.

In 1880, Henry Swan and his son Will F. Swan sold out to Alexander H. and Thomas Swan, and went on their own, on the North Platte and the Snake rivers, where they ran the Ell Seven. Will F. Swan's son, Henry Swan, Denver banker, today is an honorary member of the Association, as well as a director of the Colorado State Historical Society.

Alexander H. Swan in 1883 organized the Swan Land and Cattle Company, largely with British and Scotch capital. It was incorporated for three million dollars. This company operated in Wyoming for 63 years, at one time controlling 600,000 acres of rangeland and running more than 100,000 cattle. Its main brand was the Two Bar.

Swan resigned as manager in 1887. The company was re-incorporated in Delaware in 1926 as the Swan Company, with John Clay as president. In 1947 its holdings, except for the home ranch at Chugwater—of which Curtis Templin in 1953 was still manager—were sold.

The Swan brothers brought the first Herefords into the West; Alexander H. Swan headed the Wyoming Hereford Association, which he organized in 1883. He was one of the organizers of the stockyards at Council Bluffs, Iowa, and was largely responsible for establishment of the Union Stock-yards at South Omaha. Coutant, the Wyoming historian, called him "one of the most remarkable men in the border-land."

Thomas Sturgis, who was the Association secretary from 1876 to 1887, was only a little less remarkable. Like Swan, he was a man of intellect and vision. He was eloquent in be-half of the Association, and principles he enunciated in its early days are still its guiding force.

Judge Carey brought to the organization the legal mind it needed in its formative days. He helped hold the organiza-tion together in trying times, and is also remembered for his humanitarian ideals. Carey was delegate from the Territory to Congress from 1884 till the end of the territorial period, and president of the Association from 1883 to 1887. His was the original CY ranch, near Casper.[3]

John B. Thomas of Crook-Weston counties, a member of the Association executive committee from 1889 to '94, has left his written impressions of the manner of men who com-posed the Association in its infancy. In 1915 he wrote:

"It was in the late seventies and early and middle eighties that the Association reached the zenith of its power and use-fulness. Then the open range included western Nebraska, southern Dakota, eastern Montana, southern Idaho, northern Colorado and the whole of Wyoming, with Cheyenne as the center of the range cattle business.

"The prospective profits of the cattle business and the pic-turesque life of the cowboys, who at that time were founding a type now renowned in song and story, attracted men from all walks in life and many nationalities. Englishmen like the Frewens, Irishmen like Horace Plunkett, and Scotchmen like John Clay were representative of many of their race who came to the great West to try for a fortune and with it to get a touch of real life.

[3]J. Elmer Brock says: "In the early days of Carey's operations, he had two other brands, one for the Horse Creek ranch and one for the ranch in Natrona county. One brand was SO and the other LD. When cattle were disposed of to remain in Wyoming, the vent used (to invalidate the brand) was to add the required other brand so as to make it read SOLD. The late Charles Carey told me this."

"Of Americans, nearly every city of every state in the Union had one or more of its citizens to share in the building up of a great country. Boston was largely represented, and there were so many Harvard graduates that a jocular cowboy once said that so far as he could see 'it took four years for a Boston feller to go through Harvard to fit him to come to Wyoming to learn cowpunching at $30 a month.' "

Meetings of the Association in those days, especially the annual sessions, must have been picturesque and exciting, pervaded by the color of the West and a sense of adventure and newness. Describing an annual meeting of the Association, Thomas wrote:

" 'Cattle Kings' and 'Cattle Barons' from all over the great range country, owners of thousands of cattle, and the 'little ranchman' with fifty or a hundred head, were there, all united by the one desire to do the best they knew for the business . . . Also came the managers and general freight agents of the railroads . . . the 'Texas men,' who had started their drives and 'had a few more head than they had contracted to dispose of,' and the men from Oregon who 'would sell a bunch of two-year-olds that are the finest on the range.' . . and the foremen of the various ranches, who were there to see that the roundups in their districts were arranged to their satisfaction. And the interested visitors, 'tenderfeet' perhaps, who contemplated buying into the business; and other strangers who came from curiosity to see how this great industry of cattle raising was controlled. All these made a gathering that taxed the capacity of the Courthouse. Three days were usually expended before all the business of the Association was transacted but the entire week and longer elapsed before the various elements had finished what they came for and departed."

Ernest Staples Osgood of the history department of the University of Minnesota in *The Day of the Cattleman* wrote in 1929 that from the time of the spring roundup of 1874, "the expansion of the range-cattle industry in Wyoming can be measured by the growth of the Association and the extension of its influence." For at least a decade, said Osgood, the

Association was "the unchallenged sovereign of the Territory of Wyoming," attaining a power that was never matched by similar organizations in other western states.

Another historian, W. Turrentine Jackson of Iowa State College, in a study of the WSGA dated 1946,[4] testified to the importance of the Association particularly in the period when the ranges were being opened. Its voice has been heard and its influence felt "continuously," said Jackson, but it reached the height of its influence "during the territorial period when it dominated the political scene and its will was law in Wyoming."

Jackson emphasized that the Association could never have exerted such influence had it not entered the political field. Important territorial officials, such as the governor and secretary, were in a position to block legislation essential to the cattlemen; the latter therefore set out not only to put their representatives in the Territorial Legislative Assemblies, but also to obtain the personal support of the chief executive's office. So successfully did the cattlemen function that, Jackson says, "the organization was generally considered the *de facto* territorial government."

The close alliance between the cattle industry and the state government is reflected in the fact that the first territorial governor, John A. Campbell, was also the first president of the first organization of cattlemen, whose brief existence predated formation of the Association. Furthermore, the Association was from the start well represented in the Territorial Legislative Assembly. This governing body was small; it was composed of a "Council" or upper chamber, and a lower "House." In the first session (1869), there were in the Council nine men representing four counties; in the House there were eleven members representing four counties and one representative-at-large. The eleventh Legislative Assembly, which convened in January 1890, the last session prior to statehood, had but twelve Council and twenty-three

[4]W. Turrentine Jackson, *The Wyoming Stock Growers Association: Political Power in Wyoming Territory, 1873-1890*, published in the *Mississippi Valley Historical Review*, Vol. 33, No. 4, and reprinted in *Annals of Wyoming*, Vol. 20, No. 1, January 1948.

House members, from ten counties. With a governing body this small, it was inevitable that the large and growing cattle industry, which had in its ranks so many men who were natural leaders, should be well represented. From 1875 to 1879, the Association had at least one of its members in each Legislative Assembly.

When, in March 1879, the Laramie county stockmen's organization became the Wyoming Stock Growers Association, it entered on a broader program which brought an increase in its membership to nearly 200. And by the time the seventh Legislative Assembly convened, in 1882, half the members of the Council were stockmen and at least a third of these were members of the Association; in the House, five of the eight representatives from Laramie county were Association members.

The Association thus attained political maturity. And it held this power through the territorial period. Among its members who were also in the Legislature were such men as Searight, Kuykendall, Reel, Coad, Sturgis, Irvine, Riner, Warren, Teschemacher and Adams. The results they obtained in behalf of the cattlemen may be measured in the laws the Assembly adopted during this period.

The stock bill of 1871, already mentioned, was followed in 1873 by an act regulating the branding, herding and care of cattle. This law, with subsequent amendments, provided the basic legal requirements for stock handling on the Wyoming ranges. It made stealing of horses or cattle a felony which it said "shall" be punished by imprisonment in the penitentiary not to exceed ten years and a fine not exceeding $5,000. It made misbranding, defacing or obliterating a brand a felony punishable by a $500 fine or five year's imprisonment "or both." Any person driving stock through Wyoming was to keep his cattle from mixing with those of resident stockmen. A drover responsible for driving stock from its accustomed range against the will of an owner was liable to indictment for larceny.

In the 1875 Assembly, this act was amended to permit county commissioners to appoint detectives to discover violations of the stock laws, the detectives to be paid from the county treasury. The detectives were to be selected only on recommendation of the county cattlemen's organizations. The 1877 Assembly transferred jurisdiction over the recording of brands from county clerks to a committee of three, of whom two were to be representative stockmen. Thus was officially begun what was through the years to be one of the most important functions of the Association, the inspection of live stock for the purpose of determining ownership.

The 1882 Assembly,[5] responding to a need for protecting the range from cattle diseases, passed an act to suppress and prevent the dissemination of contagious and infectious diseases among domestic animals. Here again the quasi-official status of the Association was recognized by a provision in the law requiring that the territorial veterinarian who was to execute this law should be named by the governor on recommendation of the Association. When there was evidence of disease outside the territory, the Association was to inform the governor, who was then required to proclaim exclusion of infected cattle.

The eighth Legislative Assembly, in 1884, after a fight which found the cattlemen themselves divided on some phases of the issue, enacted the Maverick Bill, which gave the Association complete responsibility for supervising round-ups. All mavericks—that is, unbranded cattle—were to be branded by the Association and sold to the highest bidder, proceeds to be turned over to the Association treasury to help pay the cattle inspectors. This law was basic in future activities of the Association.

The Association, by the end of its first decade, was riding high,—too high, some thought. The *Carbon County Journal,* in an editorial on April 14, 1885, expressed fear that the Association was seeking "to dictate to all cattle owners, whether members of the Association or not," and advised a

---

[5]Territorial Legislative Assemblies in Wyoming met in the autumns of odd years from 1869 to 1879 inclusive, but changed to January of even years beginning with 1882 and continuing through 1890, when the last Territorial Assembly was held. (Wyoming Historical Blue Book.)

more moderate course. The united cattlemen had enemies as well as friends.

Furthermore, economic troubles were piling up for them, and Nature itself was getting ready to hand them what almost proved a knockout punch. This was the winter of 1886-7.

CHAPTER NINE

WHITE DISASTER

Wyoming winters are never gentle, but the one of 1886 and '87 reached heights of horror hitherto unknown to cow country. Even the Indians, who had been there a long time, could not remember a worse one. They measured it in terms of suffering and of destruction of their pony herds, which were cut in half. Ranchers measured it in terms of dead cattle that strewed the plains when spring finally came. More than sixty years later, there was another terrible winter, but even then the losses were less.

The summer of 1886 had been hot and dry. Grass had not done well, and cattle entered the winter in poor condition. Heavy snow fell in November. In early January there was a chinook, but this gave false hope.

Blizzards began buffeting the Wyoming plains in late January and hammered away for weeks with wind, snow and cold that paralyzed ranch operations. Pinned down in their cabins and ranch houses by the merciless onslaught, men had only one thing to be grateful for: They could not hear the groans of their dying cattle, could not see the devastation that they knew was being inflicted on their herds. Those who did attempt to penetrate the storms to care for their stock were lucky if they managed to get back into their homes alive. Some didn't.

For two months, the wind blew from sun-up to sun-down. Ranch employees were found frozen to death near Sundance, Evanston and Stinking Water, according to reports in the Laramie *Boomerang*. The newspapers told of two men being blown from a handcar near Horse Creek station on the Cheyenne & Northern Railroad.

Drifting steers froze to death in temperatures twenty to thirty below zero, on wind-swept plains where snow was sixteen inches on the flat and drifted six feet deep. After the ordeal had continued for weeks, there was a brief let-up, followed by another storm that crusted the snow so hard that drifting cattle walked on top of it, searching in vain for grass, their hocks, chins and nostrils bleeding a trail of red in the vast whiteness.

When spring came, the cost could be seen, smelled and felt. Cattle carcasses littered the plains so thickly that a man could in some places have walked a considerable distance stepping from body to body. As the sun warmed the earth, the stench became so great that men going about their range work were sickened. For the first time in Wyoming's history, so far as anybody knew, there were flocks of buzzards hovering over the plains, lured from distant areas by the immensity of the fetid harvest.

Visible as the destruction was, its full extent was not realized at first. It varied greatly from place to place. John Hunton, Fort Laramie pioneer, said that probably the greatest loss occurred on the Laramie Plains and along the streams with sources in the Elk and Laramie mountain region; in the Goshen Hole country, south of Fort Laramie, which was considered ideal winter range, his loss was about 15 percent.

Thomas Durbin, a charter member of the Association, said in 1915: "The shortage of feed on the range in 1886 and the spring of 1887 made the loss from fifty to sixty percent of all cattle in Wyoming."

These figures, from assessors' books, show what happened in some areas; these are numbers of cattle assessed:

Laramie county:		*Johnson county*:	
1870	941	1881	67,351
1875	34,988	1885	174,172
1880	113,466	1886	157,931
1885	277,072	1887	141,286
1886	233,539	1888	91,740
1887	227,792		
1888	183,437		

John Clay in *My Life on the Range* said:
"It was not until the spring roundups that the truth was

discovered and then it was mentioned only in a whisper. Bobby Robinson, acute judge of conditions, estimated the loss among through cattle at less than 50 percent. It turned out to be a total loss among this class of cattle and the wintered herds suffered from 30 to 60 percent. I had gone to Europe in June, just as the roundups had commenced. I got back the first of August and for the first time heard of the terrific slaughter. It was simply appalling . . . The Continental Company was a shadow of its former self. The Worsham folks never attempted to gather their remnant. We gathered Major Smith's four-year-olds. Out of the 5,000 three-year-olds we got 100 head . . . The cowmen of the West and Northwest were flat broke. Many of them never recovered."

Dr. T. A. Larson, chairman of the history department at the University of Wyoming, after a study of the subject which was published in the *Annals of Wyoming,* January, 1942 (Vol. 14, No. 1), said that "although accuracy is impossible [because few official records were kept in those years] one is prompted to venture the opinion that estimates placing the Wyoming losses at 80 and 90 percent are fantastic. Some herds suffered losses of 80 and 90 percent; but loss for the whole of Wyoming Territory would seem to lie somewhere not far above 15 percent. A more specific approximation seems unwarranted by the evidence."

Assessment figures, in Dr. Larson's opinion, are unreliable in this instance, for one reason because some cattle growers through political influence obtained lower assessments than they should have had. The decline in numbers does not tell the whole story, he added, because many animals that survived were set back months. This probably contributed to the decision of the assessors to slash the valuation of cattle from $14,651,125 in 1886 to $10,186,362.75 in 1887, a reduction of 30 percent in value as compared with a decrease of only 15 percent in number. The assessment figures in numbers of cattle (from the territorial governor's report for 1886-89) :

1884_____749,569
1885_____894,788
1886____ ____889,121
1887_____753,648
1888_____724,737

"A summary statement," Dr. Larson wrote, "must recognize that the winter of 1886-7 had a terrific impact upon Wyoming. Losses were magnified by the fact that those who lost were often hard pressed by creditors and had to liquidate as best they could in a market ruinously low. Between 60,000 and 70,000 head of stock were shipped during the summer and fall of 1887." That winter, in Larson's words, "brought Wyoming stockmen back to earth." There were one third as many cattle in the Territory in 1894 as there had been in '86.

For one of the conditions that helped bring them back to earth when the tragic winter struck, cattlemen themselves were to blame. They had overcrowded their ranges.[6] Eager to cash in quickly on the "big bonanza," some ranchers had purchased young eastern stock at high prices and thrown them in with their native cattle. There was some mismanagement, and there was much absentee ownership, involving speculation and lack of intimate knowledge of conditions. In some instances, huge sums had been invested in cattle on "book count," that is, on paper figures which were inflated, for one reason or another, far beyond the actual number of cattle on the ranges involved.

[6]A letter from F. E. Warren to Thomas Sturgis, American Cattle Trust, Room 12, at 120 Broadway, New York, dated Cheyenne, Wyo., July 10, 1887, is in the Association files; it says: "From all I hear, fully half the cattle in the Powder river country, as well as from the Platte over, perished the last Winter. This arose from two causes: Eaten out ranges and hard winter. Neither one alone could have produced such havock (sic). A few years ago when I was conversant with that northern country from Ft. Fetterman to Montana, everybody was throwing cattle north, and Powder river, Ft. Fetterman, etc., had a reputation from Oregon to Texas, and the consequence was the worst overstocked ranges probably in Wyoming. The past Winter has done two things, in fact three: Reduced the number of cattle to a point where they will winter safely; frightened the whole country from driving cattle in there; and gives a splendid growth of grass this year which really renews the range."

High interest rates were a factor. Struthers Burt in *Powder River* wrote: "The open range didn't last long; it couldn't. The interest on your money was too high; the life was too alluring and, in most ways, too easy; the handling of cattle was too negligent and grandiose." There might be some argument over parts of that statement, but there is ample proof of high interest rates. Three percent a month, or 36 percent a year, was standard in the 1870s. C. F. Coffee in 1915 said his cattle company was "almost tickled to death" in 1873 when it was able to make a loan at two percent a month or 24 percent a year.

Depression had begun to hit the cattle industry in the autumn of 1886. Even a normal winter would have been hard on the business. The savage winter of early 1887, coming on top of already adverse economic conditions, knocked many cowmen out of the ring and set them all back on their heels.

CHAPTER TEN

CHAMPION OF THE COWMAN'S CAUSE

Liquidation that hit the ranges in the summer and autumn of 1887 saw from sixty to seventy thousand cattle shipped out of Wyoming alone. Disposing of the survivors of the disastrous winter cleared some of the ranges completely. Prices at Chicago were down, as the result of enforced sales and crowded markets. There was a lessened demand for cattle, due to a falling-off of industrial activity in other parts of the country, and to strikes, as well as to a dry summer and resultant small corn crop, a lack of ready money and the prevalence of commercial failures. Some of the ranchers who went broke at this time regained their riches later, though the general depression of the late '80s and early '90s delayed recovery.

Elwood Mead, Wyoming's first state engineer, in his third biennial report (to Gov. William A. Richards) dated November 30, 1896, and covering the years '95-'96, gave figures which graphically show what happened to the range industry. In 1886, the assessed value of Wyoming cattle was $14,651,125. In 1896, it was $3,732,558, an average loss for the ten years of over a million dollars a year. Cattle diminished in numbers from nearly 900,000 in 1886 to less than 300,000 in 1896. There was an increase of two million dollars in the assessed valuation of sheep, which partly offset the eleven million dollar shrinkage in cattle, leaving a net loss in the valuation of range stock of over nine million dollars, or nearly a million dollars a year. Engineer Mead commented: "All this shrinkage has been in range stock. Irrigated land supports more cattle than it did ten years ago. There are less cattle because there is less grass. In many parts of the state, ten acres will not (in 1895) furnish the feed supplied by one acre a decade ago."

The period of disaster was followed by a transitional era which brought many changes to cow country. The open range was still there, more than 80 percent of Wyoming being in the public domain in 1890. But the stock growers were forced to develop many new methods, in which use of the open range was only a part of the program. The days of easy profits and rapidly expanding herds were gone. The Laramie *Weekly Sentinel* on July 1, 1876, had quoted Horace Greeley as saying that in Wyoming a steer could be raised as cheaply as a chicken, but this was suddenly no longer true. Cattlemen faced the necessity of reducing the size of their operations, eliminating waste, and turning to the production of hay and the improvement of pastures and forage crops instead of depending solely on natural grass. Acreage devoted to hay increased more than tenfold in Wyoming from 1880 to 1890. Some of the larger operators began raising sheep, combining, as they did with their cattle, the summer pasturage of the open range with the winter feeding of hay. Development of irrigation began; in some instances crop production under irrigation was combined with stock raising. Small farmers—grangers, the stockmen called them—were infiltrating the ranges, plowing up quarter-sections and planting crops,—and coming into conflict with the cowmen, in some cases (as in Johnson county) with tragic consequences.

With the rest of the West, the Association fell on desperate days. Its annual meeting in 1887 was sodden with discouragement. The president, vice-president and secretary did not even attend. Membership had dropped from 443 to 363. Abandonment of the organization was considered.

But instead of folding, the Association held together around a few stout-hearted leaders. Thomas B. Adams, who became acting secretary, was one of those who emerged as leaders in the period of crisis.

"It is in times like these," he told the cattlemen, "that all who have the welfare of the Association at heart should rally to its support." And Alexander H. Reel, accepting his sixth term as treasurer, at the annual meeting in 1889, said:

"I do not feel discouraged. All businesses have their depressions and reverses, and we had no right to expect ours would be an exception. We have seen our darkest day, and if this Association will take hold we can protect one another. There is no use in lying down or giving up."

His words of assurance were needed, for no longer did the Association have control of the legislature. There were too many grangers in the Assembly, and too many cattlemen who opposed the Association. Thomas Moonlight, territorial governor[7] from 1887 to '89, was himself a granger. He rejoiced at the plight of the Association and aided the political opposition that sought, now that the organization was weak, to kill it off. The "unchallenged sovereign" of the Wyoming ranges was being challenged to a fight for its life.

Repeal or amendment of the Maverick law, which gave the Association control over roundups and cattle inspection, became a threat. Facing this, Adams and other leaders of the Association fought to save the law by rewriting it and adjusting it to the changing times. They worked out a bill which established a territorial board of live stock commissioners, making the roundup foremen territorial officers and providing for enforcement through territorial authorities. The legislation was enacted, over Governor Moonlight's veto, thus transferring protection of the range to an official board on a basis accepted by the Association, and proving that there still was life in the organization. The legislature of 1888 did, however, considerably curtail the powers of the cattlemen, and increased taxation of live stock on the open range.

Furthermore, it granted no funds to the live stock commission which it had created.

The Association, through its executive committee, provided the commission with money to conduct the spring roundups of 1888, and at the annual meeting in 1889 instructed its legislative committee to draft an act bolstering the commission and placing it on a sound financial footing. In the 1890 Legislative Assembly, the Association succeeded

[7]While Wyoming was a territory (1869-1890) its governors were appointed by the President of the United States with the advice and consent of the Senate. Of the ten territorial governors, all were republicans except Thomas Moonlight, who was a democrat. (Wyoming Historical Blue Book.)

in restoring many of the laws which the previous session had repealed, and paved the way for reorganizing, simplifying and codifying all stock legislation of the territorial period then ending.

The leaders of the Association were adaptable enough to accept their changed status. By curtailing political activity and by such measures as riding to the rescue, so to speak, of the stock commission and the roundup system, the Association regained friends and prestige.

As Wyoming entered statehood, in 1890, the Association was at the low point of its career, with a membership of only 183 and a treasury of but $29.

But it was still in the ring ready to fight its way back to greatness as guardian and champion of the cowman's cause.

Powder River Cattle Company. Limited.

P. O. ADDRESS: SUPERIOR, WISCONSIN.

RANGES : Powder River and Tongue River, Johnson Co., Wyoming, and Mosquito Creek, Alberta, N. W. T.

ALSO, OWN BRANDS

97, —<∨, ꝏ, KC, CDK, ꝏ, Ⴀ, I, K, ꓘ, WPH, ꝏ, WH, WH, WH, Ⴑ

ON LEFT SIDE OR HIP.

Letterhead (1887) of one of the pioneer Wyoming cattle companies. Moreton Frewen was manager of the Powder River Cattle Company

PART THREE

RUSTLERS AND RUNNING IRONS

CHAPTER ELEVEN

THE OLD HANDS DID THE BRANDING

I like the old cowman who always told his men at branding
time, "Put it on good, boys, she'll wear it all her life!"

—Inspector Murphy.

All the lore and legendry of the old days of the open range
is there, for those who can feel it, in the brands that still are,
even in these days of tourists and dude camps, so much a
part of the Wyoming scene.

There are brands burned into the woodwork of the bars
and cafes; brands are the decorative motif on luncheon sets,
napkins and cocktail glasses sold in the gift shops. The covers
of western books are printed over with brands thick as tracks
in a horse corral. Brands are on signposts that stand beside
pole gates where lonesome dirt roads lead from paved highways toward ranches hidden in the hills.

Brands are not an affectation. In the days of the untamed
range they were as necessary as grass and water. Tourists
—did they but know it—can do more than smile amusedly
at the brands they see broadcast through Wyoming: They
can reach out and touch them, and when they do, they
touch yesterday.

Use of brands as a means of identifying live stock goes back
into the mists of antiquity. The word itself comes from
Medieval and Anglo-Saxon times. Today in America, brands
are usually associated with western states; they came in with
the cattle the Spaniards brought into the Southwest in 1540.
But they are not exclusively western. General George Washington, in a letter to his dragoon commanders on October 25,
1777, directed that "all the horses in your corps, in the use of
non-commissioned officers and privates, not already stamped

69

with the Continental brand, are without loss of time to be brought to the Quartermaster General to receive that brand." There is said to be, somewhere else in Washington's writings, a reference to his having sent "1 bull, 18 cows and 5 calves to Dogue Run. In all 24 head, branded on ye buttock G. W."

Some of the early Wyoming cattlemen, when it came to burning ownership marks into the hides of their herds, were more original and imaginative than George Washington was. They had to be. There were a great many more cattle and cattlemen in Wyoming in the 1870s than there were in Virginia a hundred years previously, and the herds intermingled far and wide on the unfenced ranges. For his brand, a man needed something distinctive, difficult to alter or imitate, and easy to remember. If a symbol, number, letter or combination of elements could be devised which was readily associated with the owner, so much the better.

Thus Richard Ainsworth, when he located in 1880 on the site of the Pitchfork ranch in present Park (formerly Sweetwater) county, had recently come from his native England and so he chose the royal crown, or a fairly reasonable facsimile thereof, as the mark to go on "ye buttocks" of his cattle. It looked like this:

Another Englishman, who for years was prominent in the Powder river country, was Moreton Frewen, and his brand is said to have represented the year he first became interested in the American cattle country. It was just a hundred years after George Washington sent his twenty-four head to Dogue Run. The Frewen brand—now owned by George S. Hesse of Buffalo, Wyo., whose father was Frewen's foreman—was

76

When, like Washington, they did use their initials or letters from their names for their brands, the men of the plains usually gave it some kind of a twist. Joseph M. Carey, first

United States attorney for Wyoming, later United States senator and governor of the state, in 1872 founded a brand after which CY avenue was named, in the city of Casper, which was laid out on one of the Carey ranches. Carey used the first and last letters of his name, but in later years one of them was laid down and the brand was called the C Lazy Y:

J. W. Iliff, first of the "cattle kings" of the plains ranges,[1] who operated mainly in Colorado but in 1867 trailed a herd into Wyoming from Texas, in partnership with Snyder brothers, also used two letters from his name but turned one of them around, thus creating the Reverse LF Connected:

Many of the early brands were derived from familiar objects, such as the Hoe (this ranch was established near the mouth of Nine Mile creek on Powder river in 1880; its foreman George Wellman was one of the victims of the Johnson County War in 1892) ; the Umbrella (1878, range La Prele creek, Upper Box Elder and Bed Tick) ; the Door Key (1884, Frank M. Foote, a member of the Wyoming constitutional convention) ; and the Hats, of which there were two:

In Mexico, in the early days, brands frequently took graceful, artistic lines whose stem or foundation stroke was

[1]For an interesting and documented account of Iliff's career, see "John Wesley Iliff," by Edward W. Milligan, in the Annual Brand Book published by the Denver Westerners in 1950 (University of Denver Press). Milligan says Iliff at his peak had nine separate ranches, a range a hundred miles long and 26,000 head of cattle. He could travel from Greeley to Julesburg and eat and sleep on one of his own ranches all the way.

Hogarth's classic "line of beauty." Among such Mexican brands were Las Loreles and Flor de Tulip:

In 1857, John Walker Myers settled on Bear river in Wyoming at what was later known as Myers Crossing. He had a few horses and cattle, and when he felt the need of a brand he turned, at a friend's suggestion, to a shorthand system's M hook, embellishing it first with a quarter circle and later giving the ends of the quarter circle a little upturn, arriving at these flowing lines, which surely Hogarth would have liked:

This was meant to be known as the M Hook brand, but some called it what it looked like to them: Yoke Nine. It is still in use—the oldest Wyoming brand of which that can be said, although many in the state are being used by the third generation.

Two historic Wyoming brands made use of the letter M. One was the Rolling M on stock owned by Eliza A. Kuykendall, wife of the first secretary of the Wyoming Stock Growers Association. Judge Kuykendall in his memoirs says his wife "brought a few cows and other cattle with her when she and my two sons, then small children, crossed the plains in wagons to Denver in 1866. The cattle were driven to my ranch when the family moved to Cheyenne in 1867." The Rolling M—

M

was transferred on March 27, 1884 to the Wyoming Stock Growers Association to be used on the left side of the neck in marking mavericks in the roundups, and hence came to be known officially throughout the state as the Maverick brand. Transfer of the brand to the Association was in accordance with a law enacted by the Eighth Legislative Assembly of the Territory of Wyoming convened in January, 1884.

The M Bar brand, variously written

$$ \text{M--} \qquad \underline{\text{M}} \qquad \text{M--} $$

was originally the property of J. K. Moore, post trader at Fort Washakie, who started using it there about 1875. Later he took Captain R. A. Torrey into partnership, and when this brand was first listed with the Wyoming Stock Growers Association in 1881 it was in Torrey's name. Years later the brand was listed as belonging to the Embar Cattle Company of Duluth, Minn., and Embar, Wyo.

Other towns—such as Kaycee, JayEm and Ucross—took their names from early-day brands, of which there were an endless variation, including the Olive Leaf of the Brock family, the Revolving H or Damfino brand of Russell Thorp; the TY Connected, the Hog Eye and the Flying Circle of the Keelines, second oldest in the state in point of years under the same brand and family ownership; the O Ten Bar of the Coffees, the Searight Goose Egg, the Bug brand of Mary E. Carter, wife of Judge W. A. Carter and first white woman to become a permanent resident of Wyoming; Teschemacher and DeBillier's Duck Bar, Tom Sun's Hub and Spoke, the Tillotson Fiddleback, Sturgis and Lane Bridle Bit, Count Thomas Creighton's Boot brand, the Circle Dot of Gilchrist, Plunkett and Newton, and Spectacle brand of H. W. (Hardwinter) Davis.

As the variety and complexity of the brands increased, in the days when the cattle industry was growing up, it became necessary to have some sort of registry. This was provided as early as 1869 by the Territorial Legislature which in that year enacted a law requiring not only that "every person having cattle, hogs, sheep or other live stock shall have a mark or brand, different from the mark or brand of his neighbors," but also that every such owner "shall deliver to the county clerk a description of their brand or mark, and such clerk shall record same in a well-bound book kept by him for that purpose."

In the files of the WSGA there is a large ledger in which A. M. McIntosh, clerk of what was then Sweetwater county, began recording cattle brands in pen and ink on May 6, 1872, the first brand so registered being that of James Reed, a heart with its lines curled outward at the bottom.

County Clerk McIntosh kept his record book till 1876, by which time better methods had come into use. In Laramie county, during this same period, brands were being similarly registered in a smaller book which does not bear the name of the official who compiled it. Also it was customary in the late '70s for ranchers to run illustrated advertisements in the newspapers, showing their brands and defining their ranges. The Cheyenne *Daily Leader* on October 5, 1877, called attention to this service in an item reading:

"Stock growers will find on our second page a column filled with cuts of shapely Texans, marked with each owner's brand. We are prepared to get up cuts and brands as shown in the column referred to on short notice. Every stock owner should advertise his brand in the mammoth Weekly Leader, which has an immense circulation among the ranches of the frontier . . . "

In 1882, after long and serious work by some of its members who had been appointed under a territorial law to serve as brand committee for Laramie county, the Association published a little book bound in cowhide which listed 156 brands then in use in Wyoming. This was the first Brand Book; it was printed in Chicago. The Association issued new editions in 1883, '84, '85 and '87. By 1890, the Board of Live Stock Commissioners had come into being, so the Association brand committee was discontinued.

In 1909 the Legislature passed a law requiring state brand recording, and made this a function of the State Board of Live Stock Commissioners. All brands of record in counties were certified to the Board, resulting in many duplications in the state records. The Legislature of 1933 consolidated the Board of Live Stock Commissioners, the State Board of Sheep

74

Commissioners and the office of State Veterinarian into the Wyoming Live Stock and Sanitary Board, giving the new board supervision over all live stock sanitary matters, with authority to establish quarantines when necessary, and to record brands, and supervise both brand and sanitary inspection at the live stock auction sales within the state. The law under which this board functions has been taken as a model by several other states. The late Dr. H. D. Port was for many years secretary of the board and chief veterinarian. Upon his death in 1944 Dr. G. H. Good, who had been his assistant and also had the experience of private practice, became chief executive officer and chief veterinarian, and he still holds the office. Among his accomplishments was establishment of the Wyoming State Veterinary Laboratory in co-operation with the University of Wyoming in the Veterinary-Parasitology building at the University Stock Farm, Laramie.

State law now requires re-recording of brands during each year that ends in 5. The next re-recording will be in 1955, the fee five dollars. Publication of an official brand book is also required, following each re-recording. The first state brand book, published in 1912, listed 9,427 brands in Wyoming. In 1916, the number was approximately 14,400; in 1919 it was 22,000; in 1927 it was 16,000; in 1946 it was 19,500. In 1953 the actual number of brands on record in Wyoming was 22,500.

•

Putting brands on cattle "so they could be read by moonlight" was and still is an important part of the cowman's work. Out of long experience, he evolved a set of rules.

Use a hot iron, the oldtimer will tell you—but don't let it get red hot, or it will set the hair afire. An iron the color of ashes is just right and ready for use—and it works best when heated in a wood fire. Don't use a thin or burned-up iron; it will cut too deep or make a thin scar that covers with hair. Burn just deep enough to take off the hair and the outer layer of skin.

When you lift the iron, the brand should be the color of a new saddle.

Use big brands—as big as they will go on the designated part of the critter, jaw, ribs or hip.

And don't put a hot iron in the hands of an amateur—let the pistols (cow country lingo for beginners) do the calf wrestling and holding, while the old hands do the branding.

CHAPTER TWELVE

THE ROUNDUP WAS THE PAYOFF

No. 26. Known as Bitter creek roundup, meet at Fort Steele, May 26, working all the country between Sage creek and the railroad, as far as the mouth of Muddy creek, in connection with No. 25, and then divide, roundup No. 26 working as far west as Green river and back on north side of the Union Pacific railroad to Bell Springs. Fall roundup to begin October 1. W. S. Weaver, foreman.

—Roundup directions for one of the
31 Wyoming districts, 1884.

Once the cattle were branded and turned loose to graze, their owner saw little of them, in the open range days, except at roundup time. This came twice a year,—spring and fall.

This was when the rancher counted his calf crop, when he branded, ear-marked and castrated his calves; when he gathered the beeves to be sold and trailed them off for shipping to market. It was semi-annual inventory and payoff, the twice-a-year climax in the process of growing cattle, when every cow on the ranges had to be tallied and accounted for.

This was when students of cowcraft passed their finals. Horse, man and equipment were put to the test. It was exciting, it was "glamorous," of course. There was fun in it, and risk and suspense and drama: Men were often hurt, riding the rough country, and many a horse's neck was broken in a roundup tumble.

Basically, however, it was hard work, and vital work that had to be done right if a cowman was to realize the profit that was his due for capital and labor invested; it was for this reason that one of the first acts of the Association was to bring order and system into the chaotic roundup methods that first existed.

The cattle drifted far, in many cases into neighboring states, and intermingled with the herds of other ranches. They all had to be hunted out and gathered on big flats where the herds could be worked. The cowboys rode in wide circles to find them, dividing the work among crews so that every foot of ground was searched for strays. Sometimes cows had to be dragged from mudholes; sometimes they had to be driven from dense brush. No secluded spot, no dry creek bed or badland arroyo, no wooded hill dared be overlooked. Sagebrush flats and verdant valleys alike were combed for cattle.

Cows of each owner had then to be cut out from the gather, branded and tallied. Kicking and bawling, calves were dragged to the branding fires in a maze of dust and smoke and a medley of human and animal noises, given the works and then turned loose till the next roundup.

It took four or five weeks, sometimes more, to complete a roundup. The chuck wagon fed the crews; the wranglers kept the horse herds together, fed and watered—a string of six to ten horses per man, for only by frequent changes could horseflesh meet the demands of roundup time. It was taken for granted that the men could do so.

Foremen were paid (in 1880) $8 a day. The Association gave the foremen full authority to exact obedience to orders from all men taking part in the roundups, penalty for not carrying out orders to be exclusion from participation in future roundups. Dates for the roundups were set as early in the spring as the grass and the condition of the cattle allowed their being handled.

•

In the beginning, in Wyoming, roundups were individual or neighborhood affairs,—a neighborhood in this instance of course being a couple of hundred square miles or so. As the cattle industry grew in size and importance, a better pooling of efforts had to be arranged. Individual roundups had already been prohibited by law in the older state and cattle country to the south, Colorado, "with the increase of safety and profit to all cattlemen," the Association pointed out in support of its program for systematizing things in Wyoming.

The Roundup was the Payoff

The Territorial Legislature began injecting order into the cattle industry when, accepting the suggestions of the Association, it passed laws, in the late 'seventies, governing marks and brands, organization of the roundups and determination of maverick ownership, and otherwise controlling cattle on the ranges. Individualism gave way to economic necessity, and cooperation was forced upon the "sooners," the rugged individualists who had been rounding up and branding whenever they felt like it, often without giving neighboring ranchers an opportunity to examine cattle before they were driven to market, or to check the ownership of calves before they were branded.

The first organized roundups in Laramie county were held in 1874, the spring following formation of the county association. (In Albany county, it was three years later that the first organized roundup was held.) Rules governing the roundups were drawn up by a committee, and approved by the Association members assembled on April 6. The roundup was divided into two parts, Upper and Lower, John Snodgrass being foreman of the former and Andrew Kerr of the latter. The same set-up prevailed in 1875.

Minutes of the meeting of April 3, 1876, show that on motion of Snodgrass that year S. K. Johnson was to have control of the Upper roundup, which was "to commence April 25 at Johnson and Walker's ranch on Horse Shoe and round up all cattle north of the Laramie river, roundup to begin again at the mouth of the Chug May 25 and round up to the Colorado line under control of A. H. Swan; Lower roundup to begin at the A. H. Reels old ranch May 20 and to work east to Pine Bluffs, thence to Pawnee Buttes and there meet the Weld county roundup, thence go to Antelope Station and meet the Cheyenne county roundup, thence work north under the control of John Snodgrass."

By 1878 it had become necessary, due to the increase of cattle, to have four roundups for Laramie county; they were known as the Northwestern, Southwestern, Pole creek and Lower Horse creek roundups. Mitchell Oxarart was foreman in the Northwest, W. C. Lykins (who became famous as a stock detective) in the Southwest, D. E. Brown on Pole creek and G. B. Goodell on Lower Horse creek.

In two more years there were six roundup divisions, and by 1884—the Association in 1879 having become the Wyoming (rather than the Laramie county) Stock Growers Association —there were 31 roundups covering Wyoming cow country.

The area in each district was defined by natural boundaries which usually followed the watercourses. District 15, for example, covered the Cheyenne river and all its tributaries west of Hot Springs, South Dakota. A. A. Spaugh was foreman and Curtis E. Spaugh assistant foreman "to the mouth of Black Thunder; Lee Moore foreman and J. B. Moore assistant foreman from the mouth of Black Thunder to the end of the roundup." A. A. Spaugh, in a letter written just fifty years afterward (May 14, 1934) and printed March 1, 1946, in *Cow Country,* said the district No. 15 roundup alone gathered and worked 400,000 cattle in six weeks, in 1884. Twenty different cattle outfits took part, represented by 200 cowboys with 2,000 horses. The crews started from Hat Creek station on Sage creek, on the Cheyenne-Black Hills stage line.

•

Edgar Beecher Bronson came to Cheyenne by train in the early 1870s as pretty much of a tenderfoot, to learn to be a cowboy in the hard school of a roundup on the N. R. Davis horse ranch on Owl creek (in later years, Bronson was a member of the executive committee of the WSGA). In his *Reminiscences of a Ranchman,* Bronson relates the instructions Davis gave him as they drove out to the ranch in the Davis buckboard:

"I'm not going to favour you. You've got to take your medicine with Con Humphrey's outfit (said Davis), and he's about as tough a rawhide as ever led a circle. But he always gets there, and that's the only reason I keep him. It's lay close to old Con's flank, Kid, and keep your end up or turn in your string of horses. On the roundup no soldiering goes; sick or well, it's keep up with the bunch or be set afoot to pack your saddle; there's no room in the chuck wagon for a quitter's blankets, and no time to close herd sick ones . . . . Don't start out unless you have the guts to stand it."

The roundup on which young Bronson cut his eye-teeth was to go down Willow creek to the Pawnee country. When Bronson finally reached the roundup crew, he says:

"A merry fire blazed at the tail end of the chuck wagon. About it were sitting sixteen punchers, feeding from tin plates and cups, gorging on beans, beef, and baking-powder biscuits, washed down with coffee strong enough to float an egg, men with the ferocious hunger of the wolf and the case-hardened stomach of an ostrich. They were of all ages, from sixteen to sixty, but most of them under thirty, all grimy with the dust, and several reeking with the blood of the day's work in the corrals."

After a night's sleep on "the lumpy mattress of buffalo grass," Bronson began taking part in the early-morning roundup activities, which he described thus:

"Breakfast over, in twenty minutes camp kettles, war sacks and beds were loaded into the chuck wagon, horses caught and saddled, and we were mounted and headed southeast for Willow Creek.

"N. R. had assigned me a string of five horses, all kind and gentle, and unusually good ones, I later realized, to intrust to a tenderfoot.

"Average hands were never assigned less than four horses each for range round-up work, and top hands who had the heavy work of 'cutting' the round-ups, separating the cattle wanted from those not wanted, rarely less than seven or eight horses. And there were never too many horses, seldom enough. Lacking corn and all other fodder but the native grasses, it was only by frequent change of mounts and long intervals of rest for each that they could be kept in fair flesh, strong of wind and limb and sound of back. In the saddle from dawn to dark, and then riding a two to three hours' turn at night guard round the herd in hand, fifty to seventy miles a day was no more than an average distance daily covered by the average cowboy on the round-up; and throughout a third to sometimes more than half the day the pace was the ponies' top speed, handling and turning wild cattle bent on escape.

"Thus by the noon finish of a morning circle sides were lathered, flanks drawn, strength and wind gone, and fresh mounts necessary, while during the afternoon's work of 'cutting' the herd, the pace was so killing for the top cutters, with the terrible shock of sudden sharp turns and short stops, that one or two changes were always desirable."

•

In those years cattle sent to market each year from Wyoming ranges would run from 120,000 to 180,000 head, according to a memoir of Thomas F. Durbin, an early member of the Association, written in 1915. Durbin added: "It was said of the Association when it had its greatest meetings that its membership represented a value of one hundred million dollars." This statement may be checked against figures preserved in the Association minute books, from a report made by Thomas Sturgis, secretary in 1882, covering an assessment levied on Association members that year. The figures used as a basis for the assessment (the report calls it a one-mill tax, and says it was levied by the Association to meet expenses caused by the necessary killing of livestock because of an outbreak of pleuro-pneumonia) showed the total number of neat cattle in the six counties then comprising Wyoming to be 476,274, of which the largest part, 190,963, were in Laramie county. Total value of the 476,274 cattle was given as $6,942,851.50. Secretary Adams' report said these figures might not be exactly correct but that they were considered accurate enough to serve as a basis for the assessment.

It was in the year (1884) of the first of the big general roundups on the open range that the Maverick law went into effect (Laws of Wyoming Territory, 1884, Sess. 8, pp. 148-152). This defined mavericks and made them the property of the Association, to be sold at auction during the roundups, each maverick thus sold to be marked immediately with the brand of its purchaser. Money derived from the maverick sales went to pay the inspector-detectives hired by the Association to enforce the law and otherwise guard the interests of the members.

This was the beginning of the system of market brand inspection which is still so vital a part of the Association's work.

The roundup system instituted under the Association continued through the 1880s to the time of the disaster and depression that hit the ranges in the last years of that decade, and on through the 1890s and early 1900s as the industry regained its feet. The passing of the open range gradually eliminated the necessity for statewide organization of districts but the pattern established by the Association was long used.

The last big general roundup was held in June, 1905. This was the Platte River Pool, organized in 1901 by George Rhodes, Howard N. Carey, Albert Fly and the Engelking brothers. G. F. Engelking in a letter dated at Glen Rock, March 14, 1946 (printed in *Cow Country*, April 8, 1946), has described some of the events of this "last roundup."

"I worked with a few of the oldtime T7 boys, like T7 Joe, and Spike Lavering, and old T. Burleson, who was running a bunch of steers with the T7 at that time.

"In June, 1905, after working in Wyoming, George Rhodes, our wagon boss of the Platte River Pool, and I had dinner at the T7 wagon with Al Kenney, an oldtime roundup cook. In 1897 I was with the CY wagon No. 2, and Al was cooking at that time for J. M. Carey & Bros. He was a good old roundup cook.

"Wyoming's last big general roundup was about the fifteenth of June, 1905, the Platte River Pool or George Rhodes' wagon. Our outfit was camped at the mouth of Duck creek, on the Dry Cheyenne river. The Rhodes wagon was to meet the George Amos 4J Keeline outfit, the T7 Matthews outfit and the 21 J. L. Baird outfit, at the old Fiddle Back road crossing or the 74 pens, on the Cheyenne.

"We had good grass that spring, but did not get any flush rains to fill the water holes and the buffalo wallows on the range for cattle. There was not much water at the road cross-sing on Cheyenne river. The water comes up, then is lost in the sand farther downstream. We camped on or about June 15, and the next morning started out on the drive down river, at the same time looking for the other three wagons. We were about halfway to the 74 pens when we saw the riders coming up river, looking for the Platte River Pool or Rhodes outfit. We met, and a quick decision was made to work our herds that day, and to go down the next day to work the other three herds. 'That is,' said one of the wagon bosses, 'if we can hold the cattle.' For it was burning hot, dry weather, and no water for the cattle. There were not less than 6,000 cattle, and about 650 head of work and saddle horses, and all burning for a drink of water. They had been rounding up for some time and the larger the herds got, the more water it would take for the stock.

"We got back to our outfit and it did not take long till we were at work on the Platte River throwback herd, and the sun was getting hotter.

"We could see the dust of those 6,000 or more cattle, milling for water and the riders riding hard to hold them. Then along in the afternoon of that day (June 15), as we were working the herd, a little black cloud came out of the sky from nowhere, and not another cloud any place in the sky. It just got bigger and bigger right over where the cattle were. And then about 3 o'clock that afternoon it started to rain right over the cattle. The cowboys told us next morning that the cattle just stood where they were and drank, for the rain came down in torrents. So the cattle were held and we worked those three herds. Rhodes and I worked together cutting cattle coming up the North Platte river. It was a great sight to see 75 or 80 riders working those 6,000 cattle; riders, reps from Montana and South Dakota and Wyoming being represented.

"And so came to a close the last big general roundup in Wyoming."

CHAPTER THIRTEEN

BETTER OFF IN BROOKLYN

"I would do it all over again" (said the Virginian). "The whole thing just the same. He knowed the customs of the country, and he played the game. No call to blame me for the customs of the country. You leave other folks' cattle alone, or you take the consequences."

'The Virginian,' by Owen Wister, Macmillan, 1902.

There were various ways of stealing cattle or horses in the early days. You could run them off on a dark night, you could slap your brand on an unbranded animal when you thought nobody was watching, or you could, in some secluded spot, with a running iron* or a red hot cinch ring, change the brand already on somebody else's critter to make it look like yours. Whatever the method, it was rustling, and it still plagues honest ranchers, on a minor scale, however, to that which prevailed in the lawless frontier days.

The comparative ease with which it was possible, early in the game, to acquire other people's cattle often led to this form of stealing by men otherwise honest. Many of the pioneering cattle companies were huge concerns operating under foreign capital and absentee ownership. It was not unknown for a local employe of one of these outfits to build up his own herd gradually on the side, by putting a brand of his own on some of his employer's calves, and thus eventually branch out on his own. Just as today there are those who see no harm in pilfering small items from big concerns on the theory that "they'll never miss it," so in the open range days persons who were by no means the criminal type rationalized the occasional acquisition of stray unbranded calves that they knew belonged to someone else who happened to be far away.

*A running iron was a branding iron with a straight edge, used for illegitimately altering legitimate brands.

The little man did his rustling furtively. There were big operators who were bolder, and who sought security through alliance with accomplices. The rustler gangs, large or small, were the hard ones to handle.

Before the courts began functioning and efficient enforcement became at least theoretically possible, it was the custom of the country to deal quick and drastic justice to those who didn't leave other folks' cattle alone. The consequences were shooting or hanging. There was no tender way to meet the problem.

•

Owen Wister fictionized the cattle rustler, and the man who hunted and hanged him (friends though they were), in the first of the novels of the West, a story laid in Wyoming. The Virginian, first of the strong, silent, straight-shooting plainsmen who have become part of the American tradition, was a figment of a story-teller's fancy, but his counterpart existed, many times over, in the factual record.

You can find him in the files of the Wyoming Stock Growers Association, in the official reports of the early inspector-detectives who, after Judge Lynch's days, in the era when the task of coping with rustlers was entrusted by the territory to the Association, brought at least some of the rustlers to justice. For thoroughness and efficiency in dealing with desperados, and for economy of words in telling about it, some of these men rival any imaginary character in the wide field of western fiction.

There were some thirty such detectives in the years between formation of the Association and 1900. Sharp-eyed, goateed Ben N. Morrison was one of the first of these. He was in the Association's employ from 1879 through '82, and his life was in danger much of the time.[2]

---

[2]An episode illuminative of Morrison's personality is told by Robert B. David in his book *Malcolm Campbell, Sheriff*. Morrison was one of the invaders, or regulators, in the Johnson county war (see Chapter 20.) During one phase of the fight at the TA ranch, Morrison was in the embattled ice house. A companion-at-arms called to him, through the hail of flying bullets, "Hey Ben, want a drink of water?" Morrison called back, "Hell no, I'm on ice now."

Here, in his handwriting on two ruled pages apparently torn from a ledger, is the report Morrison submitted to the Association on April 3, 1880, for the seven months ending March 31; one must read between the lines for the full force of the restraint and taciturnity with which his story is told:

"Sept. 12, 1879: Left Cheyenne in search of horses owned by Mr. T. A. Kent. Followed trail to Grey Bull creek in the Bighorn basin, there lost trail. Picked up 3 head on my return trip, arrived in Cheyenne October 19.

"October 28: Left Cheyenne for Council Bluffs on inspection duty, returned by way of Lincoln. Visited the penitentiary on business of the Association and arrived in Cheyenne November 9.

"Nov. 10: Time was occupied in inspection of range hide houses in town and one trip to Plum creek, up to December 1.

"December 1: Left Cheyenne for Pine Ridge Indian Agency (South Dakota). Remained there during the 'big issue.' (Beef issue to the Indians) Found everything all right. Returned to Cheyenne January 17, 1880.

"January 24: Left for Deadwood on inspection, found everything all right. Returned via Camp Robinson and Fort Laramie. Inspected hides at latter place, found everything all right. Brought from Fort Robinson Hamilton, U. S. mule thief, and U. S. mules. On the way captured Cress and J. Hain, also U. S. mule thieves. Arrived in Cheyenne February 9."

Then came this terse summary of the first chapter in a tragic happening that was to become a public issue and the cause of much discussion and some excitement:

"Feb. 13: Left to arrest J. J. McGinnis, captured him at Fort Laramie. On the trip to Cheyenne he attempted to make his escape and met his death. Arrived in Cheyenne February 20." The charge against McGinnis was not stated.

A coroner's jury went to the spot where the shooting occurred and where McGinnis was buried by cowboys from a nearby ranch. The coroner's jury disinterred the body and "sat upon it" (as the Cheyenne *Daily Leader* put it at the time), afterward officially reporting that the man had come to his death during an attempt to escape from an officer who had been authorized to arrest him. "As a matter of form," the *Leader* added, the coroner likely would enter proceedings against Morrison "and the grand jury will discharge him beyond doubt. There can be no question raised as to the justifiability of the shooting."

However, the newspaper proved a poor prophet. A question was raised.

It was raised by McGinnis's widow, who went to Cheyenne with an affidavit from two Fort Laramie soldiers who had been assigned to escort Morrison and his prisoner. Although the two soldiers had been riding ahead, and were out of sight over a hill when the shooting occurred, their affidavit said it looked to them like murder.

Morrison meanwhile was off on the trail of some horse thieves in South Dakota, when, as he phrased it later in his yearly report, "I was compelled to abandon the pursuit for the time being as my presence at the spring term of court which convened at Cheyenne May 25 was imperatively necessary for reasons which I will not mention here as I presume they are well understood."

These reasons were that the authorities at Cheyenne, in response to demands by McGinnis's family and friends, had filed against Morrison an information (request for grand jury investigation). It was because of this that Morrison turned back from the horse thieves' trail.

When the grand jurors filed their report, on June 27, they commented on the clean condition of the jail, remarked that the court-house roof leaked, warned that certain butchers and hide dealers were growing careless about observing the law,—and uttered not a word of indictment against Morrison.

This entire affair prompted Morrison, when time came to submit his report covering the year, to become unusually wordy for him:

"I have this to say, that the duties of the position which I hold is full of perplexities and inconveniences such as are not and cannot be fully understood except by those who have had personal experience in the matter."

That the officers seeking to bring law and order to early-day Wyoming cow country had a rough row to hoe is also indicated by this paragraph from the Cheyenne *Daily Leader* during the time that the McGinnis affair was in the limelight:

"Deputy U. S. Marshal W. R. Schnitger arrived in Cheyenne on Tuesday evening from a trip to Fort McKinney. He says the condition of affairs in the northern part of Albany county (adjoining Laramie) is very bad. Criminals stalk broadcast without the slightest fear, and as a consequence life and property are jeopardized."

The Cheyenne *Leader* on February 22, 1880, recorded this impression of Morrison:

"He is a man of a medium stature, heavy set, and wears an open, generous countenance. In deportment he is calm, and speaks with an air of honesty that is convincing. He much regrets the killing and is sorry it was necessary."

•

Another Association detective-inspector in the '80s was a fabulous character whose name at that time was Frank Canton. He was a Texan who came northward in his youth for motives similar to those that kept many men on the move in the old West. In Canton's case, there were several killings and other crimes in Texas that he didn't like to talk about. He became in turn cattleman, sheriff, live stock detective, deputy United States marshal, secret service man and National Guard officer. His trail stretched from Texas to the Klondike and back to Oklahoma, where he died in 1927.

Canton was still wanted in Texas while he was sheriff of Johnson county, Wyoming. After the Johnson County War, in which he played a part the full story of which does not show in the records, he went back to Texas to clear his record there. One story is that when it was time for him to be interviewed by the governor, Canton after meditating a while slid an extra six-shooter between his shirts with the remark that he would have a pardon or Texas would have a new governor. He got the pardon.

A Jekyll and Hyde of the Plains, Canton was feared as a peace officer, and hated by many as a ruthless killer. One

Wyoming old-timer who now lives in another state has said: "Canton was out to collect rewards. He was always looking for someone, always suspicious of a stranger, always wanting to get something on somebody. He often came to me for information about people, for I knew everybody in the Powder river country in those days. All he thought about was guns and killing, and he dreamed at night about the men he was going to get, or that might get him. I have slept beside him on the ground and heard him toss in his blankets and mutter, 'Did you hear them yet?' and 'Do you reckon they're coming now?' "

The Cheyenne *Leader* of February 2, 1884, in reporting one of Canton's exploits, adopted the same sort of brevity that marked the literary style of the reports by the early stock detectives—or perhaps this was all the *Leader* could get Canton to tell:

"About two weeks ago, Sheriff Frank Canton (he was concurrently sheriff of Johnson county and WSGA detective) received information that two persons answering the description of Tee Haines and Jim Baker, two of the parties charged with having been connected with the stealing of 70 head of cattle from the Little Venture Cattle Company on Powder river last summer, were coming across the country in a westerly direction from the Black Hills. They are now in custody in Buffalo."

Canton cleaned up the Teton Jackson horse-stealing gang; Jackson afterward escaped from the penitentiary and disappeared, leaving a list of men whom he planned to kill, with Canton No. 1 on the list. Canton ended Indian depredations against cattle herds in Johnson county, by trailing and capturing two Arapahoes, Samuel and Beaver. He performed many other feats which helped give the Association and its detectives the reputation of being the scourge of stock thieves.

Edward Burnett's memoirs in the Association files tell of an incident of those days in which Burnett was an unwilling participant. The Burnett ranch was in Johnson county, and Burnett, who was then quite young, knew Canton well.

"Canton carried a gun, perhaps sometimes two of them,"

Burnett writes. "I never knew of his using one. His eye was sufficient. When Canton got his steel gray eye on a man, that settled it."

After Canton had served two terms as sheriff of Johnson county—which then ran to Montana on the north, the Platte on the south and the Bighorn on the west—he declined to run again. His deputy, Johnnie McDermott, became sheriff and McDermott named as his deputy a jolly, blue-eyed Swede named Chris Gross.

Gross was sent into the Bighorn country after a horse thief. He found his man in a cabin and got the drop on him.

"The horse thief would have surrendered to Canton," says Burnett. "But he said he wouldn't give up to any damned Swede, and kept talking and edging over to the corner where his gun was. Chris had to kill him." Burnett continues:

"Chris threw the dead h.t. over a saddle and tied his head and feet together and to make him safe and comfortable put a double diamond hitch on him and started down the mountains, 25 below zero. The trail then came down to Crazy Woman canyon, and I lived at the mouth of the canyon. We were just sitting down to supper and Chris walked in.

" 'Come and help me unpack a horse,' said Chris.

"I got a lantern and led the way; when I shone the lantern on the pack I dropped right there. Chris persuaded me to hold the lantern and he undid the pack rope but he couldn't make me help lift the dead h.t. off the saddle, so he rolled him off like a cowboy unloading his bed, and the h.t. fell with a thud, frozen solid, round as a horseshoe. I ate no supper that night."

Burnett adds that the deputy was fired for having killed this man, and implies sympathy for Chris.

"It wasn't his fault," says Burnett, "that he had the playful, joyous, jolly blue eyes of his race, the face that does not count. Bat Masterson (Dodge City peace officer) had a round, jolly face, too,—but he had the eye. Frank Canton had the face AND the eye."

•

It was this kind of an eye in the head of this kind of man

that made one outlaw leader remark that he wouldn't give a damn for all the sheriffs in Wyoming, if the Association would just let him alone.

The man reputed to have said this was Doc Middleton, who was wanted in three states when he came to Wyoming in the late 1870s. He was tall, with a fair complexion, long hair and a fierce-looking mustache. He had a steady nerve and was a natural leader of men. The trouble was that the men he led were, like him, unwholesomely interested in other people's horses.

William C. Lykins was a WSGA stock detective in 1878 when the Middleton gang ran off forty head of horses from the W. C. Irvine ranch on Horse creek, and headed for Kansas with them. Lykins with a small posse overtook Middleton and his men near Julesburg, Colo. The horses were recovered, and Middleton and an accomplice named Smith were captured. The two men escaped that night. Smith was recaptured in the Black Hills and sent to prison. A tip from him put Lykins back on Middleton's trail, which this time led to Nebraska. Lykins and a posse of four[3] flushed the rustlers at a house in the Niobrara valley. The rustlers carried the attack to the officers, coming at them with guns ablaze. One deputy was unhorsed and wounded. Lykins' rifle let him down; four times the detective fired and four times the cartridge failed to explode. Lykins pulled his Colt, closed in and got Middleton in the stomach. Their leader down, the other outlaws fled. While Lykins was aiding his wounded deputy, Middleton crawled into some underbrush, where his gang picked him up and got him away.

Lykins followed, and eventually Middleton was cornered again, in a house where his wounds were being cared for. He was recaptured and taken on a buckboard to Sidney, Nebr., to await legal permission for his transfer to Wyoming.

Middleton's friends sent a warning to Lykins against trying to take his prisoner away. When the necessary papers arrived, Lykins broadcast the word that any attempt to interfere with

[3]Russell Thorp says that Gene Hall, who in 1953 was still living at Alliance, Nebr., in his 90s, was one of those deputies.

him would result in Middleton's sudden death. Then two armed stretcher-bearers carried Middleton from the house and down the street to the railroad station where he was put in a baggage coach bound for Cheyenne. Lykins led the little procession with a shotgun in his hands and a six-gun on each hip.

Back in Wyoming, Middleton was sent up for five years. After doing his time, he ran a saloon at Ardmore, South Dakota, for a while, and in 1914 was operating an illegal gambling establishment at Orin Junction, Wyo. Stabbed in a fight, he died in jail—from erysipelas.

Russell Thorp, who knew Middleton, says it was common knowledge that Doc stole horses from emigrants and settlers coming into Wyoming. There was a Robin Hood streak in him, for Thorp tells of an occasion when Middleton encountered an emigrant family whose horses had played out, some of them dying. Doc the bad man saw the emigrants on their way again with a complete outfit of fresh horses,—which he had stolen from ranchers.

There were many others of the Lykins type—Nathaniel K. Boswell, who picked off three outlaws from three different roundup crews so quietly and effectively that none of the roundups knew the men were gone; and Sam Moses, who trailed one of the George Wellman slayers for ninety days before he caught up with him in Indian Territory—to name two.

To name a third, there was James Dahlman, who was known as James Murray when he was appointed an Association live stock detective in 1884, and who later left cow country to go to Omaha where he put in twenty years as mayor of that city. Dahlman was another Texan who had come north in a hurry; the story is that he appealed to the Association secretary at one time to write to Texas to find out if he was still wanted. The reply came back from Texas that he was not wanted—the man he had shot had not died— although he "needed killing."

Dahlman showed what manner of man he was in many ways, while in Wyoming. One revealing incident was his firing of a roundup cook for disobeying orders by camping on the near side of a river. Whenever a trail crew or roundup outfit came to a river, the thing to do was to get across and then camp. That way, Dahlman figured, if a storm came up and flooded the stream, or any other adverse circumstance occurred, at least you were across the river. A minor note, perhaps, yet a significant one. It was the spirit that builds any country, gains any goal: Getting across the river before you make camp.

And as for the people who couldn't leave other folks' cattle alone, and who took the consequences at the hands of the men with the steel gray eyes,[4] it was as the Virginian said in Wister's Wyoming novel, after trailing and hanging his friend Shorty the bungling rustler:

" . . . Back East you can be middling and get along. But if you go to try a thing on in this Western country, you've got to do it *well*. You've got to deal cyards *well*; you've got to steal *well*; and if you claim to be quick with your gun, you must be quick, for you're a public temptation and some man will not resist trying to prove he is the quicker. You must break all the Commandments *well* in this Western country, and Shorty should have stayed in Brooklyn."

[4]For example, Scott Davis, who was detective-inspector for the Association 1890-95, had been officially thanked by a resolution adopted by the Territorial Legislative Assembly, 1877, for his "indefatigable exertions and signal bravery" in capturing two road agents. These were Dunk Blackburn and one Wall. Russell Thorp knew Davis as captain of the shotgun messengers guarding treasure coaches on the Cheyenne-Black Hills Stage and Express Line, and later as body-guard to W. C. Irvine, whose life had been threatened by rustlers. To Thorp and others who knew him, he was Quick-Shot Davis.

CHAPTER FOURTEEN

THE INSIDE OF THE HIDE

OGDEN: Inspector Burgess reports: Steer removed from through shipment from Wheatland, destination Los Banos, Calif. Shipment stopped at Ogden to feed and rest. Estray removed. Brand not listed on local inspection certificate out of Platte county. Proceeds, $121.83, to Horace Wilson. This steer was one of a shipment of 982 head of cattle consigned to Bing Crosby.

OMAHA: Inspector McVicker reports: Cow and calf, and one steer, loaded at Riverton, when inspected and clipped proved to be estrays. Proceeds of cow and calf to Moseley Land & Cattle Co., Jackson. Proceeds of steer to Wind River Indian Agency for account of Wallace St. Clair. These cattle were loaded more than 100 miles from their home range.

—From Inspectors' Estray Reports, 1949, WSGA.

There were six head of cattle in the bunch that a small Wyoming rancher had sent to a shipping point for sale. Brand inspectors were checking the brands to make sure the cattle were the property of the man selling them.

Five of the animals were found to be branded on the left side with the seller's brand. On the sixth, a bull, no brand could be found. The bull was about to be entered on the books as an estray, which meant that the money from its sale would be withheld from the shipper until or unless he could prove ownership.

One of the inspectors, however, was not yet convinced. The one was Frank Brainard, then in the prime of his 44 years service as a detective-inspector for the Wyoming Stock Growers Association.

"He's too gentle for a maverick," said Brainard. "He must have a brand some place."

So they sheared the bull,—and sure enough, there was a

95

small brand on the right lower foreleg. It proved the shipper was the legitimate owner of this animal as of the other five—and thus an acute and experienced inspector saved a distant rancher from paying the penalty of his own carelessness in sending poorly branded cattle to market. The episode demonstrates the importance both of clear brands and of skilled inspectors,—the kind who will examine the inside of a cow's hide if that extreme becomes necessary to determine ownership.

Brainard was one of the best inspectors the Association ever employed. He could spot a worked-over or defaced brand as soon as the animal bearing it walked into the yards, or so his friends said. He served the Association as inspector from 1883 to 1927.

Another of similar stripe was Claud L. Talbot, who started working for the Association in 1885 and retired in 1931. In 1891, when there were 5,000 brands in the Association brand book, Talbot knew most of them so well that he seldom had to look one up to see who owned it.

•

The nature of the work that these men and the other detective-inspectors performed for the Association changed as the cattle industry changed. As the frontier era faded, and the worst of the rustler gangs were broken up, running down thieves on the ranges became a less important part of their work, and the inspecting of brands at shipping points grew in importance. This was less spectacular than trailing thieves in the hills, but brand inspection in the yards soon became—and still is—one of the greatest services rendered to the cattle industry of Wyoming by the Association.

Actually, the Association, as soon as it was formed in 1873, began its inspection work, on a small scale, checking the brands on trail herds coming in to stock the ranges or passing through to other range states. In 1881 the Association, in addition to the detective work it was doing at home, began the inspection of cattle at railroad points where the stock was unloaded for feed and rest. Inspectors were placed in '81 at Council Bluffs (Omaha), Pacific Junction, Boone and Clin-

Family hearthside in 1891 on the A. L. Brock ranch at EK mountain near the North fork of the Powder river. In the picture, Julia A. Brock, John E., Genevra S., Ernest A. and A. L. Brock. (Photo from J. Elmer Brock.)

Women voted in Wyoming before they did so in any other state. This photo, taken when Teddy Roosevelt was up for President, in 1900, shows Mrs. J. C. Thorp about to vote, in Raw Hide Buttes precinct. The clerks were A. D. Reed and a Miss Chalfant; judges were Mrs. M. E. Mayes, H. B. Hargraves, and the young fellow with the bow tie, who was Russell Thorp, later for many years secretary of the Wyoming Stock Growers Association.

This was downtown Cheyenne, in 1868.
(Wyoming State Historical Department.)

Masculine interests—including surveyor's instruments stacked in the corner right of the fireplace—dominated the scene when this photo was taken in 1885 in the Sturgis and Lane home ranch on Horse creek. (Colorado State Historical Society photo.)

In the swank Cheyenne Club (see Chapter 16) in the early 'eighties gathered cow country's elite—the titled Britons, the eastern bluebloods —for their caviar and champagne, and their big cattle deals. This picture is from a contemporary drawing. By contrast, the old photo below shows cowboys on a Laramie Plains ranch enjoying a game of monte on a saddle blanket. (Robert H. Burns, from the Axel Palmer collection.)

Bert Mills Studio, BUFFALO, WYO.

More than a picture of three cut-ups in a Buffalo, Wyo., photo studio,
this group includes a portrait of a man whom General Crook called
one of the greatest scouts of the Sioux war of 1876: Frank Grouard.
He stands on the right. Son of a Polynesian woman, Grouard lived
for years among the Sioux, who called him Standing Bear and nick-
named him The Grabber. Man seated on right is Dan Mitchell, early-
day marshal at Buffalo; other man unidentified. (J. Elmer Brock
photo.)

A photo of 1882, by C. D. Kirkland, showing (left to right) in the rear row Roy Robinson, Newt Abbott and William H. Ashby of the Bridle Bit; and in front Shockey Hall of the Bridle Bit, Bartlett Richards of Richards & Comstock, and John Harris of the Circle Block. (From Association files.)

'Stage driver saved by a woman's interposition,' was the caption on this gaudy illustration in an eastern periodical in the '80s. It was based on an affair at the Fred Schwartz road ranch, between Ft. Laramie and Cheyenne, when a bunch of drunk cowboys shot up the ranch in Schwartz's absence, terrifying his wife and children. One of the cowboys decided to shoot the stage coach driver, but the woman kept him from it, as you can see.

Behind the scenes in the Postoffice at the rear end of the J. K. Moore post trader store at Ft. Washakie in 1905. J. W. T. Gray, assistant postmaster, in the checkered shirt. Indian shawls and blankets hang overhead in the store part of the building. (J. K. Moore, Jr., photo.)

ton, Ia.; Kansas City, Mo.; Fort Sheridan, Nebraska, and the Rosebud Indian Agency in South Dakota. By the next year, there were 13 stock inspectors, under whose keen eyes in one season passed 200,000 head of cattle.

In 1883 the first market brand inspection was begun, at the Minnesota Transfer, St. Paul. The system was gradually extended to other open markets where Wyoming cattle are sold.

By legislative enactment, the Association since 1931 has been recognized as a quasi-public organization vested with authority to represent the state of Wyoming outside the state in inspection of live stock to determine ownership, the Association books being audited annually by the state examiner.

From its inception until 1924, cost of the inspection system was borne entirely by members of the Association, the money coming from dues and assessments based on numbers of cattle owned. The burden on members was heavy at times, as hundreds of thousands of dollars were paid to owners of recovered estrays, many of the owners not being members of the Association and contributing nothing to the inspection costs.

Following enactment by Congress of the Packers and Stock Yards act, which became effective in 1924, the Association was registered as a marketing agency and authorized by the United States Department of Agriculture to post tariffs and collect inspection fees on all cattle originating in Wyoming, regardless of last loading point, which come into any market outside Wyoming in which the Association maintains inspection.

Brand inspection is the backbone of the Association, and today is carried out co-operatively through the Association and the state Live Stock and Sanitary Board. Wyoming law contemplates that no cattle or horses shall be removed from their home county without inspection for brands and ownership at some point before Wyoming surrenders jurisdiction. At open markets outside the state, this is done by inspectors representing the Association; at Wyoming sales rings, it is done by inspectors employed by the Board. Shipments consigned to points other than open markets are inspected at the points of origin or loading points by officers of the county.

The Association as of 1953 had eight inspectors: Three at Omaha, two at Denver; and one each at Idaho Falls, Ida., and Ogden, Utah, and one special inspector. In addition to these, through reciprocal agreements, the Association has inspectors of other states act as its agents. This is the case at Rapid City, Sturgis and Belle Fourche, South Dakota; at Billings, Montana; Sioux City, Iowa; Chicago; Scottsbluff, Alliance and Harrison, Nebraska. The number of cattle inspected by all these during the calendar year 1952 was 331,597, of which 282,545 were Wyoming cattle.

During the state fiscal year ending March 31, 1953, thirteen live stock sales rings (auction markets) were licensed in Wyoming and operated all or part of the year. Brand inspection was maintained at each sales ring by inspectors employed by the Live Stock and Sanitary Board. That inspection force in 1953 included one chief inspector and eleven inspectors. These had all served apprenticeships with the Board or the Association.

During the 1952-53 fiscal year, 166,937 cattle (including 56,036 calves) and 3,934 horses were inspected at sales rings. There were 3,227 cattle and 353 horses held for proof of ownership. The proceeds from 34 cattle and 79 horses remained unclaimed sixty days after dates of sale. Proceeds from all unclaimed estrays except animals consigned as estrays by county live stock inspectors are turned over to the Association for determination of ownership.

An estray is an animal that does not belong to the shipper claiming it. It often happens that stock belonging to someone else is by mistake included in a shipment; some times it is not a mistake. When an inspector discovers an estray, he removes it from the shipment. It is then sold at the market price and the proceeds are sent to the Association office for delivery to the rightful owner when and if he is found. Sometimes ownership is quickly established. On the other hand, there have been instances of estray claims being paid as long as 28 years after sale of the animal. This service, incidentally, is supplied to all stock men in Wyoming, regardless of membership in the Association.

A tabulation of estray money cleared through the Cheyenne office of the Association in the 57 years of market inspection prior to January 1941 showed the amazing total of $40,000,000. Since that date an additional total of $1,009,-673.33 in estray money has been remitted to the Cheyenne office. This includes only markets outside Wyoming and does not include auction sales within the state.

In addition to the foregoing, the law requires that each Wyoming county employ a county live stock inspector and such deputies as are needed. Appointments are made by the county commissioners. In about half the counties, the sheriff doubles as county live stock inspector. In all counties, inspectors are law enforcement officers, and work from or in close co-operation with the sheriff's office. During the calendar year 1952, inspectors for the counties cleared for shipment 249,500 cattle and 18,500 horses. Inspections in the counties are coordinated by the Live Stock and Sanitary Board which is given "general supervision" by the law but takes no direct part in appointment of inspectors.

Inspection services of the Association are financed by a 15-cent inspection fee collected on each animal inspected at the central markets, plus a special mill or tax levy on cattle and horses in the state, which is calculated to cover the deficit, if there is one, in the preceding year. The Association is limited to a levy of three mills. It has never touched that limit; in 1953, a levy of only one-half mill was required to make up the deficit.

At Wyoming sales rings, the brand inspection fees are 20 cents per head on horses and cattle and four cents on sheep and hogs. The service is as nearly as possible self-supporting, and deficits when they occur are met from the appropriations to the Board. County inspection is financed by appropriations in the annual county budgets. The legal fee in the counties is now 15 cents per head on horses and cattle, which goes into the county general fund.

The inspector who carries out his duties today in the yards

is as much of a detective as was his predecessor who scanned the ranges for rustlers. He watches for stolen cattle, for altered brands, for false bills of sale, for intentional and unintentional diversion of valuable property from its rightful owner. His methods have changed, but his functions are the same.

An example of the changed methods is the use of photography. Not many years ago, as an instance, Inspector Earl W. Carpenter at the Denver stock yards saw two cows whose brands appeared to him to have been altered. Photographs were made and examined, creating increased suspicion. Finally the animals were slaughtered, and then examination of the flesh side of the hide revealed clearly that the middle character in the brand 7PC had originally been a Flag, which was the brand of the rightful owner. These cattle had been trucked from their range in Nebraska into Wyoming, where the brand altering was committed. Through the WSGA, proceeds from the sale of these cattle eventually reached the man to whom they belonged.

The Wyoming Legislature in 1947 enacted a law providing for the training of live stock inspectors and prohibiting employment of any inspectors not so trained. Ten thousand dollars were appropriated to set up the training program and provide an inspector-at-large (Russell Thorp) to act as instructor, under the State Live Stock and Sanitary Board. Purpose of this move was to standardize and otherwise improve the brand inspection service. Experience in the live stock industry, a knowledge of brands and an ability to read them, were among the requirements established for all inspector candidates. On one occasion, as a test, the members of the Association executive committee took the examination for stock inspector. Experienced cattlemen though they were, none of them were able to answer correctly all the questions asked of inspector candidates.

•

Dean of the Association inspectors today is the head man at the Denver Stockyards, Earl W. Carpenter. Born in 1897 of pioneer parents, Mr. and Mrs. W. S. Carpenter, whose ADA ranch adjoined the Carey ranch in Laramie county twenty-five miles north of Cheyenne, Earl began work with the Association at Long Pine, Nebraska, in 1918, at a time when too many cattle were somehow disappearing from the Long Pine stockyards. Carpenter helped clear this up, then was moved to Omaha, where he trained for a year under Claude L. Talbot (who was an Association inspector 47 years). In January 1920, Carpenter was transferred to Denver, where he has been stationed ever since. W. W. McVicker of Shoshoni, Wyoming, the chief inspector at Omaha, is second in years of service. At Ogden, the inspector is Warren Burgess; at Idaho Falls it is Lee Dull.

With one assistant, C. E. Maddox, Carpenter inspects an average of 75,000 cattle a year in the Denver yards. They have checked as many as 100,000 in a year. A brand inspector's job is a seven-day-a-week responsibility when shipments are running heavy, as they usually do in the autumn. The market opens at 9, but the inspector, if the run is heavy, is up at 4 and out to the yards to check his waybills and get his papers in order. He spends most of the day in the yards, sometimes on horseback though in modern times this is often not necessary. He frequently discovers obscure or suspicious brands, which call for tying an animal up and clipping it to facilitate an accurate check. Photography is often resorted to; sometimes a brand is studied for days before it is finally identified. Carpenter tells of having to kill one animal and preserve the hide for study. "I had that hide in my office a week," said Carpenter, "before I figured out what the brand was."

When his work in the yards is finished, the inspector returns to his office in the Livestock Exchange and does his paper work. Tallies are made out in triplicate, one for the commission firm that sells the cattle, one for the Cheyenne office of the Association and one for the inspector's files. The shipper is not paid until the commission firm has received its tally. Carpenter is informed each month by the Live Stock and Sanitary Board as to new brands and transfers, so he is always within thirty days of having a complete and up-to-date transcript of all registered brands. These are kept in a modern filing device, listed three ways—alphabetically, by numbers, and by characters such as anchor, anvil, hat and so forth.

An incident at the Denver stockyards in the fall of 1945 demonstrated the efficiency of the inspection system. Carpenter recovered an estray for Lester Walck of Saratoga, Wyo. The cow was one of seven head that had jumped out of a truck when the tail gate opened. It was night, and the driver lost the cattle. Six were recovered in the subsequent ten days. The seventh was advertised for but not found—until Carpenter caught it as an estray in a shipment arriving at Denver. The animal weighed 1,570 pounds and the proceeds net to Walck were $209.37.

Wyoming's brand inspection system today is the best that any of the stock growing states have devised, and has been recognized as such by the fact that other states have used it as a model. Inspection is necessary because there simply is no other way of proving ownership of cattle except by the brands burned into their hides. From the early trail-driving days to now, this service, rendered to all Wyoming stock growers regardless of membership in the Association, has been of prime importance to Wyoming cow country.

PART FOUR

COW COUNTRY CAPITAL:
OLD CHEYENNE

CHAPTER FIFTEEN

HELL ON WHEELS

Notice to Bullion Shippers
The spring cleanup (from the gold mines) will leave for
Cheyenne on the regular stage at 7 A.M. next Monday. Wyatt
Earp of Dodge will ride shotgun.
        —Black Hills (South Dakota) Pioneer, June 1877.

The city of Cheyenne has been capital of Wyoming cow
country ever since the day in 1872 when the five men in the
livery stable laid the groundwork for organization of the
Wyoming Stock Growers Association. Cheyenne and the
Association grew up together.

The city rose almost overnight from the raw prairie, in the
Indian days. At one time it was so deep in frontier dust and
mud that people wondered whether it wouldn't be simpler to
move the town than to clean it up. They didn't move it,
and they did clean it up, and the Magic City, which first ruled
the ranges as a rough cow town and railroad center, became
in surprisingly short time something of a cultural influence
as well. There is rawhide at Cheyenne's roots, but there has
always been something of a softer nature there, too, making
itself manifest in unexpected ways, as we shall see.

The Union Pacific Railroad, poking its rails westward, in
1865 sent its chief engineer into Wyoming (then Dakota
Territory) to survey a route for the tracks. This chief
engineer was a young army general, Grenville M. Dodge, on
leave from the service for this purpose. Reconnoitering along
Crow creek, a tributary of the South Platte, he and his men
were chased by Indians, and during the flight Dodge shouted
to his guide, "If we save our scalps, I think we've found the
route for the railroad." They had. Two years later, on

105

July 4, 1867, General Dodge officially located the first Wyoming terminal or division point of the Union Pacific at the spot on Crow creek where the Indians had chased him, and named it Cheyenne, after the Indians. Wyoming's population centers at that time were Forts Laramie and Bridger, with a total of fewer than a thousand persons.

Before the first building went up at what was to be Cheyenne, a cemetery was started, for two members of a Mormon emigrant train killed by Indians while Dodge was still camped there. The first white residents of Cheyenne lived in tents. Some slept under their wagons. Then, as one of the tent dwellers said, "We woke up one morning and found that half of us had built board houses." So swiftly did the town grow, in anticipation of the coming of the railroad, that by the end of 1867 it had 4,000 residents, many business houses and two newspapers.

The tracks reached Cheyenne on November 13, 1867. The first train in brought a load of railroad equipment and workers, plus a lot of adventurers of both sexes from the last division point eastward, a notorious frontier outpost. The train was dubbed Hell on Wheels, and as the people of Cheyenne saw the characters it was bringing, "Here comes Julesburg!" was the cry. The lawless flocked in, along with the other kind. But the other kind in due time took charge by forming vigilance committees that maintained order of a sort, until courts were set up.[1]

A city government was formed in the late summer of 1867, with 350 votes cast. This was followed by organization of a Laramie county government. In December, the people

---

[1]G. E. Lemmon, an old cowman who as a boy lived in Cheyenne, says in a manuscript in the Association files that he and his family arose one morning from slumber in their house on the west bank of Crow creek "to behold three men hanging by their necks, one at the west end of Main street, another at the west end of about Fifth street, and a third under the railroad bridge spanning Crow creek. The first two were hanging under tripods made of three clothes-line poles, with the clothes lines for hangman's ropes. Soon thereafter the Vigilantes went to Laramie and captured seven toughs, loading them into a government eight-mule wagon, transporting them to the Dale street bridge and placing ropes around their necks, tossing the ropes over cross ties of the bridge and tying them, and driving from under, leaving the men dangling."

elected a school superintendent and by February school was being held. When Wyoming Territory was organized, in 1869, Cheyenne became its capital.

The town's floating population drifted on westward with the railroad tracks, but the car shops and the cattle industry, then just beginning to boom, were permanent fixtures and by 1881 Cheyenne was a substantial little city of 4,500 persons, with many good homes and public buildings.

Six theaters were thriving there by 1886, plus numerous variety houses. The Opera House, built in 1882, seating a thousand persons, echoed to the silver voice of Lily Langtry and to the tread of Edwin Booth. Theater audiences saw Sarah Bernhardt and Modjeska. The theatrical best came to Cheyenne from the outside world. In return, Cheyenne gave the world a new type of outdoor entertainment,—the Wild West Show. Colonel W. F. Cody assembled his rough riders annually at Cheyenne from 1882 on, trouping from there across the country and the Atlantic. Something of the Buffalo Bill tradition is preserved in modern Cheyenne, in the annual Frontier Days celebration, which set the pattern for western rodeos from the time of its first show in 1897. Cody, incidentally, was a member of the Wyoming Stock Growers Association, and served on the executive committee 1902-1903.

The Headquarters Saloon was one of the largest buildings in early Cheyenne. It was 36 by 100 feet. Next door was a two-story hotel. A building 24 by 35 feet was adequate for the first postoffice. Churches began going up in 1869. In 1872 there was a shed beside the railroad tracks, 175 feet long, 60 feet wide and 30 feet high, packed full of buffalo hides for shipment east. Squatters from Julesburg seized some lots and started to build houses on them; Cheyenne's police department was outnumbered, but a battalion of troops from Fort D. A. Russell, which had been established nearby at the same time Cheyenne was born, came in and turned the rascals out.

The dirt streets were loud at night with the whisky-voiced cheers of the variety-house audiences. There were restless cowponies tossing their heads at hitchracks, there were six-shooter slayings on the board sidewalks, there were lynchings in behalf of law and order.

So young Cheyenne booted and brawled its way up from the raw plains, and those who knew it in those days called it, even from its infancy, Old Cheyenne because they loved it so.

CHAPTER SIXTEEN

GAY LIFE ON THE PLAINS

The cattle kingdom was a world within itself, which, though
of brief duration, was complete and self-satisfying.

—The Great Plains, by Walter Prescott Webb.

In the center of the crude Cheyenne of the 1880s there
bloomed in the lush days of the cattle industry a club where
titled Englishmen and sons of some of the first families of the
eastern seaboard foregathered to feast on champagne and
caviar. They dressed for dinner—some of them—and they
played whist and billiards. Smoking was allowed, but not in
the dining room between 7 a.m. and 7 p.m.,—and no pipes,
please, in any of the public rooms! For those who wished to
while away an hour in the library, Harpers and the Atlantic,
and the Boston Sunday Herald, were on the reading tables.

Here in the incredible Cheyenne Club, within sight of a
plains area over which still roamed the Indians and the buffalo, monocled Englishmen hobnobbed with hell-raising
ranchers fresh off the range. Some of the members rode their
cowponies to the clubhouse, which provided nineteen hitch
racks for their use, but others dashed up in style in a tally-ho
imported from England and drawn by six prancing horses.

There was contrast in the personalities of the Cheyenne
Club, but a common interest drew them together: the need
for a social gathering place where the rigors of the range could
be forgotten for a while, and where mutual concerns could be
discussed. It was primarily intended for sociability, but soon
became a center for transaction of much of the business done
by cattlemen. Many a big deal was cooked up over a scotch or
bourbon in a quiet corner of the Cheyenne Club. Its dues
were high, for those times, and its membership was restricted.

The Cheyenne Club was for the wealthy and the influential. One of the major purposes served by the half dozen sleeping rooms it provided was to make it unnecessary for the British and other absentee ranch owners to stop at ordinary hotels on their occasional trips to and from their holdings.

The cowmen who congregated at the Cheyenne Club in the good old days were men of taste and judgment when it came to food and drink. One of its members has recorded the statement that more high-priced liquor was sold to the Cheyenne Club in its heyday than to any other club in the country. The caviar and the champagne had to be the best. The members didn't mind paying twenty cents for a cigar, but they thought the Reina Victorias a bit small for the price. Furthermore, two quarts of a shipment of champagne were "badly corked, neither bottle full," on one occasion which prompted a complaint to the dealer who had dared palm off inferior goods on the Cheyenne Club.

The building itself cost some $20,000—and that much and more frequently changed hands in a night within its walls. The club was incorporated September 22, 1880, and went for a short time under the name of the Cactus Club. That same autumn, work was started on the clubhouse, a rambling brick structure with a mansard roof and a "lantern" or skylight over the main hallway, and with wide verandahs fronting on two streets. Inside were lounging, dining and game rooms, the library, and a few private dining rooms available only to groups of four or more. Upstairs were six "chambers for use of members." It was "a good club, on an eastern basis," as a letter from the secretary to one prospective member put it. The landmark stood at the corner of 17th street and Warren avenue long after the days of its glory had passed. In 1936, when it was tottering and dilapidated, it was torn down to be replaced by the trim brick home of the Cheyenne Chamber of Commerce, which eventually emerged from the various transformations through which the Cheyenne Club passed after the turn of the century.

The paintings and other art objects that once graced the walls of the club are largely lost, but a few remain. One interesting relic hangs in the State Museum at Cheyenne. It is a large oil painting of a bull, a copy of a painting done by Paul Potter, seventeenth century Dutch artist. The copy was made by Thomas Mesker in 1885. One of the Cheyenne Club members—John C. Coble of Albany County—was displeased with the Dutch artist's handiwork; the Holstein bull didn't look like any critter on Coble's ranges. After brooding over this affront to animal life, Coble one night pulled his .45 and took a bead on the malformed bull. The bullet hole still shows. Coble was suspended by the club, and resigned. The by-laws didn't specifically forbid shooting holes in pictures but they were broad enough to cover the case.

The Cheyenne Club was at its best from 1880 to 1885. Then it began disintegrating, so far as its original and distinctive membership was concerned. The depression and the blizzards that set the cow business back on its haunches in 1886-7 practically ended the unique institution that was the Cheyenne Club in the days when Biddles, Blairs, Fords, Plunketts and Frewens brightened its membership roll and its dances, horse races and wolf hunts.

Even the servants employed by the Cheyenne Club grew to have for it a fondness that went beyond the call of duty. Like the liquor and the caviar, these servants were imported, and were of the best. One of them was known to most members only as Thomas. He came to the club as a waiter, and later was made steward. He presided over management of the clubrooms with such efficiency, and showed such a sense of the fitness of things, that he became a general favorite. As for Thomas, the Cheyenne Club was his life. When the club's sun set, Thomas went to a distant city and put a bullet through his head.

CHAPTER SEVENTEEN

HI KELLY'S HOUSE

History is the essence of innumerable biographies.

—Thomas Carlyle.

Tall, broad-shouldered, handsome Hi Kelly—"straight as a pine tree," John Clay called him—was never a member of the caviar-consuming group of Wyoming cattlemen, but he built a house that outlasted that of the Cheyenne Club. Kelly's house was one of many mansions erected in the city of Cheyenne in the 1870s and '80s by Wyoming cowmen with the quick profits they made on the free grass range. In 1954, Kelly's home is one of the few such dwellings that still stand.

In Kelly's life there was no tally-ho, no foreign capital or influence. Whatever it was to which he aspired for his family or for himself, as exemplified by the loveliness he built into their house,—whatever it was, it came right out of the soil of America.

Kelly—he signed his name Hiram B.—drove an ox team from Independence, Mo., to California in 1849, when he was 15. Thereafter for 21 years he rattled around the West, teaming, haying, woodcutting, carrying mail, driving a stagecoach, running a store. The spring of 1870 found him in Cheyenne, 36 years old with little more accumulated than a lot of experience and a few work cattle. These cattle he sold, to be shipped to Europe—it was the time of the Franco-Prussian war. They were the first cattle loaded and shipped from Cheyenne by railroad.

Then Kelly went into the cattle business, buying a few hundred head and establishing a ranch on the Chugwater, some fifty miles north of Cheyenne. He caught the cattle business on its way up. He made money fast—so fast that in 1884 he sold out for $250,000 and moved to Cheyenne to give his family a better living than he had had.

Kelly had married when he was in his thirties. Like numerous cattle men and other pioneers, he had chosen for wife one of the Indian women of the area. She was fifteen when he married her. Her father was a French trader named Reshaw, her mother a full-blood Sioux. She and Hi had eight children, one of whom, William H. Kelly, was elected on the Democrat ticket to the Fourth State Legislature convening in 1897. His portrait in the Wyoming Historical Blue Book portrays a young man who had inherited Hi's handsomeness and his mother's distinctively Indian appearance. He was living in Denver in 1954.

In Cheyenne, Hi Kelly bought a quarter-block of ground at the northwest corner of what is now Carey Avenue and Twenty-fourth Street. His wife's signature to the papers is written "Elizabeth Kelly, Her Mark."

The Kellys built a three-story house on this site, which is across the street from where, two years later, construction of the present State Capitol building was started.

There was a tower on the Kelly mansion, which has since been removed. But the rest of the house can be described in the present tense, for the family that bought it in 1902 still maintains it much as it was when Hi Kelly and his half-Indian wife and their eight children lived there.

It is surrounded by an iron fence in which Indian symbols —tomahawks and arrowheads—predominate. There is a stable on the rear of the lot. The house has five high-ceilinged rooms downstairs, and six on the second floor. There is a finished third story. There are crystal chandeliers, high plate glass windows with inside wooden shutters, and colored glass squares above the doors. The woodwork is hand-carved cherry and black walnut. The staircase is hand-carved walnut. Hardware is brass. In the library are mounted heads of elk, deer, antelope and bighorn sheep. Each of the six fireplaces has cherrywood mantel and little shelves for such art objects as porcelain figures from Dresden. Each fireplace is framed in imported tile. The tiles around the fireplace in the library depict characters from Shakespeare, except that the center tile above the opening is a picture of William Cullen Bryant.

There is nothing in the record to show that Kelly or his wife even knew who Shakespeare and Bryant were. But this is the house they built in the city that was the capital of Wyoming cow country in 1884. This is the house in which Mrs. Kelly, who was born in a tepee,[2] sat on the parquetry floors painting Indian pictographs on buckskin—some of her work is preserved in glass cases in the Colorado State Museum at Denver. She died in Denver, in 1922; Hi followed her two years later. In 1954, two of their eight children were living.

The reason Hi Kelly had to sell his mansion in Cheyenne in 1902 was that after he left the cattle business, which he knew from the sod up, he went into real estate and mining investments, and others who knew more about those things than he did soon had his money. A former employe of Kelly's went to see him in Denver when Kelly was an old man. Kelly was not home; his wife bade the visitor welcome and invited him to stay and see Hi. When Kelly came home, he was carrying a shovel. He was broke, and working as a laborer on the city streets. The former employe offered him financial help which Kelly declined. No charity for him. He could still make his own way. Later, the friend, learning that Kelly still owned a little land, leased it from him. The land was of no use, but the old friend made Kelly think it was.

The Kelly home in Cheyenne was one of many such built there by the Kents, Careys and others who made fortunes on the shortgrass ranges of early Wyoming. It is in a way a living memorial to the stalwart spirit of the old-time independent cowmen of whom Kelly was only one shining example.

[2]She loved flowers and trees. When the Kellys sold their Cheyenne house, the yard and garden were full of growing things. Mrs. Kelly asked the new owner if she might take with her a certain white lilac bush. The new owner said yes. Later, some misunderstanding arose between the two, and the gift of the white lilac bush was withdrawn. Mrs. Kelly as she walked away in anger put an Indian curse on the bush. Although surrounded by other trees and shrubs which always bloom, and given the best of care, the white lilac bush has never bloomed since.

114

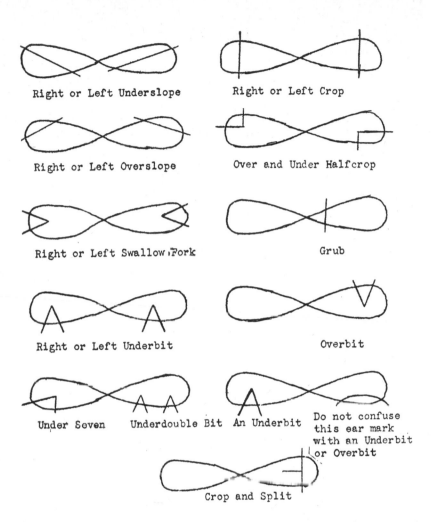

Right or Left Underslope

Right or Left Crop

Right or Left Overslope

Over and Under Halfcrop

Right or Left Swallow Fork

Grub

Right or Left Underbit

Overbit

Under Seven   Underdouble Bit   An Underbit

Do not confuse
this ear mark
with an Underbit
or Overbit

Crop and Split

This chart, from *Cow Country,* shows the ear marks sometimes used on calves, largely as a matter of local convenience among neighbors. Inspectors do not determine ownership on ear marks, though sometimes they take them into consideration. (There was, in the open range days, a roundup cook whose nickname was Overslope, because the tops of his ears had been frozen off.)

When Kelly had to sell, the buyer was another ranch family, that of Edgar Boice, owners also of the old PO Arbuckle ranch near Cheyenne. The Fred D. Boices, Sr., who occupy the Kelly house today, have two sons, Fred Jr. and Robert, who carry on the ranching business. Mrs. Fred Boice, Sr., who has presided graciously over the fine old home since 1916, is a former Cow-Belle president. Russell Thorp, for nineteen years secretary-treasurer and chief inspector of the Wyoming Stock Growers Association, has occupied an up-stairs apartment in the home for many years. Hi Kelly would be happy over his old house, if he could see what good hands it is in nearly three-quarters of a century after he came in from the ranges and built it.

PART FIVE

SHEEP AND OTHER TROUBLES

CHAPTER EIGHTEEN

WAR WITH THE WOOLLYBACKS

Every year, when the medder larks come back, an' calves begin to show up, the Wyoming cowmen git together. They have done this for 77 years. In the old days they didden have much to talk about. Most of the meetin' was given over to sheep, the railroads, cattle rustlers an' the packers. Decidin' what to do about sheepmen and rustlers took mighty little time!

—Neckyoke Jones, in Sheridan (Wyo.)
Press, June 7, 1949.

Sheep began infiltrating cow country in the 1870s,[1] and there was conflict at times between cowmen and sheepmen, in some parts of Wyoming, although in other parts the two interests managed to get along without bloodshed. By the early 1900s, however, when Wyoming was well on the way to becoming one of the greatest sheep states in the Union, war on a fairly large scale hit the ranges.

Some of the cattlemen drew deadlines, across which they warned sheepmen not to venture. Some of these deadlines were carefully observed. Where they were disregarded, there was trouble for the woollymonsters, as early Wyoming cowmen called sheep.

In 1904, Lincoln A. Morrison, a sheepman, while at a

[1]Probably the first permanent flock in the state was that of William A. Carter, post trader and sutler at Fort Bridger, according to R. H. Burns, head, wool department, University of Wyoming, who says Carter's flock showed up on Uinta tax rolls in 1869. That same year, William Tweed of Lander shipped some Cotswold sheep from Iowa to Point of Rocks, railhead at that time, and trailed them to Fort Brown, near Lander. Later these sheep were taken to his Red Rock ranch, where they were maintained for many years, first under his ownership and later by the late William Macfie. Many sheep were trailed westward through Wyoming 1847-56.

camp near Kirby creek (a tributary of the Bighorn, south of Tensleep) was shot and killed and his sheep were stampeded. The next fall a band of sheep belonging to the Lynn brothers was dynamited after it had crossed a deadline onto a cattle range. Bands of masked riders terrorized the Wind river, Owl creek and Bighorn basin country. In the spring of 1909, Joe Allemand and Joe Emge, disregarding warnings, placed 5,000 sheep on Spring creek, which flows into the No Wood, north of Tensleep. Armed riders attacked the camp at night, killed the two owners and a herder, ran off two other herders, burned the wagon and camp. There was great excitement over this affair. A grand jury summoned witnesses, one of whom killed himself. Arrests were made, the militia guarded the jail against mob violence, and five men went to prison.

Enforced peace between the two conflicting range interests was finally brought about, in part due to the operations of a federally-organized force of armed and mounted officers called the United States Rangers—predecessors of the U. S. Forest Rangers.

In some parts of Wyoming, cattlemen and sheepmen got along well together. This was the case in Albany county from the time that sheep began invading that area, which was about 1870. Lola M. Homsher, who is authority for this statement, says the Albany county tax roll in 1870 assessed Hutton and Company for 2,500 sheep worth $3,000. Hutton was also in the cattle business at that time, and had 4,000 head of cows worth $48,000. Other sheepmen of the time were Thomas Alsop and Latham and Coates. "There seemed to be no distinction laid down between sheepmen and cattlemen in Albany county at the beginning of the industry or later," Miss Homsher wrote in 1949. "Ranchers raised both animals and when specialization became the order of the day, they amicably divided the range."

There is actually on record an instance of cowboys helping sheep men to get their herds into Wyoming. Frank Abbott tells about it in the story of his experiences trailing cattle down from Oregon (Chapter 3) in 1882. Abbott and his crew had brought 500 head of cattle from Pendleton into Wyoming:

"Just before we reached Green river, a horseman came riding fast, and asked the boss if someone could bring the saddle horses ahead, and drive them through a band of sheep that had balked, and would not cross the river. They had been held on the gravel beach for forty-eight hours, trying to starve them into crossing, but they wouldn't take the water at all. About this time our mess wagon arrived. Big Ed drove about halfway across and stopped to let his horses drink. When he started on again, we put the saddle bunch into the stream, and the sheep followed right along. In a few minutes the whole band had crossed. Then we learned they were the same men we had helped across a small stream in the mountains of eastern Oregon. They had started from New Mexico the year before with nine thousand of the woollybacks in one bunch. They had expected to sell them in Oregon, but as they didn't find a market there, they were on their way to Cheyenne to sell them there."

In August of that same year, the Cheyenne *Daily Leader* said 100,000 head of cattle and 200,000 head of sheep were being driven eastward from Idaho, Oregon and Nevada. Herds were also brought from California to Wyoming, some of them being driven through to Nebraska, in the early 1880s. A sheep that cost $1.50 in Oregon was salable in Wyoming for $3 or more. Even if in bad condition from three to four months on the trail, a sheep would bring more than twice its cost. Sheep could travel long distances between water, and could be kept moving by fewer men than the same number of cattle would take. In 1882 Hartman K. Evans and his partner, Robert H. Homer, drove three bands of sheep, 23,000 in all, from near Pendleton, Ore., to Laramie, some 850 miles. It took them four months. Evans as trail foreman supervised movement of the three herds, each of which had a foreman, three helpers and a cook who drove the grub wagon. This was the year that trailing sheep into Wyoming reached its peak; thereafter, the price differential between Oregon and

California, and Wyoming, declined so that sheep trailing was
no longer profitable.

The sheep man and the nester, or small farmer—who often
was a cattle rustler—brought new woes to the cattleman,
who had first had the ranges to himself. Sheep grazed the
ranges clean, cropping the grass close to the ground; their
sharp hooves cut the grass roots.[2] They took over the water
holes. The depression in the cattle industry in the late '80s
plus the nester and sheepman invasion drove some individual
cattlemen to such extremes as raiding the sheep camps, burning herders' wagons and killing some of their flocks. In 1893,
numerous sheep outfits were raided by such men, who, because of the disguises they donned, were dubbed Gunny-
sackers. This went on until, as we have seen, the warfare
reached its height in the early 1900s, since which period cattle
and sheep men have learned to live side by side, dividing the
ranges between them.

Once convinced that sheep were here to stay, some cowmen
went into the business. A. A. Spaugh, who came up from
Texas to Wyoming with a trail herd of cattle in 1874, remained to become manager of the Converse Cattle Company
and eventually went into business for himself, buying among
others the 77 and Horseshoe ranches. Sheepmen crowded his
pastures, around 1902, and Spaugh rather than trying to
battle them bought them out, and was in the sheep business
until 1910, after which he devoted his profits from sheep and
cattle to banking and other investments.

Wyoming's sheep population was only 6,409 in 1870. It
hit its peak in 1910, with almost five million head, and in
1950 had declined to a million and a quarter head. However,
R. H. Burns, University of Wyoming sheep expert, in figures

[2]The old time cowman's attitude toward sheep is well expressed in a
verse by Frank Benton, "How I Love Sheep," one verse of which as given
in D. F. Krakel's MS *South Platte Country* goes:

> A sheep just oozes out a stink
> That drives a cattle man to drink.
> Its hooves leave flavors on the grass
> That even make the old cows pass.
> Sheep ranges cattle sure won't graze—
> But cowboys hate sheep anyways!

he prepared in 1951 on the natural resources of Wyoming, showed the important place that the sheep and wool industry held in 1948, the latest year for which these comparative figures were available. In spite of a record oil production in that year, the percentage of total income from different resources in Wyoming in 1948 was:

Agriculture and Minerals			100.0
Agriculture		100.0	50.2
Live stock	100.0	77.0	
Cattle & calves	59.4		
Sheep & wool	24.6		
Dairy	7.6		
Poultry	3.6		
Other	4.8		
Crops		23.0	
Minerals			49.8

Wyoming for a number of years has led the states in average fleece weights. In 1953 the average fleece weight amounted to 10.1 pounds. The 1953 wool clip was estimated (USDA BAE "Shorn Wool Production in 1953") at 20,594,000 pounds and exceeded the 1952 clip by 25 percent. The 1953 clip was the largest since 1947 but even so was 13 percent below the 1942-51 average. Only Texas, with a total production of 41,101,000 pounds, exceeded Wyoming production in 1953.

Wyoming's sheep population was founded on Merinos, Rambouillets, Cotswolds and Lincolns, and there has always been a good amount of fine wool blood in the flocks of the state.

The affinity of interests between cowmen and sheepmen was first recognized at the 1932 convention of the Association at Green River, when officials representing the two different groups sat together. This was repeated at subsequent conventions. In 1947, at Lander, this demonstration of unity was increased by the appearance of the head of the Wyoming State Grange. Only the State Farm Bureau head was absent, and he had planned to attend but was unable to do so.

CHAPTER NINETEEN

FEVER RIDES THE RANGE

There were no fences in the open range days, and that was good. But likewise there were no barriers to disease, and that was bad. The early-day ranchers were defenseless against animal ailments that could decimate their herds or wipe them out.

Cattle coming in from other states brought fever with them. Little was known in those days about such matters—amazingly little compared with the mass knowledge now available and the highly scientific safeguards in modern animal husbandry.

Texas fever, tick fever or splenic fever, as it was variously called, spread into the western range states with the herds that came up the long trail from the Southwest. It is a protozoan disease, transmitted by ticks that the southern cattle carried north on their bodies. Dropping off in the brush or on the grass along the trail, the ticks were picked up by other cattle. The disease these tiny carriers inflicted on their victims started with fever, anemia, enlargement of the spleen and ended in the animals' complete collapse and possible death. The months from June to September were the period during which the disease was most likely to spread. Kansas, Missouri, Colorado and Nebraska between 1875 and 1880 passed quarantine laws restricting the movement of cattle dusing the summer months.

In 1881, Wyoming cattlemen became apprehensive over the threat of Texas fever, and the Stock Growers Association was successful in getting the Territorial Legislative Assembly in 1882 to enact a law empowering the governor to appoint a state veterinarian. It was his duty to inspect incoming cattle and to notify the governor when he found any disease among them. The governor was then required to issue a proclamation forbidding movement of cattle from the locality where the disease prevailed, under heavy penalty, including liability for damage to the stock of other owners. James D. Hopkins was the first territorial veterinarian. He was recommended to the governor by the Association, for the law gave the WSGA this responsibility.

The Association sent emissaries to nearby states, urging the cowmen there to prevail on their legislatures to enact laws similar to Wyoming's new one, and several of the states did follow suit.

Disease threatened Wyoming's herds from another direction the next year, when an epidemic of pleuro-pneumonia broke out east of the Mississippi. This disease had spread westward from the Atlantic seaboard after reaching this country from Europe. The peril convinced the Wyoming stockmen that preventive action on a wider scale than state or area basis was now necessary. Hence the annual meeting of the Association, at Cheyenne on April 2-3, 1883, adopted a resolution calling for a committee to procure the co-operation of other live stock associations in holding a "congress" at Chicago for the purpose of obtaining federal legislation to combat the pleuro-pneumonia epidemic as well as Texas fever. A committee went to Washington, to lay the situation before the Commissioner of Agriculture.

When the Chicago meeting was held, November 15-16, 1883, there were 175 delegations present from twenty states and territories. Mostly they came from feeding and dairy states of the Middle West. The range-cattle industry of the plains had one delegate each from Texas and Arizona, six from Colorado—and sixteen from Wyoming. Thomas Sturgis, secretary of the Association, was chosen secretary of the convention, and he and Joseph M. Carey, who was then Wyoming's delegate in the national Congress, were named to represent Wyoming stock growers on a committee of eight preparing a bill for presentation to Congress.

Against strong opposition from Texas cattlemen and from other interests including Chicago stockyards, commission men and packers, this committee succeeded in getting legislation through Congress to protect the cattle industry. A bill was passed, and signed by the President on May 29, 1884.

It was watered down and weakened, and Osgood in *The Day of the Cattleman* says the economic and political pressure exerted by the Wyoming Stock Growers Association was all that kept it from being killed. But the bill did create within the Department of Agriculture a Bureau of Animal Industry.

This was a great step forward. The Bureau was to be headed by a veterinarian, and was to issue rules and regulations to suppress cattle diseases, inviting the states and territories to co-operate in making rules effective. The states and territories that did co-operate could receive help from a $150,000 federal fund set up for the Bureau.

This movement set in motion by the Wyoming cattlemen primarily to protect their own interests grew into action which benefited the entire country. For this was the beginning of improvements in food protection which a few years later led the government to institute the inspection of meat products. This in turn was extended to cover other foods, and eventually resulted in passage of the pure food and drug act (1906).

There was another important result from the 1883 meeting in Chicago. The delegates at that meeting resolved to convene again at Chicago a year later, to form a nation-wide organization of cattlemen. Thus in November, 1884, came into being the National Cattle Growers Association of America, which later became the American National Cattlemen's Association.

•

In 1884 Texas fever became widespread in Wyoming. The Association, through its executive committee, got the legislature to revise the quarantine law of 1882 and put more teeth in it. This brought opposition from the cattlemen in eastern states, notably Illinois and Missouri, as well as from those in western states such as Idaho who were sending stock into Wyoming, and who feared loss due to prolonged quarantine. State officials and the Association stood by their guns, insisted on inspection and on quarantine when necessary, doing all they could to prevent blockades and delays. The Association financed construction of quarantine yards near the railroad at Cheyenne, and the Union Pacific co-operated by building a switch track, and by disinfecting the Cheyenne stock yards and cars in which diseased cattle had been transported.

So successful were all these efforts to protect Wyoming's cattle industry against disease that although 52,791 head of cattle were brought into the state during 1885, contagious diseases were non-existent among the cattle of the state that year. Of the cattle brought in, nearly 10,000 came from Texas and more than 15,000 from New Mexico and Indian Territory, and none of these had to be detained, as they were shipped from areas in which the disease was not prevalent. Only eight herds, totaling 485 head, from Illinois and Missouri, had to be quarantined. So smoothly and effectively did the process function that cattle commerce was not seriously disrupted and, as the territorial veterinarian, James D. Hopkins, reported:

"The inconvenience and expense, such as it was, fell chiefly upon the residents of the Territory who were bringing valuable stock from the states east of the Missouri, and was felt by them generally to be a small burden for the immunity from danger thus secured."

And Thomas Moonlight, territorial governor in 1887, said in his annual report that year: "There is no state or territory where animals are more healthy than in Wyoming and there is no state or territory where more care is taken to prevent the introduction of contagious or infectious diseases among the domestic animals."

There was another outbreak of Texas fever in October 1891, and several hundred cattle died on the trail from the Belle Fourche to the Little Missouri. These were cattle raised and gathered on the Platte river and driven over the same trail previously occupied by Texas cattle. An early frost killed the germs and saved the herds on that part of the range from serious losses. To prevent a recurrence of this disease, the Board of Live Stock Commissioners, on re-

quest of the cattle men, obtained from the governor a proclamation embracing such quarantine regulations as would
effectually keep the state free from Texas fever. Provisions
of the proclamation were carried out under direction of the
state veterinarian, Dr. A. A. Holcomb, with the result that
there was no reappearance of Texas fever the following year.

PART SIX

ME AND NICK WAS GETTING BREAKFAST

CHAPTER TWENTY

THE JOHNSON COUNTY WAR: ITS CAUSES AND CONSEQUENCES

Whose was the right and the wrong?
Sing it, O funeral song,
With a voice that is full of tears!

Longfellow (Revenge of Rain-in-the-Face).

There's a strange thing about the Johnson County War of 1892: Even in those accounts which pretend to some historical accuracy, it reads like fiction. It doesn't sound real even on the lips of men whose fathers were in it.

But there is a geographical point in northern Wyoming —an old building on the former TA[1] ranch on Crazy Woman creek, south of Buffalo—at which the Johnson War becomes real—as real as a .45 slug in a barn wall.

The barn is on what is now the Clarence Gammon ranch. In the board siding of the gable end there is a roughly rectangular opening, four inches each way, made by knocking out the wood inside four auger holes drilled at the corners of a square. There is a row of such openings, rifle-shoulder high. A similar row of sinister square eyes looks out from the walls of an old log bunkhouse and icehouse nearby. There are smaller holes, too, in the old log walls, splintering, slashing holes, made from the outside, and not with augers.

The square openings are hurriedly-contrived portholes

[1]The brand was T Open A Connected and originally belonged to Thomas Alsop, who used it on his pioneer Laramie Plains ranch. Alsop about 1880 sold out to Dr. William H. Harris of Buffalo who moved the cattle to his own ranch on Crazy Woman, continuing use of the TA brand there. Alsop died in 1889.

knocked in the barn and bunkhouse walls on an April day more than sixty years ago. Through these were thrust the rifle barrels of the besieged Johnson County Invaders—or Whitecaps, or Regulators, or cowmen, as you please. It was here that a band of fifty hard hombres to their own amazement found themselves grimly fighting to stay alive, on the losing side of a showdown fight in which they had never imagined themselves as anything but top dogs. Here the Invaders were halted by the invaded, the Rustlers, that is, or the Nesters, or Grangers, or settlers, whichever name you prefer. Here the attackers, suddenly thrown into the role of defenders, might have been wiped out to the last of their fifty men had not the President of the United States sent the U. S. Cavalry riding to the rescue.

It sounds like fiction but it was fact. It happened. The portholes and the bullet holes in the log walls are lingering visible reminders of the time when the struggle between old and new, between little and big, between two concepts of right and wrong and two eras in Wyoming's history, was written off in rifle smoke. To this barn, and no farther, rolled the high tide of the Johnson County War. It all comes real again, on the ground of its Gettysburg.

•

Cattle stealing was only the immediate cause of the Johnson County War. Rustling had been a rangeland worry ever since the coming of the first herds, but in the boom days it had created less concern than it did when hard times set in. In the late '80s and early '90s, it increased both in volume and in its damaging effect on the stock growing industry.

But this increase in stealing was only part of a whole series of economic and social changes that affected the ranges at this time. These changes were the deeper and more fundamental causes of the trouble that finally found its explosive climax in the Invasion.

Many of the natural forces that operated against the big ranchers during this transition period were distant and intangible. The rustlers, however, were close at hand and visible, and against them the ranchers turned the full fury of their rough-hewn wrath.

Other live stock states had the same problems, to a greater or less extent, but met them differently. It was only in Wyoming that the inevitable period of transition from a single open-range cattle industry to a more diversified and complex economy erupted into violence.

The catastrophic winter of 1886-7 was part of the prolonged disaster. So was the economic depression that had already been felt in other parts of the country and hit the ranges in the wake of the hard winter. So were the changes that resulted from the invasion of the sheep herds, and the coming of the small ranchers, the homesteaders or nesters, with their plows and their fences.

These changes were disastrous to the big cattle companies that had opened up the country and prospered on the free range. They were natural and inevitable changes, anybody can see now. But the men who had been there first had a hard time seeing it then.

As the cattle raising industry reeled under the shock of first one blow and then another, the fortunes of the Wyoming Stock Growers Association likewise were shaken. Many ranchers and companies were driven out of business by the decimating of their herds, in the winter of '87, by the selling off of many cattle that did survive, and by the effects of over-grazing[2] and other practices which added to the difficulties of the changing times. The Association membership, its treasury and its prestige went dangerously low.

Creation of the Board of Live Stock Commissioners in 1888 by the Territorial Legislature did little to check the

---

[2]"Pasture was eaten too close and too continuously. It could not seed itself. Areas that should have been preserved for winter were used in summer." From *The Rustler Business,* by Charles B. Penrose, 1914. The Penrose manuscript, in the Association files at Laramie, is the source of much of the information used in this chapter. Penrose was the doctor who accompanied the invaders. He was a brother of Senator Boies Penrose of Pennsylvania, and had come to Wyoming for his health; he left Wyoming for the same reason, after taking part in the Invasion.

downward course. It placed control of the roundups, sale of mavericks and inspection of brands in the hands of the Territory rather than of the Association. Personnel of the Board was made up of Association members, but its functions were no longer those of the Association, although WSGA funds were turned over to the Territory. The Board ran into difficulties; its control over the industry was weaker than that which had prevailed under the strong hand of the Association.[3] This further contributed to the increase in cattle stealing and mavericking. Osgood, in *The Day of the Cattleman,* says "the situation was so bad by the spring of 1891 that no man's cattle were safe."

A contemporary observation by the Cheyenne *Daily Leader* summed it up on July 25, 1891:

"Men who before this year have borne and deserved good characters are now openly engaged in preying upon public ranges . . . All their neighbors and acquaintances are perfectly aware of the fact and the practice is oftentimes not merely winked at, but applauded . . . Efforts have been made by some of the larger cattle companies to bring the offenders to justice.[4] In some cases the grand juries have refused to indict; in others, petit juries have brought in verdicts of not guilty in the face of evidence as conclusive as any ever submitted in court . . . There are only two horns of the dilemma, either the thieves or the cattlemen must go."

In a way, the big cattlemen were reaping a whirlwind they had helped sow. For many of them had long been

[3]From the annual report of the Board of Live Stock Commissioners, Wyoming, 1892: "A thief in charge of a herd of cattle trailing from Utah to North Dakota stole cattle all along the route from the time he entered the state. . . In several instances, parties from South Dakota and Nebraska have come into Wyoming and worked the ranges ahead of our roundups and taken away with them on one drive over a hundred yearling cattle and horses, all unbranded. The Board heard of these raids, but were powerless from the fact that they had no inspectors where they could get after the raiders in time."

[4]A letter from W. C. Irvine in the Penrose MS says: "75 cases were nolle prossed by the Johnson county attorney at one time because the county was too poor to stand the expense of prosecuting."

guilty of mavericking, that is, of putting their own brands on stray young cattle that they knew were not theirs. John Clay, in *My Life on the Range,* tells of buying in 1883 a bunch of cattle from a rancher whose range was "towards the head of Powder river." Clay says: "We bought his cattle at $32.50 per head counted out. A good many of them had been mavericked, a practice we all followed in those days. There are a number of very respectable cattle owners of the present day who did likewise and some went further."

In a letter written in 1953, a 90-year-old man who at one time worked for Frank Canton recalled one of the evil effects of this practice: The changing times brought seasonal unemployment to an increasing number of cowpunchers, as the big ranches tightened their belts to weather the economic storm. Cowboys laid off for the winter would hole up in line camp cabins and ride out the lean months, picking up a little money now and then by finding mavericks and branding them with the brands of their erstwhile employers. Standard pay was three to five dollars for each animal thus acquired. Some of the cowboys got to thinking it over, and concluded they might better form their own outfits,—then, as one of them put it, "The mavericks we brand will be our own." This concept led to the formation of at least one cattle outfit[5] whose brand is still in use—in honest hands now—on the Wyoming range. The Board of Live Stock Commissioners in its report for 1892 said: "Instances have appeared where one thief, who never owned a cow acquired honestly, has come into market with more yearlings of an even age and size than could be obtained from the largest herd on the ranges."

The big ranchers blacklisted those who thus came in competition with them, that is, they barred the upstarts from the Association roundups. The men thus ostracized then got together with their sympathizers and other small

[5]"This outfit was started with the purchase of 23 cows and at the end of four years had 1,500 head, meanwhile having sold many, including 200 trailed to Idaho." (Penrose MS.)

operators and rounded up what they called their own cattle. In Johnson county they even formed a competitive organization, known as the Northern Wyoming Farmers and Stock Growers Association. John R. Smith—he of the Crazy Horse fight at Horseshoe Station in 1868—was president of this association when it met in the spring of 1892, in the town of Buffalo, with thirty members present, to organize its own roundups.

Buffalo, on Clear creek, at the foot of the Bighorn mountains, had become known as the rustlers' capital, just as Cheyenne was spoken of as the cowmen's capital. Cowmen and farmers came into the country around Buffalo in a wave soon after the Indian country was opened up. Buffalo itself was founded in 1879, by cattlemen, nesters, miners and freighters. Moving in, as they did, practically at the same time, the ranchers with their roving herds and the farmers with their fences came inevitably into conflict.

"It is a question of life and death," John Clay said in the president's address at the 19th annual meeting of the Wyoming Stock Growers Association at Cheyenne on April 7, 1891. "The trouble comes mostly from our getting no help from the state. Every cattle company here pays enormous taxes into the treasuries of the counties, and so far as I am concerned there is not a single company that I have to deal with that gets one iota of help from the counties in which they are taxed."

Later that same year the Association, through the Board of Live Stock Commissioners, took the initiative by instructing brand inspectors to seize cattle sent to market bearing certain brands which were listed as those in use by rustlers. These cattle were then to be sold, the receipts going to the Board. Resentment over this move helped drive more of the small ranchers and farmers into sympathy if not co-operation with the men who were actually rustling. Newspapers took the side of the "little people." The Cheyenne *Leader* decried "the revival of the old spirit of intolerance in the Wyoming Stock Growers Association."

Wrong was committed, undeniably, by both sides. Then the shooting began.

•

But first there were some hangings. One of these, even though it was a link in the chain of events that produced the Invasion of Johnson county in 1892, actually took place three years before the Invasion, and in Carbon county. There, in Spring Creek gulch on the Sweetwater, not far from the famous Independence Rock landmark on the Oregon Trail, a posse one night in July, 1889, hanged Jim Averill and Cattle Kate Watson from the same tree.

Averill kept a little store on Horse creek; one of the wares in which he dealt was whisky. One of his associates— sometimes known as his wife—was Ella (Cattle Kate Watson) Maxwell, whose profession, part-time at least, was the oldest one in the world. Cattle Kate took her pay in calves, and she and Averill acquired quite a herd. Their neighbors, including some big ranchers whose names were then and still are known throughout cow country, resented the incursions on their herds. Their attitude toward Averill and the woman was not softened by letters Averill wrote to newspapers, denouncing the big ranchers as tyrants and land-grabbers.

This part of the story came to an end with the hanging of Averill and Cattle Kate. There was a sequel, but it was anti-climax: Six ranchers were arrested when a coroner's jury named them as the lynchers; they were never brought to trial.

Next was Thomas Waggoner, who had a horse ranch forty miles southwest of Newcastle, in northeastern Wyoming. Contemporary newspaper accounts say he was "quite freely charged" with being a rustler and a fence for stolen horses. Three men rode up to his ranch house door one June day in 1891 and took Tom to a place since known as Dead Man's gulch. Tom died there, at the end of his own rope, with his boots and spurs on. ("I helped cut him down ten days after he was hung from his top horse, a flea-bitten gray," wrote D. J. Nelson of San Diego, Calif., to *Cow Country* in 1947.)

And in November of 1891, the people who had assumed the role of Regulators tried to get Nate Champion. Old-time saddle stiffs in Wyoming even today go sentimental when the talk gets around to Nate. He was for a time foreman of the EK (Horace Plunkett) ranch on Powder river. He worked for other outfits at times.[6] Champion was one of the best horsemen and gun handlers in cow country. His worst enemies never tried to take that away from him, nor did they deny his leadership qualities and all-round manliness. It was, in fact, because of these attributes and the wide following they brought him, that, when the cattle men drew up a list of rustlers who had to go, Nate Champion's name led all the rest. And they did rub him out, eventually, but not the first time they tried. That was on the morning of November 1, 1891, in the Powder river cabin of W. H. Hall, where Champion and Ross Gilbertson were staying. Six men raided this cabin at dawn. Champion deferred his own death by grabbing his six-shooter and driving off the men who had thought they could kill him in his bed.

But they did get Orley E. (Ranger) Jones. On November 28, 1891, Orley, who was 23 years old, was driving home from Buffalo on a buckboard drawn by two horses. He was shot by someone hiding under a bridge at a crossing of Muddy Creek fifteen miles south of Buffalo. The horses were cut loose, and the buckboard was used to haul Orley's body to a gully where it was left.

Two days later, John A. Tisdale, 39, another rancher, was driving home from Buffalo with a load of supplies and

[6]J. Elmer Brock tells this: "Champion was engaged by my father one year to look after our house on the EK ranch while father and the family were away. Champion boarded himself. Father came back, and Champion invited him to eat, and during the meal apologized for not having any potatoes. Father asked why he didn't have any, and Champion replied that he had been unable to get to town to buy any. Father said there were two or three tons of potatoes in the cellar, why didn't he take some of those, the door wasn't locked. Champion replied, 'Yes, I know, but they weren't mine.'"

Christmas gifts for his wife and three children. He was shot from ambush at Haywood's gulch, eight miles south of Buffalo. His body was found by Charles E. Basch, who rode up by chance practically as the shots were fired. Basch took the news to Buffalo, whence the sheriff, W. H. (Red) Angus, led a posse to the gulch to bring in the body. That same night, Jones' body was found.

People in Wyoming today will tell you that these killings were committed by gunmen hired for the purpose by big cattlemen. But nothing was ever proved. The only one ever legally accused of murder in connection with these cases was Frank Canton, the former sheriff and stock detective. In his autobiography *Frontier Days*, Canton says he was arrested at his own insistence, "to refute the slander" that he had done the killings. The case against him was dismissed.

Jones, who was murdered on the Muddy, and Tisdale, who died among the toys he was taking home for Christmas, were, like Nate Champion, well known and popular. Tisdale had graduated from a little Texas college and had come north trailing Texas cattle. For a time he was Theodore Roosevelt's foreman on the Elkhorn ranch in North Dakota. Tisdale came into Wyoming with money and took up a ranch on the Red fork of the Powder. He was a man of education and high ideals. By background and instinct he belonged on the side of the big cattlemen, but the strange alignment of forces on the ranges in '91 found him with those who were against them. This was due in part to bad blood that developed between him and Frank Canton, and this was due originally to the fact that two of Tisdale's friends, an elderly couple, were on the list of persons supposedly, at least, slain by Canton in Texas. The first time Tisdale laid eyes on Canton, on the streets of Buffalo, he recognized him as the killer of his friends. Tisdale's first impulse was to avenge these deaths forthwith. With this intent, he followed Canton into a store; Canton went out the back door as Tisdale went in the front. Tisdale cooled off, but after the attack on Champion and Gilbertson, in the Hall cabin, he talked about what should be done to those who tried to kill people in their beds (he and Champion had been boys together in Texas), and this is believed by old ranchers in Johnson county today to have been what led to the dry-gulching of John Tisdale. Dry-gulching, incidentally, was scorned by most of the rustler element; they said they could have killed off all the men in the big outfits had they been willing to descend to that mode of killing, but they always felt that their code of ethics was above that of the big cattlemen. The fact that Tisdale disapproved of shooting people in the back, and said so, led to his own death by that very means.

Like a low-lying cloud, the "life or death" issue that John Clay had spoken of hung over Wyoming as the year 1892 came on. A state of dangerous excitement pervaded cow country. There was an ominous undercurrent of suspense. Then the cattle men decided to take the law into their hands, and launched the Invasion.

It was not an official function of the Wyoming Stock Growers Association, although leading members of the Association took part in it, the secretary, H. B. Ijams, conducting some of the correspondence in connection with the raising of the invasionary force. In the records of the executive committee of the Association there is a two-line statement: "No meetings of the Executive Committee were held in 1892." The annual meeting of the Association itself, however, took place April 4, at Cheyenne, but only 43 members answered roll call. This was a one-day meeting. George Baxter presided, in the absence of John Clay, who was in Europe. Clay in his book says he was later accused of having planned and instituted the Invasion, "whereas I was innocent as an unborn babe." But he adds: "Some of my associates were in it tooth and nail," which did not overstate the case.

Clay in his book applies the word "indefensible" to the Invasion. It was indefensible, and it can be understood only when it is placed in perspective against the frontier times in which it occurred. Human life was cheap on the border. Killing was the common method of settling a dispute. It was not good, but it was so.

•

The Johnson County Invasion got under way the morning of Tuesday, April 5, 1892, with the arrival of a train at Cheyenne from Denver. It was a special train, with the blinds pulled down in its passenger coach. There was a baggage car, and a flatcar bearing wagons and camp equipment. There were three stock cars carrying horses.

In the passenger coach were some twenty-five men who had been hired for the occasion. These were mostly Texas gunmen; they included former sheriffs, deputies and marshals and others known for their cool nerves and trigger fingers.

At Cheyenne, twenty-five Wyoming men got on the train, ranchers, foremen, live stock detectives, brand inspectors. There was a doctor, and there were two newspaper men, one from Chicago and one from Cheyenne.

The original plan had been for the twenty-five mercenaries to do the job alone. Later, an equal number of ranchers and cow men agreed to go, when exhorted to do so by William C. Irvine. Irvine was a Pennsylvanian who had come to Wyoming as representative of financial interests, and managed several large cattle companies, the best known of which was the Ogallala Cattle Company with the Keystone brand.

"Our intention," said Irvine in telling about the Invasion afterward, "was to take Buffalo, seize the arms of the militia in the court house, arrest what rustlers were there, call the people of the town together, and tell them what we were there for."

J. Elmer Brock, who in a long life spent in the Powder river country has known many who were in the Johnson county war, on both sides, is convinced that the original plan of the Invaders was to enter Johnson county in a peaceful manner and not to use their armed strength unless forced to do so.

"They planned," Brock says, "to go to Buffalo, and take

141

charge of the court house and the weapons of the militia, which were stored there. This was to be done to keep the settlers from getting them. There were also some court records against those who had attacked Champion and Gilbertson in the Hall cabin which the Regulators wanted to destroy. They proposed then to call a mass meeting of citizens of the county. They intended to tell the law-abiding residents that their rights would be recognized and respected. They expected to confess that they had opposed the settlers' coming into the country, and had done many things against them for which they were sorry now. They wanted to offer to make amends and obtain the co-operation of the honest settlers in protecting property which everybody knew was being stolen wholesale. They planned, following this meeting, to post a list of the confirmed thieves and those so classified, and give them 24 hours to get out of the country on pain of death."

Canton in his book says the Invaders had warrants for the arrest of certain rustlers. There is no other evidence that this was so. The Invaders did, however, have a list of nineteen men whom they considered ring-leading rustlers, and they proceeded on the theory that the ranges would be safe if they could, one way or another, rid cow country of these men.

In command of the Invaders was dapper, nervy little Major Frank Walcott of Glenrock, whose title derived from Civil War service and who had also been a United States marshal. Frank Canton rebelled, during the march, at Walcott's leadership and temporarily replaced him. When the going got tough, however, Walcott returned to command by demand of the men, who felt safer when he was in charge.

It was an army, on a small scale, and for a time it moved with military precision along carefully planned lines. As the train chugged northward, telegraph wires north of Douglas went dead; they were cut to prevent an alarm being sounded. At Casper, nearest railroad point to Buffalo (still 125 miles away) , men, horses, wagons, guns and other equipment were unloaded and started northward, over the sagebrush hills.

After two days of difficult traveling, with sundry mishaps and adventures along the way, the Invaders reached the Tisdale TTT ranch on the South fork of the Powder river. Here they paused to rest, and here they were met by Mike Shonsey, foreman of the Western Union Beef Company ranch, who brought them news direct from the rustler camp. For Shonsey had slept the previous night in a four-room cabin, on the KC ranch, eighteen miles north, where Nate Champion and Nick Ray were staying. Shonsey told the Invaders that about a dozen of the men whose names were on their list had been at the cabin that same night.

At this point, differences of opinion as to their campaign plan split the invading force. Some of the cattlemen were for following their original plan, others insisted on pushing on for an immediate attack on the town of Buffalo.

Those who favored the original plan warned that if it was not followed, the entire campaign would fail. When this plan was abandoned, two men left the group. They were H. W. (Hard Winter) Davis, a rancher, and Penrose, the doctor.

Some of the Texans added to the crisis by showing signs of restlessness. Among other things, they demanded to see the warrants they had been told they were to help serve.

Two days later the Invaders reached their first objective, the only one they were to succeed in taking. This was the four-room cabin on the Nolan KC ranch, on the Middle Fork of Powder river, where Nate Champion and Nick Ray were living. This time they got Champion. They surprised and trapped him. The fight he put up that day, against overwhelming odds, single-handed after Ray was killed, is in itself a Western epic. It was immortalized by Champion himself, who not only lived up to all that had ever been said about his courage, but kept a penciled diary of his last hours on earth which is a border classic. "Me and Nick was getting breakfast," Nate's saga begins, continuing with a simple but graphic hour-to-hour description of the day-long fight, and ending: "I think they will fire the house this time . . . It's not night yet . . . Boys, I feel pretty lonesome just now . . . The house is all fired . . . Goodby, boys, if I never see you again." He never did. When the Invaders moved on northward, Champion and Ray lay dead and the KC ranchhouse was in ashes.[7]

The town of Buffalo, nearly fifty miles north, was the next objective. The Invaders never got there.

For by now, news of the approach of the Invaders had reached Buffalo, the Settler—or Rustler—stronghold. The town swirled with the dust of an angry army mobilizing out of nowhere. Guns and ammunition were tossed out of stores to arm those who didn't have their own weapons. Singly and in groups, defenders of the settlers' cause spurred their lathered horses toward the invading army.

Caught off guard by the swift gathering of their opponents, who outnumbered them four or five to one, the Invaders first were cut off from their supply wagons. Then their triumphant forward progress became a gallop to safety. They found it at the TA ranch, on Crazy Woman, where they took refuge and prepared to defend themselves against the hosts they had aroused. This was when they cut the portholes in the walls of the barn and the bunk house on the TA ranch, as they deployed their forces for a defensive battle. Their headquarters were in the ranchhouse.[8] They dug trenches on some of the ridges surrounding the buildings. The Settlers surrounded them, and poured lead at them. Slugs and cartridge shells are still turned up every

[7]Site of the cabin where Champion and Ray died is lost in the grass of a pasture where no signs of the old ranch show, just south of the town of Kaycee.

[8]From the Buffalo *Bulletin*, June 2, 1892: "The largest dance given in the winter of 1888-9 was at the now celebrated TA ranch. It was a large, roomy house, and had just been built. The floors were smooth and nice to dance on. Charley Ford (foreman of the ranch) had been married but a short time, and he acted as the genial host to perfection. It seems strange that three years afterward he should be barricaded in the same ranch, with 47 other murderers, fighting nine out of every ten men who were there at the dance that night."

Buxom Cattle Kate sometimes took her pay in cattle, and some of the cattle were rustled, so Kate died a rustler's death, at the end of a rope, in 1889. Her partner, Jim Averill, went with her. Their hanging was one of the events that preceded the Johnson County War of 1892. which is discussed in Chapter Twenty. (Photo of Cattle Kate from WSGA files.)

Thomas de Beau Soli, a French trapper, came into Wyoming Territory and became a cowman, building in 1872 a one-room log ranchhouse on the Sweetwater river. His name was Americanized to Tom
Sun, and in the days of the open range, in the late 'eighties and
early 'nineties, was widely known in the Sweetwater country. His son
still runs the old ranch, living in a modern home adjoining the log
cabin of 1872. (Photo from Tom Sun.)

Robert Foote, whose general store is shown in this photo, of the east side of Main street, Buffalo, Wyo., in 1883, figured prominently in the Johnson County War on the side of the settlers. Buffalo today is a trim, modern little town, alive in the summertime with tourists traveling US Highways 16 and 87 (Photo from Wyoming State Historical Department.)

Nate Champion, killed in the fight at the KC ranch in the Johnson County War, stands behind the man with the gauntlet glove in this photo of the Bar C roundup wagon in 1884. Left to right, standing, Hank Devoe, foreman; Ray Peters, George Gordon, Chester Morris, Nate Champion, Joe Vincent; sitting, Buck Jackson, Jack Donahue, Hall, Rice, McCarty, Al Allison, Bill Rankin, Jack Flagg. (From WSGA files.)

In this tiny cabin on Powder river, November 1, 1890, Nate Champion and Ross Gilbertson were attacked by six men, including Frank Canton, who surprised them in their beds. Champion and Gilbertson were too quick with their guns; they drove off their attackers, and Champion temporarily thwarted the fate that caught up with him in April of 1892 at the KC ranch. (J. Elmer Brock photo.) Right, Capt. John R. Smith, who fought Crazy Horse at Horseshoe Road Ranch (Chapter Five) in 1868, and was a prominent resident of Johnson County at the time of the War in 1892.

A Jekyll and Hyde of the Plains, in the days of the open range, Frank Canton (above) was feared as a peace officer and hated as a ruthless killer. See Chapter Thirteen. (Photo from Association files.)

THE INVADERS

JOHNSON COUNTY CATTLE WAR TAKEN AT Ft. D.A. RUSSELL
(FRANCIS E. WARREN) MAY 4TH 1892.

No. 1. TOM SMITH
" 2. A.B. CLARKE
" 3. J.N. LESLIE
" 4. E.W. WHITCOMB
" 5. D. BROOKE
" 6. W.B. WALLACE
" 7. CHAS. FORD

No. 8. A.R. POWERS
" 9. A.D. ADAMSON
" 10. C.A. CAMPBELL
" 11. FRANK LABERTEAUX
" 12. PHIL DUFRAN
" 13. MAJOR WOLCOTT
" 14. W.E. GUTHRIE

No. 15. W. McIRVINE
" 16. BOB TISDALE
" 17. JOE ELLIOTT
" 18. JOHN TISDALE
" 19. SCOTT DAVIS
" 20. FRED D. DEBILLIER
" 21. BEN MORRISON

No. 22. W.J. CLARKE
" 23. L.H. PARKER
" 24. M.A. McNALLY
" 25. B.C. SCHULTZE
" 26. W.A. TABOR
" 27. J.J. GARRETT
" 28. W.A. WILSON

No. 29. J. BARLINGS
" 30. M.A. McNALLY
" 31. MIKE SHONSEY
" 32. DICK ALLEN
" 33. FRED HESSE
" 34. FRANK CANTON
" 35. W.H. LITTLE

No. 36. JEFF MYNETT
" 37. BOB BARLINGS
" 38. S. SUTHERLAND
" 39. BUCK GARRETT
" 40. G.R. TUCKER
" 41. J.M. BENFORD
" 42. WILL ARMSTRONG

Barn on the TA ranch, Crazy Woman Creek, where the Johnson County War ended when the besieged Invaders were rescued by U.S. cavalry. Three portholes show in upper part of barn. (Photo, taken in 1892, from Clarence Gammon, present owner of the ranch.)

now and then on the ranch grounds. The bullet holes in the walls are still there.

In the buildings and corrals of the TA ranch, and in the earthworks they dug, the Invaders held off the Rustlers long enough for horse-back messengers, who slipped through the lines in the night, to get word back to Cheyenne of the desperate plight of the army. Wires were kept hot between Cheyenne and Washington, while the battle at the ranch went on for three days. The Rustlers once tried heaving big shot at the ranch buildings from an improvised howitzer which blew up at the first blast. Then they rigged up a movable breastwork, which they called the Ark, and tried to push dynamite close enough to blow up the buildings. This too failed.

On the morning of the 13th, three days after the siege had begun, three troops of the 6th cavalry from Fort Mc-Kinney, near Buffalo, reached the scene, under command of Col. J. J. VanHorn and on orders from President Benjamin Harrison. The Invaders surrendered to the troops,[9] the Rustlers withdrew. The shooting stopped.

The fifty prisoners of the troops were taken to Fort Mc-Kinney, then to Cheyenne, where they were held for three and one half months, and eventually to Laramie, under charges of murder. After more months of legal skirmishing, and of technical custody, they were finally all released, in January of 1893, on their own recognizance, because the county had run out of funds for their care and maintenance in custody and for their further prosecution. So far as the law was concerned, that was the end.[10]

[9]One of the Texans with the Invaders, seeing the troops ride up and not understanding exactly what was going on, exclaimed: "My God, have we got to fight the Army too?"

[10]Battle casualties for the War included several men slightly wounded and two of the Texans ironically killed by their own guns. One died when his rifle was discharged as he and the gun were thrown from a snorty horse; the other was shot in the stomach by his own sixshooter falling from its holster as he crawled on hands and knees through the ranchhouse door. Also, Champion killed one of the men at Kaycee. His diary told of his shooting at "that duck in the stable door," and added "Don't know if I got him or not." Men who were there said he did.

It would be pleasant to be able to say that sweetness and light settled down over cow country in the wake of the Johnson County War. Actually, however, another decade was to pass before Wyoming's agony of evolution was to end and the sanctity of human life was to be restored and acknowledged. Federal troops moved in and stayed for several months following the Invasion. There were more killings—notably, the ambush murder of George Wellman, on May 9, 1892. Wellman was foreman of the Hoe outfit, and a United States marshal, well liked. His murder was at the time attributed by each side to the other, but in later years has been, to the satisfaction of close students of the affair, laid at the door of a rustler gang called the Red Sashes (because they wore strips of red flannel under their cartridge belts to keep the bullet grease off their clothes).

It was typical of the times that when the Rev. Charles E. Duell conducted Wellman's funeral, in St. Luke's Episcopal church at Buffalo, the pastor wore a brace of guns underneath his vestments, and the Masons who helped conduct the service were similarly armed. When Nate Champion and Nick Ray were buried, also in Buffalo, tension was so high that the church organist declined to appear, and the organ was played for the occasion by a young girl who was not afraid. The girl was Lillian Hogerson Baker, who died in Buffalo in 1953.

Some ranchers, their plans for mass purging of the rustlers thwarted, turned again to individual killings and hired gunmen to eliminate, one by one and at so much a head, the men the ranchers named as thieves. The fiction-like figure of Tom Horn moved through this period, even unto the gallows that ended his life—but not the controversy over him—at Cheyenne in 1903.

There was also the Hole-in-the-Wall trouble. This centered in a desolate Powder river area which became the rendezvous of gangs of real criminals, including train robbers as well as large scale rustlers. For a long time, honest cattle men's roundup crews feared to penetrate the Hole-in-the-Wall country to work the cattle there. Then Bob Divine, foreman for the Carey CY ranch, came along. He had the courage to ride into the desperadoes' stronghold and work the cattle. There was some gunplay, in which one of the rustlers was killed and Divine was wounded. Worse trouble was averted by intercession of A. L. Brock,[11] whose EK ranch was on the north fork of the Powder. In the range wars, Brock (a member of the Legislature) had been aligned with neither side and was respected by both. This gave him an influence which he exerted quietly but effectively in behalf of the law and order that were eventually established in cow country. Men of this type were the ones who did succeed in accomplishing what the ill-conceived Invasion failed to do.

The Invasion failed because the cattle men did not perceive that vigilante days in Wyoming were over, that a blood purge would not accomplish a moral reform. They sadly misjudged popular sentiment; apparently they had no idea that the Settlers had so many on their side, or that the Invasion would arouse such swift and spirited resistance. They did not recognize the "rhythm of change" that was at that time affecting the whole country. They were not the only ones who were unaware of what was happening. It is only with the perspective of time that historians have come to call this period "the Watershed of the Nineties." On one side of the watershed lay pioneer America. On the other side was the beginning of the modern era. It was a time of the breaking up and re-shaping of communities and institutions, and not only Wyoming.

J. Elmer Brock has put it this way:

"It is easy to see how the feeling between the owners of the big cattle companies and the homesteaders came about. The big outfits were mostly outside capital, much of it foreign. Many of the English and Scotch companies had their *field* offices in New York or Chicago. Their animosity

[11]A. L. Brock settled in Johnson county in 1884 on Kelly creek and in 1890 located near the EK mountains on the North fork of the Powder. He was the first chairman of the historical committee of the Wyoming Stock Growers Association. He died in 1946, aged 88.

toward anyone invading what they had appropriated as their range was not illogical from their viewpoint. Their employes, in direct contact with the homesteaders, were able to differentiate and looked upon the settlers with mixed feelings. There was also a differing viewpoint among the large ranchers. To some of them, the poor homesteader who settled near them, and who was honest and left other people's cattle alone, became a moral responsibility and they saw to it that neither he nor his family suffered. However, the matter was complicated by the unholy alliance that developed between some homesteaders and the professional cattle rustlers, many of whom were men who had left Texas for their own good and that of Texas. Through association with the honest ones, the rustlers acquired a false background of integrity and honesty, which they overplayed in pursuit of their rustling. As it finally wound up, the big cattle outfits were largely driven out, and the honest homesteaders were the ones who had to clean the matter up."

So far as money was concerned, the Invasion cost the cattle men $105,000—W. C. Irvine's figures, in a letter to Dr. Charles B. Penrose, February 22, 1914. As of January 1, 1895, Johnson County had paid out, in litigation fees, court transcripts, judgments and interest, $10,482.46, and there was $17,295.92 still owing. Johnson county was practically broke after the Invasion, and was later aided by a state relief bill passed by the legislature on the initiative of W. J. Thom of Buffalo.

Rerouting of a proposed railroad line was one of the economic effects, old-timers in Wyoming say today. The railroad was being laid across Wyoming from the South Dakota state line to the Montana line in the range war era. The original intent was to go from Gillette, Wyo., to Sheridan via Buffalo. Bonepickers went ahead, gathering up carloads of buffalo and other animal bones along the route. A grade for the railroad was run as far as the bone piles, but the steel was never laid; instead, the railroad switched to a route that took it around the northeast corner of Johnson county, the explanation being that the road wished to avoid an area as heavily in debt as Johnson county then was. The line was laid by the Grand Island and Northern Wyoming Railroad Company, and is now a part of the Burlington system.

Consequences of the Invasion were felt for years. Many of the men who took part in it left Wyoming, some of them permanently. Cattle owned by participants were for a long time unsafe on the ranges; many of them were killed. There were political repercussions too. The Republican party, to which most of the cattle men belonged, temporarily lost much of its power in the state. Churches and fraternal orders were, for a time, split down the middle.

When the Wyoming Stock Growers Association held its annual meeting in 1893, John Clay, back from Europe and again in the president's chair, found the situation still depressing and forbidding. In the preceding two years, he said in his address to the convention, the cattle industry had labored under many difficulties:

"Low prices have prevailed and during the winter of 1891 and 1892 serious losses occurred. Credits were strained and under these unpleasant circumstances many herds were sold out in whole or in part. Not content with the imposition of financial and climate troubles, another burden had to be added to our lot. After a long period of forebearance and patience from range depredations, both petty and wholesale, the trouble culminated a year ago and the so-called Invasion of Johnson County took place, which ended unfortunately and gave rise to an almost interminable amount of bad blood politically and socially. It developed and brought to a head the feeling held and openly expressed by many people in the state that stealing cattle is a proper and just way of making a living. No state can survive such a morality and we have before us a young and what should be a thriving community, gradually retrograding. If you will observe the towns of this state, if you go into the great valleys, you will see unmistakable signs of decay. Nothing else can be expected. If you endeavor to do business in a community that has no respect for property, success can only be short lived. The world is wide and people move away gradually, almost imperceptibly, to other fields of enterprise and labor. The policy of the majority in the state is to pull down its principal industry. It has sunk to a low ebb, so low that in my opinion it has touched bottom. Late events, particularly in the Legislature, prove this to be the case. Some convictions for cattle and horse stealing in the local courts have taken place and it is sincerely to be hoped that they will continue.

"While the Invasion is now consigned to history, it developed, during the progress last spring, and the long weary summer months which followed, a spirit of admiration, from all classes, of the men, the very flower of Wyoming's citizens, who had taken part in the expedition. Under the most trying circumstances they stood shoulder to shoulder, scarcely a murmur escaping them. Gentlemen, I am not here to defend these parties. Technically, legally, they did wrong, but I consider it no mean privilege to stand in this prominent position today and to say that I count every one of them a friend. . . "

W. C. Irvine succeeded Clay as president of the Association in 1896, and held the office for fifteen years, during which the Association slowly regained its position, its influence, and its membership.

•

The sixty-two years intervening since the Johnson County War have done much to close the wound. Sons of men who were on one side have married daughters of men who were on the other, and some of their children and their grandchildren are running ranches and managing farms side by side along the Crazy Woman and the Powder with never a thought of reaching for their rifles to settle their problems. In another generation, the healing hand of time will have obliterated the few remaining fragments of the hatred that turned some peaceful gulches into graves.

But there are grizzled old cow men in Wyoming today who still bristle at certain versions of the Johnson County

War, even when it is their friends and associates who relate the tale. "That's the way *he* sees it," such a man will snort. "*My* father was on the other side, and *I* see it *his* way."

A veteran rancher nods at his wife across the breakfast table. "Yes," he says to the guest in the house, "when we were kids, I used to throw rocks at her, because her folks were Settlers and mine were cow people." He smiles when he says that now.

Not long before her death in 1953, the little old lady who as a girl had dared to play the organ for Nate Champion's funeral looked back into her girlhood and said: "We never went to the door to answer a knock, in those days without a gun in our hands."

And an old man who started punching cows on the Powder in the eighties, and who fought with the Rustlers, writes, from the sundown slope of the Pacific coast, in shaky script to a friend in Kaycee: "If I could come back, and take you to the TA ranch, I could show you where our outfit was during the fight, and I could show you something that no other man living could show you." Whatever secret[12] is possessed by this one of the few survivors of the Invasion will probably die with him, for at 90 there is no coming back.

And the bitterness and animosities of the frontier days in Johnson county have drifted away like pistol smoke.

[12]In the Association files at Laramie there is a tightly sealed package, apparently a manuscript, which is said to pertain to the Johnson County War; it is heavily labeled: "Restricted to December 15, 1973." In 1954 there was only one known survivor of the Invaders; he was Mike Shonsey, of Clarks, Nebraska.

PART SEVEN

A DROUGHT IS LIKE A DYING WOMAN

CHAPTER TWENTY ONE

THE DIRTY THIRTIES

There was a great drought over Wyoming in 1935; a dreadful drought. The summer pasture went; the winter pasture. Men saw their sheep and cattle starve, weaken and die. The markets were overstocked. Yearlings, seed cattle, everything, sold for what a man could get. Drought is like a dying woman, wide-eyed, staring, never moving, fever on her lips.

From 'Powder River: Let 'er Buck,'
by Struthers Burt (Farrar and Rinehart) .

Indians, rustlers, sheep, Texas fever, grasshoppers, blizzard and cloudburst—all these the cowmen had to fight: And drought.

Each demanded a different defense. Against human enemies, the ranchers needed courage, a steady nerve and a sure aim. A storm you could do something about, at least as soon as it was over. But meeting the long, slow droughts that have periodically plagued the Plains has called for a special kind of resistance. Courage, yes, but patience, too, and far-sightedness, a willingness to learn from past mistakes, and an ability to work with others for a common end. You can't sight down a rifle barrel at a lack of moisture. It has to be met some other way, and only bitter experience teaches how.

Cow country has passed through many periods of drought, but the one that hurt the worst was the one that came along hand in hand with the depression of the 1930s.

•

By this time, fortunately, the Association had recovered from the worst effects of the turbulent '90s and had regained some of its prestige and influence. It had hit a low mark in 1900, with only 28 members at the annual meeting (143 sent proxies). There were no speakers, no banquet. Problems discussed were the encroachment of the dry farmer and the sheep man, and intensified horse thievery. The boom days were gone, and modern scientific ranching was in its infancy. The Association at the turn of the century lacked vitality but it kept alive under the guidance of a succession of presidents who included, after W. C. Irvine's fifteen-year incumbency, John B. Kendrick, Robert D. Carey, James C. Shaw, J. C. Underwood and John L. Jordan. These were stalwart cattlemen, most of them trained in public service through experience in the legislature or other civic duties. Kendrick's career, for example, included service both as governor and United States senator.

Nevertheless, as the 1930s came on, the Association was far below its full effectiveness. As Agnes Wright Spring's *70 Years Cow Country* makes plain, "the stock industry was facing one of the most trying decades in its history. The full impact of the 1929 'crash' had just hit the West."

The Association had only 262 members and but $565 in the bank when, in 1930, J. Elmer Brock was elected president. But this was a turning point for the Association. Its fortunes started upward again, so that by the end of the 1931 fiscal year there were 971 active members and 29 bank members, including the Federal Reserve Bank. The membership owned approximately 375,125 head of cattle, or more than 55 percent of the range cattle in Wyoming.

When Brock took charge of the Association's affairs its executive committee had not met for several years. It met four times in 1930, and before it Brock laid the unpleasant facts as he found them, consulting the best business men and the most experienced cattle growers in the state, and planning and executing one step after another to aid the industry and restore the Association to its position of leadership.

By legislative enactment, a $55,000 obligation to the state was wiped out. This was money for estrays, which the law required the Association to turn over to the state.

Because it had already turned over more than $100,000 in estray money, and this had gone into the state general fund in spite of a supreme court ruling that these funds were intended to be used for the benefit of the cattle industry, the Association withheld the $55,000. At the same time this was wiped out by statute, the state appropriated $30,000 to the Association from the $100,000 it held, and the rest of the $100,000 was turned over to the Association inspection fund by subsequent legislatures.

An accounting system was set up, under which the annual auditing of the Association books by the state examiner became standard practice, as it still is.

The Association acquired official recognition as a quasi-governmental institution when a law was passed, in March 1931, giving legal authority to the Association to make brand inspection of all cattle shipped from the state, whether by members or others, thus further strengthening the market inspection system which the Association had then been carrying on for fifty years.

By thus rebuilding its foundations, the Association began to grow again. It concentrated on legislative matters of importance to the cattle industry and stayed out of other people's affairs. Its regained power was discreetly but effectively used.

Russell Thorp became field secretary of the Association coincident with Brock's presidency. Thorp, member of an old Wyoming family, had become a member of the Association in 1902 and had served on the executive committee in 1927. His knowledge of the cattle industry and his understanding of its problems were so helpful that in January 1931 he was made acting secretary, and in 1932 became executive secretary-chief inspector, a position he held until 1948, when he moved up to a field secretaryship with the American National Cattlemen's Association.

The revitalized Association restored the efficiency of its brand inspection service and expanded it to meet new needs. It fought for and obtained reductions, eventually totaling 50 percent, in grazing land tax valuations, which had grown out of proportion to revenue. It united forces with the wool growers of the state on such common interests as taxation, railway rates, the marketing system, the public domain and state land rentals. The office of the Association in Cheyenne was reorganized, and Mrs. Myrna F. Agee was brought in as stenographer and bookkeeper. So expert did she rapidly become that in 1948, when Russell Thorp resigned, she served as interim secretary of the Association— and she was the first of a few women who have passed the Association examination for brand inspector, though she never served in that capacity. She is still in the Cheyenne office, as assistant secretary.

•

It is well that the Association was thus reorganized and fortified at this time for early in the 1930s, along with other problems, came the drought. The warmest, dryest years in the recorded history of the Great Plains were at hand. Waterholes went dry. Wells were driven ever deeper, until in some cases it took a gallon of gasoline to pump a gallon of water. Subsoil moisture was depleted to great depths. Topsoil blew away in powdery dust flung far and high by hot, dry winds that were in themselves devastating. Dust covered the pastures and the feed stacks. It drifted in piles that hindered train and auto traffic. People hung dampened blankets at the windows of their homes, and wore wet cloths over their faces when they were outdoors. There was darkness at noon. Humans and animals suffered alike. A few of the humans fled, leaving their homes to the dust and the wind. Cattle died from suffocation and from starvation.

The first Western states drought conference was called at Salt Lake City, in July of 1930. Charles A. Myers of Evanston represented the Wyoming Stock Growers Association. Steps were taken to begin moving cattle from the drought-affected areas to regions where feed was available.

By 1934 the situation was so bad that government purchase of live stock was begun in the counties designated as emergency areas. Due in large measure to the emergency cattle-buying program, losses that year were not excessive. Between June 1, 1934, and February 1, 1935, there were 285,697 head of cattle purchased in Wyoming under this program.

For the year 1934, cattle losses were 25,000, which was 2.4 percent of the January 1 inventory of 1,050,000 head. Calf losses that year were 27,000, which was 7.3 percent of the calf crop of 372,000 head.

Cattle bought by the government during the drought went for an average of $12.50 a head, or about a third of the cost of producing a weaner calf.

Gaunted cattle were slaughtered and buried; those suitable for canning were concentrated at loading points and shipped to slaughtering plants, where they were canned for relief purposes. This kept the affected cattle out of the usual market channels. Due to leadership exercised in this emergency by the Association, Wyoming was the first range state to complete its organization and start moving its drought cattle. Except for Hot Springs county, every county in the state was designated drought area, entitled to emergency freight rates on both cattle and feed.

Throughout the struggle against the drought and its consequences, the Association maintained brand protection for cattle owners—and Wyoming was the only range state receiving this protection on cattle purchased at markets by the government during the drought. The Association also helped obtain emergency rates on concentrates, cottonseed cake and similar essentials, and distributed information on all matters pertaining to the crisis. It originated a plan, worked out with the co-operation of Will G. Metz, state director of the Emergency Relief Administration, for construction of chutes and pens throughout the state, to facilitate unloading of live stock for brand inspection.

The Association's battle with drought was spread over a period of years. There were some places in the state where a more severe toll was taken in 1936 than in 1934. Whole herds were sold at prices that were less than production costs. Association officers and committeemen were tirelessly on the go, keeping members informed on range conditions and weather prospects, and on the many steps being taken to provide relief; locating pasture to which the cattle could be moved, and getting them there; obtaining emergency rates on feed.

Let one cowman who lived through the drought period tell what it was like in his region. This is Joe H. Watt speaking; he runs a Hereford ranch near Moorcroft, his range being in Weston and Crook counties, northeastern Wyoming:

The weather started getting dry in 1930. The grass was short, and we had a scant hay crop. The year 1931 was drier, but not too severe; 1932 was a good year, with grass plentiful, and cattle in good condition. But by 1933 the weather had turned dry again and grasshoppers had made an appearance. The spring of '34 was so dry the grass hardly started, and by May the air was hot and dry, cattle were beginning to lose weight, and some cattle were moved to market. The price of cattle at that time (in May) was four to five cents per pound for feeder cattle, and three to four cents per pound for dry cows.

In early June the grasshoppers began to hatch and to eat what little grass there was. The government started its cattle buying program the first of July, giving $4.00 to $8.00 per head for calves, $10.00 to $15.00 for yearlings and $14.00 to $20.00 for older cattle. By this time cattle were dying from starvation and thirst. One rancher who sold 400 head to the government had 75 head condemned and killed, as they were too weak to be shipped.

The hoppers became so thick that on a hot afternoon they would gather on sagebrush and the north side of fence posts until the surface was completely covered. The winter of '34 and '35 was mild, and what stock was left in the country was able to get along on very little feed; 1935 was a fair year and the hoppers didn't seem so thick. Then along came 1936, which was hot and dry early in the spring. The grasshoppers hatched out the latter part of May, eating what green feed had started. The stockmen had to find feed; some shipped into surrounding states. In July, cattle were turned into meadows on what was normally winter feed, and were living off weeds and grazing the leaves off the trees as high as they could reach.

The Mormon Crickets made their appearance that summer. They advanced like an army. The ground was completely covered in their march. I can remember moving a herd of cattle, and, when we met the crickets, spending some time forcing the cattle and saddle horses to cross them. The crickets moved in a straight line. When they came to the house they crawled up the side and over the top. The house was completely covered with them. The crickets did little damage to feed, as the ground was bare by that time, and there was little they could hurt. People at Sundance, Wyo., tried to build a tin fence around their town, and put oil at the base to keep the crickets out, but this was not too satisfactory.

The government and individuals spent a great deal of money trying to poison the grasshoppers and crickets. They succeeded in killing a great many, but it had no noticeable effect.

All through these years, we had strong southwest winds that caused dust storms, drifting dirt to the top of fences and buildings, and into houses, covering everything with a fine layer of dust.

The winter of 1936 and '37 was mild again and the spring of '37 started out dry and with lots of 'hoppers, but in June we began to get rain, and grass began to grow. In the fore part of July we had heavy rains and hail. Within a week every one began to notice that the grasshoppers had disappeared. Whether they had died, no one knew, but we were thankful to see the last of them.

Through all this, most of the real cowmen managed to hang onto their ranches and foundation herds, though I suspect few of them could tell today just how they did it. But they never thought of quitting.

This sort of thing called for co-operation with other states and with many agencies, including the federal government. It demanded much patience on the part of all concerned, in order that differing viewpoints might be reconciled and a plan of action followed. The rugged individualist who was the cowman came in contact here with governmental bureaucracy and red tape, and was duly and properly irritated thereby, at the same time that he had to accept some of the emergency benefits that stood between him and complete disaster. He took his beating, too, with a sense of humor that has always helped his kind get along as well as they have.

"We would give a lot for a three-day rain," wrote one member to the Association office during the dry times. "We may have to call on you for help along that line as it seems to do no good to call on the Almighty."

The rains finally came, and that drought period ended. But everybody knew that new ones—worse ones, perhaps—would come in the future, though scientists were saying that droughts can be measured, studied and predicted with increasing precision. However that may be, the "dirty thirties" at least provided cow country with some lessons in what to do when they do come, and much of the pattern of that period was repeated in 1953 when drought again was inflicted upon parts of Wyoming.

Presidents who followed Brock in the 1930s (he declined a third term) were Dugald R. Whitaker of Cheyenne (1933-36) and Sam C. Hyatt of Hyattville (1937-39). In 1942, when Charles A. Myers of Evanston was launched on his third term as president, at the seventieth annual convention, at Gillette, Secretary Thorp was able to report that the membership was up to 1,496. During the preceding year, Thorp added, 324 cowmen had joined the Association; this was more than the total membership at the advent of the Brock-Thorp era in 1930.

162

PART EIGHT

WOMEN OF WYOMING

CHAPTER TWENTY TWO

THE COW-BELLES

Private problems that seemed vitally important a short
time ago are beginning to take second place. We are growing up fast, we Americans, and I have a hunch we need to.
It is hitting us in many ways, this consciousness of a different
and more complicated world, with its grave responsibilities
for us all.

—Mrs. P. J. Quealy, first president
of the Cow-Belles, June 3, 1941.

The tough, bearded men at the fur trappers' rendezvous
in 1836, at the junction of the Green river and Horse creek,
in what is now western Wyoming, were treated to a strange
sight: White women. The Indians killed their fattest pup-
pies for a dog stew in honor of the white squaws.

There were two of them, the wives of missionaries, Dr.
Marcus Whitman and the Rev. H. H. Spalding, who had
come into the wilds with an American Fur Company supply
train. A monument in Rendezvous Park, at the town of
Green River (Sweetwater county) pays tribute to these, the
first white women in Wyoming.

Women rode the hard plank seats in the covered wagons
that rolled over the Oregon trail. A few women brightened
the earlier ranch houses, in the days when a cowman felt
crowded if someone came in and settled within a day's ride
of where his cattle grazed. In Wyoming, women voted before they did so in any other state. The territorial legislature of 1869 gave them the vote, and equal suffrage was
written into the constitution when statehood was achieved
in 1890. Delegate Coffeen from Sheridan county climaxed
the arguments in behalf of the bill with his classic statement

that "if consideration is given to disfranchising half our people, it ought not to be the better half."

Wyoming women served on juries and as justice of the peace even before they voted. Women have been chosen to many county offices, particularly in school positions, and six women have been elected state superintendent of public instruction. There have been feminine legislators: a woman has been governor of Wyoming.

And the wives of the Wyoming cowmen were the first to organize, on a statewide basis, an auxiliary to a stock men's association. This took place in June, 1940, at the 68th annual convention of the Wyoming Stock Growers Association. The idea is credited to Mrs. George Snodgrass of Casper, and she drafted the first constitution. The Wyoming women called themselves the Cow-Belles. A local group had organized in Arizona, on a county basis, the year before; there, as later when an auxiliary to the American National Cattlemen's Association was formed, the name was written CowBelles.

The first president of the Wyoming Cow-Belles was Mrs. P. J. Quealy of Kemmerer—the only woman who ever served on the executive committee of the Association. She was a member of the committee from 1933 to 1939. She had also been Democratic national committeewoman, and for many years was vice president of the state Democratic committee. She lived in Wyoming over 60 years, having come to Rock Springs in the early '90s as the bride of Patrick J. Quealy, who operated coal mines as well as sheep and cattle ranches and was a business and political force in the state, dying in 1930.

In 1941, at Worland, the auxiliary met for the first time in conjunction with the annual convention of the Association, and on that occasion Mrs. Quealy addressed the convention. At that time, war was looming, and Mrs. Quealy said the women, like the men, were wondering what was going to happen to them. And what could women do about it? Go on with your work, said the president of the Cow-Belles, "do what you have been doing, only do it better.

Learn about food values and food substitutes. Guard against hysteria in buying; build and develop skills against a day of emergency. Learn to handle tools well; fit yourselves for some of the things men do and women may have to do. Learn to sew and knit. . . Our job is to help keep America strong."

Subsequent presidents of the Cow-Belles and the years they served: Mrs. George Snodgrass of Casper, 1942; Mrs. Dugald Whitaker, Cheyenne, 1943; Mrs. T. D. O'Neil, Big Piney, 1944; Mrs. George A. Cross, Dubois, 1945; Mrs. John L. Jordan, Cheyenne, 1946; Mrs. Norman Barlow, Cora, 1947; Mrs. Sam Hyatt, Hyattville, 1948; Mrs. Joe Watt, Moorcroft, 1949; Mrs. Charles Kane, Wolf, 1950; Mrs. Bryan Patrick, Torrington, 1951; Mrs. Fred D. Boice, Sr., Cheyenne, 1952; and Mrs. Verne F. Barton, Upton, 1953.

During Mrs. Watt's administration, the Cow-Belles published a cookbook which sold all over the United States and brought a nice sum into the treasury. The auxiliary has supported the work of philanthropic organizations and while Mrs. Boice was president instigated a nursing scholarship at the University of Wyoming. Under the administration of Mrs. O'Neil, an annual award was established for the girl showing the best breeding animal at the state fair.

Mrs. Snodgrass has served as vice president of the National CowBelles, and is now their parliamentarian. At the January, 1954, convention of the American National Cattlemen's Association, in Colorado Springs, Mrs. Joe Watt of Moorcroft was elected first vice president of the national auxiliary.

In 1953, the Wyoming Cow-Belles were sixth in membership among the score of states having members in the national auxiliary.

One of the first members of the Wyoming Cow-Belles was Mrs. Robert Miller, of Big Piney, who was designated in the April 1953 issue of *Cow Country* as "a typical ranch woman from Green River Valley." Mrs. Miller is distinguished for a wide variety of interests,—in addition to her husband and the two sons they are rearing.

She writes, and she participates in such community responsibilities as the Parent-Teacher association, takes part in preserving the history of her region, and shares the activities of life on a ranch. She helps her husband work the cattle, and is herself an accomplished rider.

Born in cow country, she graduated from the Big Piney schools and from Rowland Hall, an Episcopal girls' school in Salt Lake City. She has traveled around the world. Her education and experience have provided the background for a life of constructive influence that reaches beyond the "little cow town" where her interests center. She is "typical" of the best of Wyoming womanhood.

How does women's life on a ranch today compare with that of frontier times? Let a Wyoming woman—Mrs. Paul C. Pape, of Pinedale—tell:

"The material changes—labor-saving devices, mechanization, and improved communication—have only broadened, rather than lessened, the work of ranch women. Today's women spend less time baking, churning and scrubbing (though these are still done, to a surprising extent) and more time taking part in community, state and national affairs.

"Women in Wyoming today may play good bridge, but this is, for the typical rancher's wife, not an avocation but merely one of the occasionally useful social graces. For the most part, such so-called leisure as she has acquired is spent in socially useful activity, its breadth limited only by her physical and financial condition. For the rest, though transportation and communication have improved almost incredibly since the day of Eliza Spalding and Narcissa Whitman, you will find the same unquestioning hospitality, the same industry, and the same courage and social consciousness that distinguished the pioneer women."

Mrs. Pape once wrote a poem which, while it was dedicated to Mrs. Robert Miller, is equally applicable to Wyoming women in general; it was composed after a world's championship steer-roping contest at Pinedale, in which Mrs. Miller carried the colors. The poem:

THE COLOR-BEARER

With quiet assurance she rides out into the dusty arena,
Rhythmic and certain and straight, bearing the flag in the sunlight,
Simple in bearing and dress, clothed with a sense of belonging,
At one with the mountains and sage, at ease in the scene that surrounds
    her,
Her gentle command of her mount born of pleasure and deep under-
    standing,
Unconsciously graceful and sure with a grace that comes from within
    her.

I am not sure I can say this thing that has touched me so deeply,
So seldom in words do we speak, direct and clear to each other,
The things of the inner perception that often concern us most nearly,
Held back by the limits of words and a strange, inarticulate shyness,
So bound are we still in the selves that we cannot reveal to each other.

But this is a thing I am feeling with every part of my being,
Feeling with eyes and with ears, with my heart and my mind and my
    senses,
A joy in beholding a thing so lovely in line and in balance,
A vicarious muscular pleasure in controlled and confident motion,
The pressure of happy tears from release of an urgent emotion,
A lift of the heart and the mind in the force of that palpable goodness,
A sense of the fitness of things so seldom met with in this present,
A belief that the world will come right with such people bearing our
    standard.

This is the feeling I have as I stand by the dusty arena,
Watching her wheel and lope past, under the rippling colors,
Breasting a wave of applause, bearing the flag in the sunlight.

A woman who in an earlier day was widely known in the Powder river country of Wyoming was Mrs. Fred Whitten. Her husband was general manager for many years for the ER Cattle Company and the ER ranch was the stopping place for many freighters and for other travelers in that area soon after the turn of the century. A brief article about Mrs.

Whitten in *Cow Country* December 1953 gives this glimpse of her life on the ranch:

"Those who had many weary miles to travel where there were few homes or humans to be found often arrived unexpectedly and stayed overnight at the ER ranch.

"In order to tell how many there would be for breakfast, they didn't 'count noses,' they counted the saddles around the corral, for when they all turned in at night there might be six or seven reps* there, and when they were up, at dawn, there might be fifteen or more. No matter how many, Mrs. Whitten cared for them all, with the help of her husband, or a 'hand.' During roundup time, when the men were all out 'gathering,' Mrs. Whitten would know when they were coming in for supper, as she would hear the cattle bawling long before she could see them. This was the dinner bell of the West!"

•

The women of Wyoming were an integral part of the whole story of the development of a wild, open-range country into the peaceful pastoral and agricultural region that is the Wyoming of today. Their early participation in elections and in affairs of government helped bring law and order into the area more quickly than would otherwise have been the case. The women matched the independence and the resourcefulness of their mates, and made a record of their own to which it is impossible to do justice in one short chapter.

*For more about reps, see Chapter 30.

PART NINE

CURSE OF THE WEST

COW-COUNTRY

OFFICIAL BULLETIN
WYOMING STOCK GROWERS ASSOCIATION
Issued for the Information
of our Members

Clarence H. Gardner, President   Manville Kendrick, Vice President
Russell Thorp, Secretary-Treasurer-Chief Inspector Norman Barlow, Chairman
Myrna F. Agee, Assistant Secretary-Treasurer   Executive Committee

| Vol. 76 | Cheyenne, Wyoming, May 1, 1949 | No. 12 |

77th Annual Convention
Sheridan
June 7, 8, 9,
1949

"Spring Roundup '49"

CHAPTER TWENTY THREE

A STRUGGLE THAT IS NOT YET WON

Together we have seen time unfold its story—from the beginning of herds of cattle on our Wyoming ranges down through the lean and the abundant years to the day of the registered bull, the fenced meadow, the Soya bean pellet and the bureaucrat.

—Charles A. Myers, at 70th annual convention, Gillette, 1942.

One reason cowmen are such rugged individualists is that they have had to fight, one way or another, for practically everything they've ever had. In recent years, their struggle has been to protect themselves and their land against what they have looked upon as governmental encroachment. It has been a bitter fight, and the end is not yet.

The cowmen have not won all their battles. The Jackson Hole affair, for instance, was a lost cause from the start.

Wyoming cowmen called it a depredation when, in March 1943, President Franklin D. Roosevelt set aside 221,-000 acres of land in Teton county as a National Monument. This was done by presidential proclamation in the face of what some at least thought was a commitment, when Grand Teton National Park was created in 1929, that this was the last land Wyoming would be asked to give up for national parks. More than half the state was already under federal control. The Wyoming legislature had repeatedly refused to give up Jackson Hole, which the government had long tried to acquire in addition to the 299,580 acres it had taken out of Teton county to establish the Grand Teton National Park.

To take 221,000 acres more off the county tax lists and away from the stock growers who ran some 14,000 head of cattle on it, and to do this by a stroke of the presidential pen, without prior knowledge to the governor of Wyoming or to the Wyoming congressional delegation in Washington, to say nothing of the commissioners of Teton county,—this, the cowmen thought, was the sort of thing their sons had gone abroad to fight against. They were aware of the value of public parks and playgrounds, but they were too close to Jackson Hole to be able to see that area as anything but a part of their economic life. If the government had thrashed the matter out in the open, with the duly elected representatives of the people, the cowmen might have felt differently about it. As it was they were stunned and hurt—and fighting mad. They brought suit in federal district court to block the action, and their representatives in Congress introduced legislation to abolish the Jackson Hole national monument. The bill passed both houses but was pocket-vetoed by President Roosevelt. Judge Kennedy in federal court ruled that he could not interfere. "Undoubtedly," said the court, "great hardship and a substantial amount of injustice" would be done to the state and its citizens by the Jackson Hole program, but the burden he said was on Congress to pass legislation to alleviate "any injustice."

The United States Chamber of Commerce, through its Natural Resources Department, joined the widespread resentment over the manner in which the monument had been created, in a report which *Cow Country* reprinted on February 20, 1945. Perhaps there should be a Jackson Hole national monument, was the gist of this statement; "perhaps the good therefrom, to all the people, would surpass the injury to local people and the state of Wyoming. But that is a matter for the Congress to decide. . . The eleven western states are, in a sense, only quasi-sovereign by virtue of the fact that the federal government still owns more than half the land, nearly all of which is in some form of federal reservation. The persuasive power of federal bureaus that administer this federal land is little appreciated east of the

Rockies. The whole tax structure, the life blood of local government, is occasionally jeopardized by and always dependent upon the federal land policy."

•

The 71st annual convention of the Association, meeting at Lusk in June of '43, elected George A. Cross of Dubois president and adopted a motion by J. Elmer Brock that it pledge "unqualified support to the Governor in his efforts to retain state sovereignty."

At various meetings during the year 1943, Association officers and executive committee members reaffirmed their opposition to the Jackson Hole "seizure," as well as to any and all talk of subsidies, ceilings on live stock and price rollbacks. They had accepted wartime regulations as essential to victory, but they wanted these restrictions removed as soon as the victory was won.

As for the use of the land, which was rapidly becoming a serious issue, Brock summed up the Association attitude in a talk that year before the Western Policy Committee at Billings, Mont., when he said:

"The curse of the West is a horde of predatory federal land management agencies. Because of them in their present form, we are denied actual statehood or political and economic independence. Most of them, created for meritorious purposes, soon forget the interest they should foster and look mostly to their own expansion and perpetuity. A cattleman in this area must now reconcile his operations with at least nine federal bureaus which show little co-operation with him or with each other. . . These agencies are changing our form of government. . . From 1937 to 1939 inclusive, they have taken over 28,459,660 acres of privately owned land. In the publication by land management agencies entitled *Our Western Range,* these agencies advocate taking over 125 million acres of now privately owned land, or one-third of all owned land in the eleven public domain states."

To Brock, as to his fellow cattlemen and to many Americans elsewhere than on the ranges, this expansion of governmental regulations was "most alarming."

•

Church bells were tolling the news of the D-day landing of American troops in Normandy on the day the 72nd annual meeting of the Association convened at Jackson in 1944. St. John's church was open all day for silent prayers.

Association membership that year was 1,941, the highest yet attained. Russell Thorp as executive secretary reported that from June 1, 1943, to May 22, 1944, Association inspectors had checked 227,613 Wyoming cattle at open markets, in addition to 40,494 cattle for other states, and that 576 estrays valued at $36,630.01 had been recovered.

That year's resolutions said "no subsidies"; opposed reciprocal trade and urged restoration of treaty and tariff-making powers to the Congress; called for retention of the embargo in diseased cattle; petitioned Congress to transfer publicly-owned land in Wyoming to private ownership "in an orderly manner, so as to promote the highest land use"; and supported United States Senator J. C. O'Mahoney in his intent to seek repeal of Section II of the Antiquities Act of 1906 under which President Roosevelt had taken over Jackson Hole.

During this summer—1944—the Association through a questionnaire obtained and printed in its bulletin *Cow Country* the opinions of a cross-section of Wyoming cowmen on the position of the live stock industry and its future. Substance of the opinions was that grass was good, rainfall above normal and numbers of cattle higher than usual, but that cost increases had outstripped price advances, and the producer should reduce numbers to available winter feed, pay off his debts and "prepare to ride out some bad years."

One of the things that was to help make them bad was the way some of the grazing laws were administered.

Russell Thorp, for nineteen years secretary of the Wyoming Stock
Growers Association, chats with Mrs. Fred D. Boice, Sr., in the Boice
home in Cheyenne. Mrs. Boice is a past president of the Cow-Belles.
The Boice home is the former Hiram B. Kelly house, built in the 1870s.
The fireplace is of imported tile, depicting Shakespearean characters,
with a portrait of William Cullen Bryant above the center. (Photo by
Hugh Bates.)

Snow buried telephone poles nearly to the top—

blocked the highways for weeks—

and stalled the railroads, in unforgettable 1949.

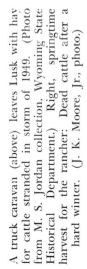

A truck caravan (above) leaves Lusk with hay for cattle stranded in storm of 1949. (Photo from M. S. Jordan collection, Wyoming State Historical Department.) Right, springtime harvest for the rancher: Dead cattle after a hard winter. (J. K. Moore, Jr., photo.)

Wyoming was blowing away, it seemed, in the drought days of the 1930s. Hot, dry winds spun topsoil as far as Chicago. (Archives and Western History Department, University of Wyoming Library.)

The brand inspection system of the Wyoming Stock Growers Association is the best any of the cattle-growing states have devised. Three of the men who have helped safeguard cowmen's interests at shipping points are shown in this photo, taken in 1937 in the Sioux City yards: Left to right, W. E. (Wild Bill) Sutter, employed by Montana, inspected for Wyoming at Billings; John R. Murphy, employed by South Dakota at Sioux City, inspected for Wyoming 1938; and R. A. (Pecos) Bacon, chief inspector for South Dakota at Sioux City, 1929-1938, who also inspected for Wyoming. (Photo from Russell Thorp.)

Above, Earl W. Carpenter, dean of Association brand inspectors, checks the files in his office at the Livestock Exchange Building at Denver. (See Pages 100-102.) Below, W. W. McVicker, Association inspector at Omaha.

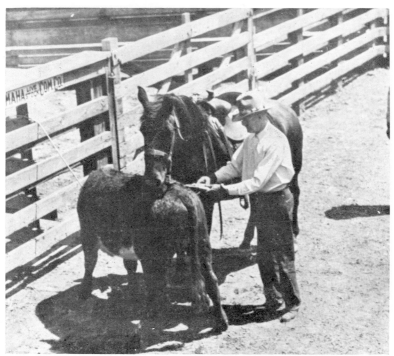

Horses are less used in brand inspection now than in former years, but occasionally they are useful. Above, an inspector's mount helps hold an animal while brand is checked. Right, Dr. G. H. Good of Cheyenne, state veterinarian and executive officer of the State of Wyoming Live Stock and Sanitary Board. Board's duties include registration of all Wyoming brands.

Denver stock yards, where many of Wyoming's cattle are marketed, on a Monday morning when the run was heavy, in late 1953. (William C. Mueller photo.)

CHAPTER TWENTY FOUR

HOME RULE ON THE RANGE.

We are not licked yet! A courageous man may not win a
fight, but he is never defeated, as the men of the Alamo
proved for all time.

—Manville Kendrick, in New Year's
message to the Association, 1951.

Although there were cattlemen among its sponsors, the
Taylor Grazing Act was opposed in the beginning by the
Wyoming Stock Growers Association, notably at its 1934
meeting, in Douglas. The act became a law that year, however, when President Franklin D. Roosevelt approved it,
on June 28.

Author of the act was Edward T. Taylor, who was a member of Congress for more than thirty years, following twelve
years in the Colorado State Legislature. He was the son
of a pioneer Kansas cattleman, and he helped put through
Congress the 640-acre stock raising homestead law under
which more than 31 million acres of "almost barren" public
land had gone to patent and into private ownership. Taylor
died in 1941, at the age of 83.

"Few laws in recent years have affected so many people in
so many ways as does this grazing act," Taylor said on the
sixth anniversary of the enactment of the measure that bears
his name. Such a law had been essential, he maintained,
because "through circumstances beyond its control, the live
stock industry was headed for self-strangulation." It was on
this basis that he had convinced Congress that the magnitude
of the problem of proper use and conservation of the public
domain, in an era of competition and in view of the "over-

use and abuse" of the land, was too great for citizens to solve without federal control.

The aim of the Taylor Grazing Act as amended June 26, 1936, and July 14, 1939, is stated in its preamble as: "To stop injury to the public grazing lands by preventing overgrazing and soil deterioration, to provide for their orderly use, improvement and development, to stabilize the live stock industry dependent upon the public range, and for other purposes."

The words "pending final disposition" were in the preamble of the act as originally drawn, and cattlemen took this as meaning that the lands were being held in trust by the federal government for the states. This idea was confirmed by reference to Article I, Section 8, Paragraph 17 of the Federal Constitution. In defining powers of Congress, this section says that these powers include the right "to exercise exclusive legislation in all cases whatsoever over such district (not exceeding ten miles square) as may, by cession of particular States and the acceptance of Congress, become the seat of Government of the United States, and to exercise like authority over all places purchased by the consent of the legislature of the state in which the same shall be, for the erection of forts, magazines, arsenals, dockyards and other needful buildings."

Furthermore, Report No. 270 to the first session of the 80th Congress (June 12, 1947) by the Committee on Public Lands, said, in regard to the history of the public lands policy of the government:

"Under (the Ordinance of 1781) the Federal Government was regarded as a trustee of the public domain to dispose of it to settlers for the purpose of building thriving states and communities. Under this policy the public domain was not to be taxed while in Federal ownership but it was recognized that Federal ownership should not continue when such lands were able to form a part of thriving States and communities . . . Your committee finds that there is a different policy from that which was originally intended and under which different policy all of the States of the United States are losing taxable lands by reason of unprecedented acquisition by the various boards, bureaus and departments of the Federal Government. Testimony established the fact that within the past ten years the Federal Government had acquired from the tax rolls of the Nation in excess of 16,000,000 acres of lands. This inordinate and un-natural growth at the expense of the normal tax base of local government has been the cause of undue hardship . . . Your committee finds that the Federal Government has abandoned any theory which holds that the public domain lands of the United States were to be held in trust to be utilized for the growth of the several States of the United States . . . Your committee cites as an example of Federal ownership in the various States the plight of the following"—

And the table recording the "plight" of the states showed that the Federal government owned 73 percent of the land in Arizona, 46 per cent in California, 38 in Colorado, 64 in Idaho, 35 in Montana, 87 in Nevada, 44 in New Mexico, 53 in Oregon, 72 in Utah, 35 in Washington and 51 in Wyoming—an average of more than 54 per cent.

All this government owned land is administered under more than five thousand separate (and sometimes conflicting) laws, rules and regulations.

•

The Taylor Act authorized the Secretary of the Interior to establish grazing districts out of 142 million acres of vacant public land in ten states: Arizona, California, Colorado, Idaho, Montana, Nevada, New Mexico, Oregon, Utah and Wyoming. Later the state of Washington was added. Within these districts, cattlemen were to be allowed to use the public land for grazing under licenses and permits from the federal government. Local advisory boards were created, through which the stockmen participated in management of allotments. In the beginning there were in all the ten original states 53 districts, which Taylor compared with "53 great ranches each the size of Connecticut." There were five of these districts in Wyoming. In 1939 in the five Wyoming districts there were 1,543 licenses and permits for use of grazing land; there were 155,357 cattle, 14,497 horses, 1,501,257 sheep. In the 53 districts of the ten states in 1939 there were 20,609 licenses and permits, 1,573,022 cattle, 106,368 horses, 10,116,322 sheep. Not all the Taylor lands are in grazing districts; the so-called "Section 15" lands are smaller parcels leased to landowners individually.

The 53 grazing districts covered a gross area of about 258 million acres of which 142 million or about 55 percent were in the public domain. The theory was that unified land control would enable the stockmen and the Grazing Service, which was created by the bill in 1935, to plan on a long-term basis for proper use of the grazing areas. Fees collected annually from the stockmen were roughly a million dollars in the early years of the law's existence. One fourth of this, under the original law, went back into the grazing districts to be used for purchase, construction and maintenance of needed range improvement; 50 per cent of the fees were returned to the states for expenditure under direction of the state legislatures.

Headquarters of the United States Grazing Service moved from Washington to Salt Lake City in 1941. Later, however, the Grazing Service was abolished by merger with the Bureau of Land Management under the Department of the Interior. Supervision and control of the federal grazing lands was thereafter under the divided control of the Bureau of Land Management, and the Forest Service of the Department of Agriculture. Today the Forest Service manages 140 million acres, permitting live stock grazing for pay on 80 million acres. The Bureau of Land Management administers the 169 million acres of public land outside the forests.

Taylor called his law "home rule on the ranges." It was that in theory, and from the beginning it gave promise of helping to bring order and stability to the cattle industry. As conferences to consider ways and means of administering the law were held, soon after its enactment, some of the Wyoming cattlemen's fears were allayed by Senator Robert D. Carey, a former president of the Association, who said he was convinced that the law would be administered in fairness and justice to the users of the land.

It did give the stockmen a chance to have a say in the management of the public ranges where their cattle ran, and many of the ranchers eventually agreed that the Taylor act, while far from perfect, was one of the best land laws the West has ever had. As Representative Wesley D'Ewart of the Second Montana district said in May 1953, "The Taylor act has been successful in assuring wise use of the land, reasonable expectancy of tenure so long as the privilege of use is not abused, and it has helped in proper conservation of the federal range."

Management of the lands under control of the Forest Service was a different story. Here, as time went on, Wyoming cattlemen became convinced that the government was doing them more harm than good. They resented the oft-repeated charge that they had over-grazed the land, and were supported in their denial of this charge by findings of University of Wyoming agronomists. They were amused when the government took credit for "recovery" of the ranges; the ranchers suspected that bounteous rains had more to do with it than the bureaucrats had. They found the grazing rules and regulations confusing and conflicting. They suffered by the "cut, cut, cut" policy of the Forest Service, reducing live stock numbers in some areas as much as 60 per cent—and they smarted under what they termed arbitrary and dictatorial methods of making grazing cuts, regardless of true range conditions. They resented the rulings of inexperienced "experts" who advocated leaving as much as 70 per cent of the grass on the ground. They wanted a fair and impartial trial of the grazing issues—they said it was un-American for the Service to act as prosecutor, judge and jury.

By December of 1945, when the Association executive committee met in annual mid-year session, at Cheyenne, the Association leaders were convinced that any softening of administrative policy on fees and grazing allotments would afford only temporary relief. They felt that the permanent stability of their industry, as envisioned in the preamble of the Taylor act, could be attained "only if and when all federal grazing lands have been passed to the States for ultimate disposition to private owners." The executive committee therefore resolved that "we urge our State officials and our delegates in Congress to use every effort to bring about the relinquishment of title by the Federal government to the various 'Public Land States,' for ultimate disposition to private owners of all Taylor act land, and all grazing land in federal forests."

The Association has joined with other western states in seeking Congressional enactment of a new land law to accomplish what it considers needed changes in existing law. In effect, these are to a great extent the application of the principles of the Taylor act to the administration of those parts of the public domain that are under control of the Forest Service.

The Uniform Federal Grazing Lands Act (H.R. 4023) was introduced in the spring of 1953 by Representative D'Ewart of Montana, at the request of the western live stock owners. It sought uniformity and stability in the management and use of the grazing lands of the Forest Service, the Taylor and the Bankhead-Jones lands, by combining into one comprehensive law the best of the laws, regulations and practices developed by long experience. Particularly the D'Ewart law, as it came to be known, provided for court review of disputes between the Forest Service and the users of the forest ranges. It wrote into law the regulations set up by the Forest Service, and already in the Taylor law, concerning ownership of commensurate property in order to qualify for range permits. It covered renewal and transfer of permits, and otherwise sought to provide for and encourage the conservation and improvement of the grazing lands by the government and the stock growers. An identical bill was introduced in the Senate by Senator Frank A. Barrett of Cheyenne, Wyoming.

Opposition to the D'Ewart bill, principally by wild life interests, killed it. The opposition was harsh and bitter.

On August 1, 1953, a new bill was introduced in the Senate. This was S. 2548, and it was sponsored by Senators George D. Aiken of Vermont, who introduced it, and Senator Edward J. Thye of Minnesota, both Republicans. (The Republican national platform of 1952 had declared in favor of legislation to define the rights of grazers and other users of the public domain, to provide the protection of independent judicial review against administrative invasions of those rights, and to protect the public against corrupt or monopolistic exploitation and bureaucratic favoritism.) An identical bill known as H.B. 6787 was introduced at the same time in the House by Representative Clifford Hope of Kansas, also a Republican.

In September 1953 the Senate committee on agriculture and forestry held preliminary hearings on S. 2548 at Albuquerque, Salt Lake City and Helena. At Albuquerque, Senator Aiken as chairman said that he and Senator Thye had introduced the bill at the request of President Eisenhower. Further hearings on this measure were held in Washington the latter part of January 1954.

The new bill made its advent at a time when there were indications of better feeling between the Forest Service and the ranchers. A step toward this had been taken in 1952, when the Forest Service, at stockmen's urging, had cooperated in setting up the first joint range improvement study in the Bighorn National Forest of Wyoming. Heretofore the Forest Service had paid scant attention to the ideas and desires of the stock men. Now it put cattle in trial pastures, to determine the best grazing rates. Stockmen and Forest officials weighed the cattle together, rode the range and in place of a policy of "cut, cut, cut" talked of range improvement and more stocking. This was progress!

Relations between the government and the stock men were further improved when Secretary of Agriculture Ezra T. Benson of Utah, himself a stock grower, recommended passage of S. 2548. His official position was that the bill "would not hamper the administration of the national forests or Bankhead-Jones land; that it would not interfere with the management and protection of the range resource; and that it would give due recognition to the multiple-use objectives of the national forests and importance of all resources and uses on the public lands under the jurisdiction of the Secretary of Agriculture."

So favorable were conditions as the new year began that, at the meeting of the American National Cattlemen's Association at Colorado Springs in January, 1954, Frank Mockler of Dubois, Wyo., chairman of the Forest advisory committee of the American National, declared:

"I really believe there is a new era of good feeling between the stock men and the Forest Service. I hope this means the end of name-calling and bitterness of recent years. We need to get together and make the most of our public lands to produce cheaper meat for our growing population."

CHAPTER TWENTY FIVE

A SQUARE DEAL FOR THE CATTLEMAN

The 1944 annual meeting of the Association re-elected George A. Cross as president, and in 1945 he was succeeded by Oda Mason of Laramie. Membership was up to 2,102, another new high. The year 1945 was highlighted, too, by presentation on May 17 of the WSGA-Russell Thorp collection of cow country relics to the Wyoming State Historical Department. The relics are now on display in the museum in the State Office Building, Cheyenne, where they have since been viewed by many thousands of persons. In the collection are more than a hundred branding irons, including rustlers' running irons, as well as many of the famous old Wyoming brands. There are also six-shooters, saddles, spurs, mess wagon equipment, dutch ovens and many rare objects of historic Wyoming cattle days. Governor Hunt received the presentation by Mr. Thorp, and Miss Mary McGrath, librarian and ex-officio state historian, spoke in behalf of the State Historical Department. John C. Thompson, editor of the Wyoming State Tribune and member of the State Landmarks Commission, was master of ceremonies.

World War II was over, when the Association held its 74th annual meeting in June of 1946, at Laramie, "the Athens of Wyoming," and the live stock industry entered the postwar period looking forward to the removal of price controls, relieving ranchers of some of the uncertainty under which they had been operating. Before the year was over, *Cow Country* reported that Wyoming was back to a normal production of about 1,100,000 cattle, an increase of about a quarter-million over the post-drought low. "There will be a decided increase this fall," said *Cow Country*, "in the number of feeder cattle marketed over the last several years, due to the fact that we now have our herds up to the capacity of our ranges."

Oda Mason, re-elected in June, 1946, as president, had told the Association that experience with governmental regimentation indicated to stockmen that "the only successful way to run a grazing service, according to the Forest Service, would be to eliminate the live stock. . . . We were here first, and, after all, priority should amount to something."

The American National Cattlemen's Association and the National Wool Growers Association as well as other range state associations had by this time joined the Wyoming Association in calling on Congress to investigate the administration of the Taylor law by the Forest Service and to return to private ownership all grazing lands other than national monuments or parks or those covered with timber, adding: "Our industry will never be stabilized till this goal is reached, and state governments cannot be stable until the industries within the states are stabilized."

•

In late winter of 1947 a shudder went through Wyoming cow country when hoof and mouth disease was found among cattle in nine Mexican states and the Federal District of Old Mexico. More than a million cattle had been exposed to the disease.

Cow country shuddered because it knew there had been seven outbreaks of this disease in America since 1900 and that they had been disastrous to the cattle industry. The most serious outbreak had been in 1914, when twenty-two states had been affected; 172,000 American cattle had been slaughtered, and nine million dollars spent, to halt the scourge at that time. There had been lesser outbreaks in California and Texas in 1924, 1925 and 1929, and at other times the disease had threatened American herds.

The United States actually had been fighting importation of foreign cattle diseases ever since 1864, when the first legislation to that end was passed. By sustained effort over the years, the North American continent had been kept free of hoof and mouth disease, except for 1914 and the other outbreaks.

So when bad news from Mexico reached the range states of America, in 1947, quick action was demanded. "The U.S.-Mexican border should be patrolled as though it were a prison camp," said the American National Cattlemen's Association. Suspected bulls in the proximity of the border should be killed and buried. The American government, in defense of its cattle industry, was called upon to furnish whatever men and money were needed to assist the Mexican government to prevent spread of the disease. And in particular the National urged consummation of "real sanitary treaties" with Mexico and Canada, to replace the inadequate ones then existing.

Dr. G. H. Good, the Wyoming state veterinarian, came back from an emergency meeting of the executive board of the United States Live Stock Sanitary Association, at Fort Worth, Texas, in February 1947, to report that the quarantine area in Mexico ran 350 miles east and west and 250 miles north and south, with a cattle population of 650,000 head. The process of liquidating the cattle by gradual slaughter for consumption would take about two years. Even this program would not eradicate the disease, and should it become established in the northern part of Mexico, the danger of its creeping across the line into the United States "would never end." The state of Wyoming, on recommendation of the State Live Stock and Sanitary Board, required permits for shipping or trailing any class of live stock into the state, in addition to the official health certificates already required. J. Elmer Brock was named a member of the National Advisory Committee to the Secretary of Agriculture and chairman of a sub-committee that was sent to Mexico to study the situation first hand. This sub-committee in 1947 visited twelve states in Mexico, traveling 2,300 miles by auto, including 2,000 miles within the quarantine area. The sub-committee interviewed Mexicans high and low, visited farms and ranches and burial pits for the slaughtered cattle. It brought back a series of recommendations which helped step up the program by which the United States co-operated with Mexico in fighting the disease, lessening its effects and preventing its spread.

In the summer of 1948, Dr. Good in a statement printed in *Cow Country* said the disease probably would continue in Mexico for a long time, and the best the American cattle industry could hope for would be its containment and eventual eradication in Mexico. Any suspicious outbreaks of disease among cattle should be reported by telephone or telegraph, he said; the Live Stock and Sanitary Board had assembled emergency kits, including rubber coats, boots, gloves and hats, and spray pumps for the use of veterinarians and others who might be called on to investigate symptoms of hoof and mouth disease. Sheriffs had been alerted to provide manpower for patrolling areas that might have to be quarantined.

In Mexico, the slaughter program eventually had to be modified to protect the Mexican economy, and a gigantic vaccination program was launched experimentally in 1948. By early 1949, in *Cow Country,* Brock was able to report that the disease had not only been kept from crossing the border into this country, but was being steadily pushed southward. The fight would have to go on indefinitely, and it would be advisable he said to keep American veterinary forces in Mexico for five years after the last known case was eradicated.

•

Clarence H. Gardner of Thermopolis was elected president of the WSGA at the 1947 meeting, which was held in Lander. Cattle prices, the Association was told by its retiring president, Oda Mason, were, if anything, higher than most producers cared to see them: "It all leads to higher overhead and higher taxes, and when cattle prices drop, it is a long, hard pull to get overhead and taxes down." He pointed out that the Association in the past year had prevailed upon the Legislature to establish a state laboratory at the University at Laramie, under supervision of the Live Stock and Sanitary Board, "to inquire into the causes of contagion, infection and communicable disease, and determine the means of preventing and curing, and collect other information of value to live stock interests."

The 1948 convention of the Association, at Douglas, was notable for two reasons: the Association membership reached 2,466, a new top; and the convention voted to raise membership dues, which had long been five dollars, to seven dollars and a half.

Clarence H. Gardner, who was re-elected president, said in his address that the public lands issue had become the most misrepresented and most misunderstood question the Association had ever dealt with, due in great part to eastern writers who were accusing the stockmen of trying to steal the public domain. So the cowmen were pleased when one writer came strongly to their defense. This was Paul Friggens, of *Farm Journal*, who with Ray Anderson traveled ten thousand miles in eleven western states to make a survey and report on the controversy between the cattlemen and the government. Their article, in *Farm Journal* for October, 1948, was entitled "Give the Cattleman a Fair Deal," and it fairly stated both sides. The cowmen, unaccustomed to having their side presented at all, had the article reprinted and circulated with the August 31, 1948, issue of the bulletin *Cow Country*.

The Friggens report showed that cattlemen in the other states were as much disturbed as were those in Wyoming over the struggle between such federal agencies as the Forest Service and the National Park Service for control of public lands; over appeals from government decisions which were heard and decided by the bureaucrats who had made the decisions from which the appeals were taken; over arbitrary reductions in grazing allotments, especially automatic cuts made in the event of transfer of ranch property or death of a permittee; over the frequently-heard charge that the ranchers were despoiling the ranges—that they were undermining their own livelihood by over-grazing; and over all the other ill effects of "inflexible dictation from big bureaucracy 3,000 miles away." What the stockmen wanted, Friggens said, was better management, including local advisory boards "that somebody will listen to"; they wanted to build up the range, protect the watersheds, save the game, and conserve the great outdoors just as other Americans did; they believed real conservation could be accomplished without hurting anybody; they wanted to produce more food and fiber, with "intelligent regulation."

About this time the House of Representatives Subcommittee on Public Lands, which had held hearings in the western states in the fall of 1947, published its report. Representative Frank A. Barrett of Wyoming was chairman of this subcommittee, whose report upheld many of the cattlemen's contentions, criticized many of the Forest Service policies, and made several recommendations for improvement. The Denver Post said editorially, "It is a good report," and with this the cattlemen agreed.

The executive committee of the Association wound up the year 1948 with a session at Cheyenne that was attended by 58 members, the largest such attendance on record. Then everybody went home for Christmas, and the day after New Year's, cow country met another one of its severest tests.

CHAPTER TWENTY SIX

ANOTHER WINTER THEY WON'T FORGET

For a few years after the drought era of the '30s had passed, Wyoming cow country had enjoyed a comparatively peaceful period. Then came the eventful days of World War II, with its tensions and agonies. The ranchers' problems in this period were much the same as those of the rest of the country. Membership, which had fallen low during the time of the range wars, rose steadily to a new high at the end of 1936, and in subsequent years went still higher. The annual conventions were well attended, and the Association made its influence felt in many constructive ways. Nature treated the ranges kindly.

During the early 'forties, the growth of grass was the most abundant in many years. But *Cow Country*, the Association's monthly publication, uttered a warning note.

"Rains and showers have continued, cloudbursts are numerous, and all this may be a forerunner of heavy snows and a long winter," said *Cow Country*. "Bear in mind it has been a number of years since we have had one of those tough winters. We advise putting up all the hay possible."

And the ranchers made hay, and the jolly voices of the Cow-Belles rang through the meeting halls, and all went merry as a dinner gong. Then came the winter of 1949.

For a standard to measure its winters by, cow country up to that time had harked back to 1886-7. Even that one is pallid now beside what happened in 1949.

The storm began on January 2 and its greatest fury was exerted in the next three days. Twenty inches of snow fell. The wind blew unceasingly at an average of 45 miles an hour. Temperatures stayed around zero. Most roads were blocked by drifts. On January 5, blizzard-battered communities began digging out as the storm eased, but then another

191

series of storms came along and whipped Wyoming intermittently until February 19. There was no thaw, no chinook. Temperatures got down to 38 below, in some instances, and the wind up to 70 miles an hour. Most areas of the state except the Big Horn basin were affected. Travelers were stranded for days in filling stations and ranch houses. Automobile traffic was stalled so abruptly and completely that in some places abandoned cars stayed stuck in drifts for weeks. One family of three persons froze to death in a car three and one half miles east of Hillsdale. A young rancher, leaving his wife and baby in a stalled truck, tried to walk to a ranch for help and died on the way.

Spearheading the Herculean effect that the emergency demanded was the Wyoming Stock Growers Association, whose office in Cheyenne became the focal point of the rescue work. Russell Thorp, executive secretary, went on continuous duty, staying at his desk for hours on end while calls for help came in and orders for action went out. State and federal workers made his office their headquarters. The Association was the driving power behind Governor A. G. Crane's mobilization of the relief program.

Governor Crane put R. J. Hofmann of Cheyenne, chairman of the Red Cross disaster relief committee for Laramie county, is charge of co-ordinating relief agencies. As soon as planes could get off the ground, the governor sent three men on a flight over southeastern Wyoming to survey the situation. The three were Fred E. Warren, veteran stockman; General R. L. Esmay, state adjutant general; and Thorp, who told what they saw: "Beneath us was only a vast sea of snow. Fences were completely buried and in many instances just the roofs of the ranch houses and the tops of windmills could be seen."

On the basis of the report from these men, the governor ordered organization of a State Emergency Relief Board with Thorp at its head. General Esmay was on the board, with Hofmann and J. R. Bromley, highway superintendent; the state legislature, which was in session at the time, added to the board Senator Leeland U. Grieve of Savery and Representative William H. Harrison of Pine Bluffs. State and federal funds were swiftly made available.

The state relief board set up a board in each county, including a county commissioner, a highway engineer, a member of the local Red Cross, the county agricultural agent and a stock grower chosen jointly by the WSGA and the Wool Growers' Association. The boards went quickly into action, some of them being in almost continuous session during much of the sixty-day emergency period. A system of priorities was set up and followed: Sick and medical cases received first attention; then food and fuel for families; then came the opening of roads to reach live stock isolated from feed; last on the list was the return of displaced persons. The Wyoming National Guard, the Civil Air Patrol, the Red Cross, the state highway patrol, police departments, federal agencies including U.S. Army units and other organizations and many individuals put other duties aside and worked for weeks to dig Wyoming out of the snow. There was heroism on the ground and in the air—300 CAP and private fliers flew more than 1,955 missions. One plane landed on a narrow ridge to get a man with frozen feet; another landed on the side of a mountain to pick up a woman stricken with appendicitis. Radio played its role. Station KFBC of Cheyenne worked around the clock, broadcasting such appeals as "A man is suffering for need of insulin at the ranch house three miles north of Cheyenne on U.S. 87. Will anyone in possession of insulin in that area please make an effort to get insulin to this man?"

"The storm pounded men, animals, and man-made things with a savage fury unmatched in the memory of those who felt its force," wrote Louise Love in her "Report of Wyoming's 'Operation Snowbound' 1949," some time afterward. "Entire communities and countrysides were immobilized while the elements made cruel and fantastic display of their strength. People in their houses were unable to get out for food or fuel; animals, both wild and domestic, drifted in the battering cold, snow and wind, many literally freezing in their tracks and others suffocating as a result of the fine snow blown into their nostrils."

"It was a white hell," said Paul Friggens, who flew over the blizzard area for *Farm Journal* in a Piper Cub equipped with skiis. "You could fly from Cheyenne to Newcastle, 220 miles away, without seeing a sign of human life or habitation. Houses were covered by drifts. I saw tops of telephone poles peeping out of drifts 300 feet long.

"Rancher Dean Prosser, 22 miles southeast of Cheyenne, had a typical experience. His stables drifted over. He had to tunnel to get to his horses. But the snow had drifted in and nearly buried the animals, in a normally tight stable. It was that kind of a storm.

"Eight thousand miles of road had to be opened to ranches. Keeping them open was in some cases impossible. They drifted shut behind the plows. I heard of a rancher who dug out a purebred bull after it had been buried in snow for ten days. The animal lived. But many died, and you saw cattle that you wished you could shoot. They were starving on their feet. There was not enough heat in their bodies to melt an icicle on a warm day. Cattle crossed over fences on the snow. Some were driven into railroad cuts and buried there until they were dug out by snowplows.

"Some of the ranches had no mail from January 2 to February 3. Mrs. Lois Schoonjans of Saratoga wrote a letter to the office of the Wyoming Stock Growers at Christmas time. It was after January 30 when she could get to a mail box to send the letter.

"Railroads rushed in the feed and hay, but trains were snowed in as fast as they dug out. The Milwaukee railroad had one train into Rapid City, South Dakota, during January.

"The Crook county (Wyoming) commissioners were unable to meet and organize their emergency relief program because the commissioners were all snowbound. Several members of the Wyoming legislature never got to Cheyenne until the session was half over.

"I saw places where ranchers had driven by teams and sleds five miles to gain one mile.

"As we flew in the waning afternoon light over the Lusk area, I spotted one fellow pulling a kid's sled behind him across the great white wilderness. Apparently he had hiked to a neighbor's for groceries or fuel. He looked like the loneliest man in the world."

There was disaster and tragedy, and occasionally there was a little grim humor. When a bulldozer finally managed to get through to one ranch, the driver asked the rancher if he wanted a road opened to a haystack near his house. The rancher pointed instead to another stack two miles off across the plains. "Let's get a road to that one," he suggested. "I'm saving this near one for when the weather gets bad."

Writing from Antelope Hill ranch to *Cow Country*, Harry H. Stevick said: "We gauged fifteen inches of snow, out of which we got a dozen ground blizzards, one of which was the worst I ever saw. When the snow was exhausted, the earth blew, putting from one to two inches of soil over the drifts, all with a S.O.B. of a wind. The cattle could hardly take it. We had one bunch, calves and older cows, that were out of the corrals but once in forty-six days, and that one day we were damn glad to get them back. Some of the younger cows just did not have the will to live after looking into those storms and winds for forty days. We had shelter for everything, but five of the corrals were so drifted over that the stock could walk out. It was tough enough to last me the rest of my life."

An example of the stupendous co-ordinated efforts that were made to help save live stock is told thus in "Operation Snowbound":

"During the period of greatest emergency, John Hay, Jr., of Rock Springs, speaking for the wool growers of Sweetwater county, telephoned Mr. Thorp at Cheyenne relief headquarters. The sheepman said that the ranchers had about one day's supply of feed on hand and were facing a desperate situation. Railroads and highways, of course, were blocked throughout the section. When Mr. Thorp consulted

officials of the Union Pacific railroad, which serves Rock
Springs, he was informed that it was entirely indefinite when
the line would be open. A suggestion was made that the
feed, amounting to about 92 carloads, be re-routed; that it
be shipped from Cheyenne via the Union Pacific, to Denver,
then by way of the Denver and Rio Grande to Salt Lake,
from there on the U.P. again to Ogden, and thence east to
Rock Springs. Both roads agreed, and went 'all out' to
facilitate the shipment. Early the same afternoon that the
idea was advanced to the companies, the Union Pacific got
the first train of feed out of Cheyenne and delivered it in
Denver to the D. & R.G., which had it under way that
evening. On the third afternoon the feed was in Rock
Springs, ready to be taken out to the range for the starving
sheep."

The ranchers and farmers who received supplies paid for
these themselves. Public agencies broke the roads open and
even, in some instances, provided the means of transportation and delivery of food, medicines and live stock feed, but
the actual supplies were bought and paid for by the persons
receiving them.

"Getting feed to the live stock on the range was one of
the primary problems," said "Operation Snowbound." "In
many instances it was necessary to open routes up to forty
miles long in order to get relief to ranchers and their stock.
With the roads closing up right behind the snowplows when
these machines did get through, a system of convoys was
established. It worked in this fashion: Ranchers would be
notified in advance, by telephone or radio, when a route
was to be opened, and instructions would be given to have
sufficient supplies and feed ready to follow the plows.
Sometimes there were as many as forty trucks to a convoy.
These would follow the plows in to the ranch, unload, and,
because the route would usually be closed again by that
time, would have to return to town in the same manner.
Whenever possible the snow-moving equipment would be
worked in pairs, since frequently a convoy starting out behind a single machine was stranded for as long as four days

waiting for repairs after the plow had broken down and the road again drifted shut."

Hay and feed were being brought in during this period by "Operation Haylift" of the Tenth Air Force. The C-47s and other aircraft carried tons of hay into the beleaguered areas. Sometimes they delivered it in the towns, and sometimes they dropped it directly on the range where weakened cattle were completely isolated from ground help. Medicine and food for humans, and other necessary supplies, were also dropped, but the main object of Operation Haylift was to get hay to the stock on the snow-covered ranges before the animals died of starvation. In some instances, the dropping of hay to animals on the range was a wasted effort, despite the skill of the airmen. They could not pinpoint their drops —and hay falling fifty feet from cattle completely stranded in the snow might as well have been ten miles away.

Wives of Natrona county stockmen took upon themselves the huge job of feeding the men of the Air Force operating the hay lift from the air base near Casper. They fed from 150 to 1,200 men daily during the time that the army crews were at the base. The group was organized and led by Mrs. Don Mosher, and set up housekeeping in the operations shack at the foot of the control tower near the main runway. Fifty or more women were on the job night and day. The Casper *Tribune-Herald said*: "Obstacles to prevent these courageous women from even getting to the air base were numerous. The roads drifted in constantly, and for some time the women had to get out in the blizzards and walk a distance over a tremendous drift not far from the base. Sheriff Louis Cooper would take them out to the drift, and would walk across with them to the other side, where they would be met by an army officer who was helping the group of women who had just come off duty and would in their turn be taken back to town by the sheriff. That one drift for a while was twelve feet high." But the women kept the air men well fed.

Many of the cattle and sheep lost in the southeast sector of the state died of suffocation. Fred E. Warren said the animals breathed in the wet snow, which filled the air for days like a fog, and that it froze in their nostrils, cutting off their air supply. He pointed out that more than one thousand sheep of a herd which was lost on one of the Warren ranches were found scattered over three or four sections of land. They were not piled up as is often the case under similar circumstances, but were found dead after the blizzard, one here, one there.

Warren called this storm the "wickedest" he had ever seen—and he had spent most of his life in that section of Wyoming. During the worst of it, the men on his 7XL ranch near the Wyoming-Colorado border tied themselves together with a rope to travel the fifty feet from the bunk house to the eating room in the main ranch house.

Late in February, Wyoming finally emerged from the terror. And Nature, as if in part to atone for the damage, blessed the land with an early spring and a gradual thaw and run-off, so that there was a more plentiful supply of irrigation water than the state had known for many years.

The financial report printed in "Operation Snowbound" showed that a fund of $125,068.74 received from the Federal Works Agency was disbursed to twelve counties for road work and to individual contractors in three counties for road work; that of one legislative appropriation of $200,000, the sum of $3,920.64 was all that was spent; and that of another state legislative emergency appropriation of $500,-000 only $245,105.22 was disbursed, $254,894.78 reverting to the general fund. The economy with which the program was handled, and the fact that so many of the funds available for relief work were returned unspent, was the source of gratification on the part of all concerned.

The Wyoming Stock Growers Association had again proved its value as cow country's guardian.

To compare the effects of the blizzard of 1949 on the cattle industry with those of the pioneer winter of 1887 is difficult because of the changed conditions existing and because in 1887 there was little official machinery for accurately tabulating the damage. In 1949 it was possible through official channels to arrive at a close figure on cattle losses.

The figures came on June 1 from the agricultural statistician in the United States Department of Agriculture's Bureau of Agricultural Economics, at Cheyenne. This office reported that cattle deaths attributed directly to the storm in the fourteen-county area where the storm was worst (Fremont, Campbell, Crook, Johnson, Weston, Albany, Carbon, Natrona, Sweetwater, Converse, Goshen, Laramie, Niobrara and Platte) totaled 20,000 head, with an additional loss of 12,000 head during this period from other causes.

This total loss of 32,000 head amounted to 4.7 per cent of 686,000 cattle and calves in the fourteen-county area on January 1, 1949. The death loss in the other nine counties was 3,000 cattle and calves from storm and weather causes, and 6,000 head lost from other causes. This made a total loss in these other nine counties of 9,000 head or 2.8 per cent of 325,000 cattle and calves as of January 1, '49.

The total death loss of Wyoming cattle and calves during the winter and spring (January 1 to June 1) of 1949 amounted to 41,000 head or 4.1 per cent of 1,011,000 cattle and calves on hand January 1, 1949. The average winter and spring loss of cattle and calves is from 1.5 to 2.0 per cent.

The winter death losses of 41,000 cattle and calves in the state were classified as 15,000 cows and heifers two years old and over; 13,000 1949 calves and 13,000 other cattle (steers, yearlings and bulls). Death losses in the fourteen-county disaster area were 13,000 cows and heifers, 9,000 1949 calves and 10,000 other cattle. In the nine less-sorely afflicted counties death losses were classified as 2,000 cows and heifers, 4,000 1949 calves and 3,000 other cattle.

The death losses varied greatly in the fourteen counties, and also between individual ranches. In some cases death losses on individual ranches were heavy and disastrous, others had relatively light losses.

Losses of all stock sheep attributed directly to the storm in the fourteen counties were estimated at 100,000 head. For the entire state, sheep losses for the storm period were

7.4 per cent, compared with a ten-year average loss of 5.9 per cent for the period from January to June.

For the people of Wyoming cow country, 1949 was truly a winter they won't forget and don't like to remember.

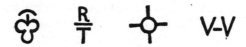

PART TEN

EVEN THE COWS ARE DIFFERENT

OFFICIAL BULLETIN
WYOMING STOCK GROWERS ASSOCIATION
Issued for the Information
of our Members

Manville Kendrick, President
Myrna F. Agee, Assistant
Secretary-Treasurer

Lloyd Taggart, Vice President
Norman Barlow, Chairman
Executive Committee

Vol. 77   Cheyenne, Wyoming, May 15, 1950   No. 9

CHAPTER TWENTY SEVEN

'WE'VE ALWAYS HAD GRASSHOPPERS'

The year after the year of the great blizzard was, for many Wyoming stockmen, the year of the grasshoppers. Not that these scourges were anything new; cowmen had endured their visitations in varying severity over all the years of their tenancy of the ranges; one old timer, asked about it in a year of drought when the 'hoppers were especially destructive, had said, "Yes, we've always had grasshoppers—but we've always had enough to feed them, up until this year."

In 1950 they were so bad that the state legislature appropriated $750,000 to be matched by federal funds, to fight the insect hordes that threatened destruction of 2,800,-000 acres of rangeland in fourteen counties, mostly east of the Big Horns and southward along the eastern part of the state.

The new president of the Association, elected at the June 1949 meeting at Sheridan, was a veteran of the grasshopper wars. He was Manville Kendrick, of Sheridan, son of the late United States Senator John B. Kendrick, who had been president of the Association 1912-13. Manville Kendrick was one of the first Wyoming stockmen to fight 'hoppers by wide-scale baiting of range lands. In 1948 he had sprayed 3,000 acres of his own holdings, in the Sheridan area; in 1949, he had participated in a federal program of 'hopper control in which 30,000 acres of his land were included. He was well aware of the importance of a continuing campaign, utilizing the most modern methods of insect warfare, against this one of cow country's enemies.

Leroy Moore of Douglas headed the state grasshopper control board, with J. Elmer Brock as vice chairman. In 1950 a total area of 2,462,320 acres were treated with 'hopper poison, at a cost of 58 cents an acre. Forty-one contract planes and two bureau planes spread 11,415 tons of bait including insecticides, between June 21 and August 17. In reporting this to the executive committee of the Association at its December 1950 meeting, Brock paid tribute to Chairman Moore, who he said literally lived in the field with the men who did the work that helped save the range from the grasshopper hordes. In 1951 the area treated was 440,610 acres in seven counties. In that year the total cost of the program was $348,963, of which the federal government paid half, the land owners a fourth and the state a fourth. It was an example of the way in which government and individuals can work together for the common good when co-operation can be based on common sense, understanding and experience.

•

The 1950 convention at Cody in June re-elected Manville Kendrick president, and maintained its stand against federal regulation and control, as well as against the ever-increasing federal spending program. The cowmen's attitude was focused in resolutions opposing the Brannan farm plan, construction of the Keyhole dam on the Belle Fourche river and any increase in taxation.

This was the year that Robert D. Hanesworth of Cheyenne became secretary and chief inspector of the Association. Russell Thorp had resigned in June of '49, to devote his efforts to the cause of the American National Cattlemen's Association, and in the interim Mrs. Myrna F. Agee had filled the secretary's job. Hanesworth came to the Association with a record of 24 years as secretary of the Frontier Days committee and 26 years as secretary of the Cheyenne Chamber of Commerce. At this time also the Association moved to new quarters in the John Bell Quarter Circle Z building at 1605 Central Avenue in Cheyenne, across the street from the Plains Hotel. And in October of 1950 the Association's Bulletin *Cow Country* graduated from its mimeographed status to that of a duded-up slick paper magazine with colored cover, halftones and advertisements. The first issue of the new magazine was Vol. 78, No. 4, dated October 15, 1951.

By the time of the 1951 convention, which was held at Worland, and at which Lloyd Taggart of Cody was elected president, the Wyoming Natural Resource Board had come into existence, and J. Elmer Brock of the Association as its president was heading another movement of benefit to the state as a whole.

•

The Natural Resource Board was created by an act of the 1951 state legislature. It began operations under an appropriation of $100,000 in addition to funds allocated to the former State Planning and Water Conservation Board, whose duties were assumed by the Resource Board. The board is composed of nine members, of whom at least one shall come from each judicial district and not more than five may be members of one political party. The board was given broad powers to make surveys, do research and develop and protect any Wyoming resource, and its first step was to begin a survey and inventory of resources, especially along the lines of water, minerals, chemicals, power, timber, agriculture, wild life and recreation. In his first report, published in *Cow Country* Sept. 15, 1951, Chairman Brock said the Board had contracted with the University of Wyoming to conduct three independent studies on the Big Horn National Forest as typical for Wyoming: A five-year study of the influence of grazing on cattle and rangelands; a study of range condition classes in the Forest; and a five-year study of the effects of intensity of use by sheep on vegetation, both below and above timberline. The Forest Service, the report noted, was fully co-operating with the University in these tests. The report showed that there were 105,705 cattle and horses and 417,802 sheep grazing in the Wyoming Forest Reserves, representing a conservative value of more than $41,000,000. The estimated annual increase from this live stock was $30,000,000. "Thirty to forty per cent reduction of live stock, suggested by forest administrators, would be a very serious blow to local economy and the industry itself, and the board believes that the depreciation in land values of areas dependent upon forest grazing would exceed, by far, other losses," said the report.

The report emphasized that "the immediate crying need in Wyoming resource development is power as well as water, and that hydro-electric power alone cannot supply the demand," and analyzed problems in connection with this and the many other phases of its investigations.

The 1952 convention of the WSGA was held at Cheyenne, with an attendance of five hundred. The membership then was 2,734; Lloyd Taggart was re-elected president.

•

News of the death of one of its oldtime members reached the Association at this time. Charles A. Myers of Evanston died at the home of a daughter in California. He was a past president of the Association, and served many years on its executive committee. More than half a century ago, he was one of those who organized the American National Cattlemen's Association. A staunch Democrat, he served in the State Senate for twelve years. He had been a member of the State Live Stock and Sanitary Board, and had received an honorary degree at the University of Wyoming.

White-thatched Charley Myers will be remembered by those who knew him for many fine qualities, including a never-failing sense of humor. Typical of this was a salty passage in cowman's language, in his address at the seventieth annual meeting at Gillette in 1942. Myers was speaking of the danger to the cattle industry from the foot and mouth disease then prevalent in countries to the south of ours.

"There is nothing that could so completely disrupt the stock men's war effort as an outbreak of foot and mouth disease," said Myers. "And yet we find our Department of State running up and down the tariff wall like a breachy steer looking for a hole in the fence, striving to find a means whereby they can bring in Argentine meat.

"Last week I helped put quite a bunch of yearlings through a dehorning chute. After you get their heads in the stanchions, some of them try to lie down, some bellow, some try to climb the side of the chute with their hind feet, but whatever they start doing they continue to do—they have just one firmly fixed idea and one set of actions which they keep until you turn them loose. It is just like that with a 'free trader.' If he was born that way, give it up—you can't talk him out of it. But then it is not to be wondered at that a babe who was cradled between two rows of cotton should pick up a few boll weevils."

O $\frac{5}{N}$ ULΛ JK

CHAPTER TWENTY EIGHT

'CATTLE BARONS'? NOT EXACTLY!

Nobody ever heard a cowman call himself or another cowman a king. 'Cattle baron' is journalese.

—J. Frank Dobie

The Association—"Guardian of Wyoming's Cow Country
for 81 Years" as the cover of its official magazine proudly
proclaimed—was still fighting rustlers in 1953. The jeep
and the truck had largely displaced the cowpony for ranch
work. The day of the big gather and the circle riding of
the open range roundup crews was gone, and the rustler too
had changed his ways. He was a rubber-tired rustler now.

In 1953 the Association paid out $500 reward for the
capture and conviction of a man who had slaughtered a
Bar Cross cow. The reward went to Eugene Morss of Cora,
Wyo. He had been driving a herd of his Bar Cross bulls to
the mountains for summer range, when the lead bulls stopped at some freshly disturbed sod and began tearing the
turf with their horns. Morss uncovered a pit four feet wide
and two feet deep in which were buried the head and hide
of a dry cow bearing his brand.

Sublette county peace officers tracked the vehicle in which
the meat had been stolen, and arrested the rustler, who went
to the penitentiary.

Earlier in the year, legislation had been introduced in the
Legislature at Cheyenne stiffening the penalty for rustling.

Twenty-one members of the Association, incidentally—
one of them a woman, and all but one Republicans—were
members of the Legislature in its thirty-second session, in
1953.

•

Moving to market: Scene on the James Boyle ranch, Spring Gulch, Jackson Hole. (William C. Mueller photo.)

Life on a Wyoming ranch today finds the Cow-Belles sometimes working alongside the boys. Above, Carole Rees, who was queen of the 1953 Cheyenne Frontier Days celebration, helps out on the ranch of her father, Dan E. Rees. Below, Mrs. Robert Miller, whom *Cow Country* has called a typical Green River Valley ranch woman (see Chapter Thirty Two), is shown while helping work the cattle on the Miller and Miller 67 ranch at Big Piney. (Melvin Thompson photo.)

Front-footing a running horse may look easy, when done by an expert, but try it some time! These photos of Dan Hanson on his ranch near Hat Creek were taken by Mrs. Hanson.

This picture turns the clock back forty years, and shows Hugh Stemler, 1953 chairman of the executive committee of the Wyoming Stock Growers Association, on a day in 1913 at Cheyenne when he rode the outlaw horse Cheyenne Red Bird.

The 1953 president of the Association, Clifford P. Hansen, is a graduate of the University of Wyoming and a member of its board of trustees. His ranch is near Jackson.

Norman Barlow, vice president of the Association, ranches at Cora, Wyo., and is a member of the State Legislature.

Executive Committee chairman 1953 is Hugh Stemler, of Glendo, veteran rancher.

Mrs. Verne F. Barton, Sr., of Upton is 1953 president of the Wyoming Cow-Belles.

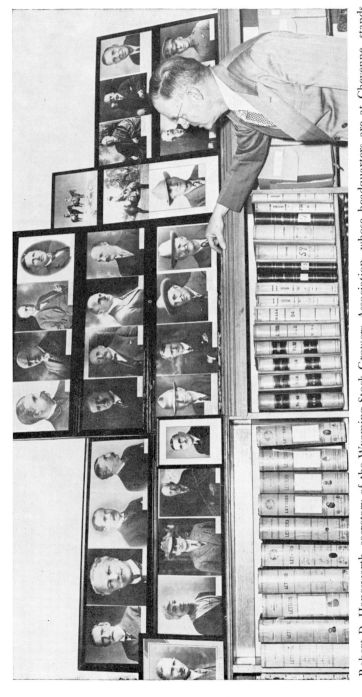

Robert D. Hanesworth, secretary of the Wyoming Stock Growers Association, whose headquarters are at Cheyenne, stands beside some of the Association's historical files in the Archives of the University Library at Laramie. On the wall are photos of some of the Association's past and present leaders—a Supreme Court justice. governors, senators, Buffalo Bill Cody—some of the men who made Wyoming. The woman's portrait is of Alice Smith, Association secretary 1896-1922.

Joe H. Watt of Moorcroft, a Weston county Hereford rancher, is a member of the Association Executive Committee, and of the Historical Committee responsible for this book.

J. Elmer Brock, chairman of the Historical Committee, has been president of the Association, of the American National Cattlemen's Association and of the Wyoming Natural Re source Board. In 1941 he was a member of the committee sent by the Carnegie Foundation for International Peace to Brazil, Uruguay and Argentine, to study hoof and mouth disease. Since 1946 he has been vice chairman of the Advisory Council to the Secretary of Agriculture on hoof and mouth disease in Mexico.

Charles A. Myers, one of the most eloquent, energetic and faithful members of the Association, was a member of the Historical Committee at the time of his death in 1952.

The trail herds are gone, the cattle wars are over, the open range is no more, but it's still cow country—and though "even the cows are different," it's a land of peace and promise. It will be that, as long as the rains come and the grass grows. This photo, by Charles J. Belden, whose camera for many years has helped preserve the Wyoming scene, is typical of the short-grass country.

One of these was Frank Mockler, of Dubois, former speaker of the house now serving his first term in the senate. It was Mockler who, at the June convention of the Association at Jackson, Wyo., gave a report on the progress in the national Congress of the uniform federal grazing lands act. Mockler, representing the Association, had recently attended hearings on the bill at Washington, and he brought back a report on some popular misconceptions such as have existed ever since the first cowboy came up the trail.

"In the East," said Mockler, "they think of the users of the range as cattle barons—and that is not exactly an accurate picture when you realize that the average grazing permit in the national forest today is for 68 head of cattle. Those of you who are in the cattle business know that on 68 head of cattle a man is a far cry from being a cattle baron. And the movies and the comics and the magazines show cowboys sitting around a bunkhouse singing through their noses to guitar accompaniment—and that isn't the way the West is today either. Today the Western ranches are family units, and it is the family unit that we are trying to protect with this legislation. There are some large ranches, but 93 per cent of the permits on the national forest, for instance, are held by permittees of less than 200 head.

"You've also heard this talk about despoilers of the range denuding the watersheds—well, that isn't true, either. When the Egyptians and the nomads in the Holy Land denuded that country (there is evidence that it was a fertile place at one time), the reason it was denuded was not that it was grazed but rather because the people were nomads with no real stake in the land itself. They moved from one place to another, and that's just the sort of thing we are trying to get away from. We are trying to tie the permits to graze on this federal land to the base property. There's nothing to be ashamed of in that. Our primary interest is to build up these federal lands by making them stable, so that the owner will be encouraged to use the proper practices and to spend his money for protecting them."

The cattlemen, through their legislative program, Mockler said, sought three things:

"We want the right to go to court if we feel we have been unjustly treated—and that's nothing to be ashamed of. Every American should be entitled to that privilege, and is in almost every other field. We want a law to define our rights in respect to the federal grazing lands, and that's nothing to be ashamed of. And we want a certain degree of uniformity in regard to those federal lands. We speak of the Taylor lands and of the Forest lands and of the land-use lands which are under the Soil Conservation Service . . . We do have a basic law with the Taylor Grazing act, and from that act a code has been worked out, but in the Forest Service we have practically nothing except for the Granger-Thye act, which was passed two years ago, and which created the advisory boards, but which does not even mention grazing as a use of the forest."

•

The uniform federal grazing lands act which Mockler talked about at the Jackson meeting was, as related in Chapter 24, replaced later in the year by the Aiken-Thye-Hope bill, S. 2548. Lloyd Taggart of Cody, retiring president of the Association, in his address at the Jackson convention pointed out a favorable sign for the attainment of a better understanding between the cattlemen and the federal government, in the fact that two western men were now members of the President's Cabinet. These were Douglas McKay of Oregon, "a friend and neighbor," as Secretary of the Interior, and Ezra Taft Benson of Utah, "a courageous and honest man . . . who agrees with us on the matter of price and production controls," as Secretary of Agriculture.

"If he," said Taggart, speaking of Secretary Benson, "is successful in removing the controls we have so long opposed and in discontinuing the subsidies that have been but a premium on laziness and indifference to the principles of independence and success, he will have earned the everlasting gratitude of us all, not excepting those from whom the subsidies and the undeserved help have been taken." Taggart continued:

"If there is some way that we can, we should do something to help him get rid of the support prices on corn, cotton, and many other products, which have been set by law, and which are now operating unfairly and to the detriment of our great live stock industry. Consider for a moment this situation: Ordinarily the growers of corn throughout the Middle West would buy our cattle and feed them out in their own feed lots, in that manner providing a market for their corn and later moving their fat cattle to market at a reasonable profit. But at the first sign of declining beef prices they deserted to the protecting umbrella of controlled and government-guaranteed prices for corn, plowing up thousands of acres of pasture land, and in some cases even their feed lots, and converting it all to additional acres of corn. This in turn will be sold to the government whose warehouses are already bulging with millions of bushels of last year's crop, much of it deteriorating to the point of worthlessness. We look in vain for justification for such an unsound and unreasonable situation, and hope for an early correction.

"I think we can and should to a considerable extent make ourselves more independent of the feeders from other states. We can feed out a large number of our own live stock. Last year I fed out two or three hundred head of cattle and from my own experience I am satisfied that, with the proper kind of agriculture, growing the proper crops such as silage and some of the cheaper feeds, we can put a gain onto our live stock equal to what the feeders in Iowa and Nebraska put on with corn . . . Every one of our larger ranches should be somewhat of a laboratory, where new grasses and feeds are intelligently tried out. If we experiment and then freely exchange with one another the information we gain, we may surprise ourselves in the extent to which we can make ourselves more independent."

Always, in the cowman's heart, that goal of independence!

Where the Association stood on this and other matters was fully stated in forthright language in the resolutions adopted by the 1953 convention; although, later in the year, cow country was to a certain extent divided over some of the issues dealt with in the resolutions, the Association as a unit stayed with them. They read as follows:

NO. 1

Whereas, demand for beef has been holding up surprisingly well in view of continued heavy cattle marketings, and

Whereas, this is due in great measure to the effective work in furthering beef sales by cattlemen's associations, meat promotional agencies like the National Live Stock and Meat Board and American Meat Institute, processors, retailers, marketing agencies, and the United States Department of Agriculture;

Therefore Be It Resolved, that we commend these agencies and urge that they do continue in their important work.

NO. 2

Whereas, we recognize the possible need this summer and fall of additional credit facilities to finance livestock producers and feeders in the present emergency,

Therefore Be It Resolved, that we urge the Federal Reserve Board and the Farm Credit Administration to prepare in advance to meet, through existing credit facilities, any such emergency as may arise.

NO. 3

Whereas, certain governmental agencies in Washington are proposing that river valley authorities be established on all the principal river valleys of the nation, thus placing the management and control of all the lands and water in those valleys under the jurisdiction of federal authorities appointed from Washington and establishing arbitrary rules as to acreage that can be owned and destroying the freedom of opportunity which exists today for the residents of those valleys to conduct and manage their own enterprises;

Therefore Be It Resolved, that we express our intense opposition to the creation of such river valley authorities as being contrary to the basic principles of our government.

NO. 4

Whereas, we have been greatly impressed with the sturdy

stand taken by Secretary of Agriculture Ezra T. Benson in his effort to put the agricultural economy of this country on a sound basis,

Therefore Be It Resolved, that we commend him for it and pledge our support to his efforts in this direction.

NO. 5

Whereas, the promotion of world trade should be on the basis of fair and equitable competition and must be done within the principle, long maintained, that foreign products produced by cheap foreign labor shall not be admitted to our country on terms which endanger the living standards of the American working man or the American farmer or stockman, or threaten serious financial injury to a domestic industry,

Therefore, if the Reciprocal Trade Act is renewed, we ask that it include strengthened "peril point" and "escape clause" provisions.

NO. 6

Whereas, the United States has been under the necessity for years past of making large appropriations for defense and for foreign aid of various kinds, and

Whereas, a continuation of that policy makes it absolutely necessary that the most rigid economy be enforced with regard to all appropriations for any purpose whatsoever;

Therefore Be It Resolved, that we commend the administration for its substantial efforts in this direction and urge the appropriations committees of the Congress to scrutinize closely the appropriations for the various federal agencies, with the purpose of ending the many needless projects, the many duplications of service and the hiring of needless personnel which has been going on for many years, and

Be It Further Resolved, that we especially recommend the complete abolishment, as rapidly as possible, of payments now being made to farmers and ranchers by the Production and Marketing Administration.

In no other way can the taxpayer stand the burden that still remains to be carried for years to come.

NO. 7

Whereas, the necessity to "Buy American" is important to the industry,

Therefore Be It Resolved, that we urge the continuation

of the "Buy American" policy which has been carried in the appropriations for the military service for several years. The government is one of the biggest consumers of domestic food products and it is only fair that, except in emergencies provided for, purchases should be on the "Buy American" plan.

NO. 8

Whereas, it is entirely clear that the production of beef during the next few years will be very heavy in relation to the production in recent years, and

Whereas, the funds now available to the National Livestock and Meat Board are entirely inadequate to meet this emergency;

Therefore Be It Resolved, that we urge immediate consideration of plans to double the present basis of contributions to the National Livestock and Meat Board for the promotion of beef and beef products.

NO. 9

Whereas, various government bureaus are still acquiring large tracts of land,

Therefore Be It Resolved, this policy of government acquisition of private land, with the resultant loss of taxes to the local communities, has long been opposed by the Wyoming Stock Growers Association; said Association again affirms its opposition to such a policy, and recommends to the National Congress that such action as necessary be taken to discontinue further land acquisitions.

NO. 10

Whereas, the Wyoming Stock Growers Association recognizes live cattle prices are in a depressed and unbalanced condition partially caused by the price support program now in force on farm products used in feeding livestock, and

Whereas, the well-being of all the Nation and the very existence of our institutions depends upon an early return to a free economy, and

Whereas, the abandonment of supports and controls must apply not only to agriculture but to every other line of endeavor, and

Whereas, it is the considered opinion of this Association that the ultimate price of supports and controls is higher than Americans are willing to pay, and

Whereas, this Association believes it is now impossible for

our animal feed and livestock economy to prosper when part of that economy is subsidized with a high mandatory fixed price support program and a part of that economy is not so supported,

Now Therefore, it is hereby resolved that the Wyoming Stock Growers Association requests the Congress of the United States to remove forthwith all price supports on agricultural products which are basic in the production of meat, or if such price supports be not removed as requested, the Congress is urged to establish a realistic system of flexible price supports on meat-producing feeds commensurate with the price of livestock to encourage a normal livestock feeding program.

NO. 11

Whereas, the increasing number of successful oil and gas discoveries with their promise of long-time production, and the varied types of strip-mining for coal, uranium, and other minerals is not only destroying the surface of the land, but also is depriving the owners of same the use thereof for an unforeseeable period of time, and is making obsolete the present system of damage recompense,

And Whereas, Congress has indicated by the tidelands legislation a fairer regard for the just claims of the Western states and their individual citizens,

Now Therefore Be It Resolved that our Senators and Congressmen be most strongly urged to prosecute their proposed legislation for a landowners three percent royalty from all mineral operations on stockgrazing homestead lands.

NO. 12

Whereas, the stockmen have attempted for three years to give wide publicity to the proposed Federal Grazing Land Tenancy Bill which they believe to be in the interest not only of the livestock industry, which is the basic industry of this region, but other federal land users as well as the public because it will mean promotion, conservation, and stability in the use of the land, and

Whereas, some newspapers in our state and general area, notably the Denver Post, the Salt Lake Tribune, the Wyoming Eagle, and the Laramie Republican, have adopted an editorial policy derogatory to the proposed grazing bill,

And Whereas these opinions seem to us to be based on misinformation as to the purposes of the bill,

215.

Therefore Be It Resolved that in order that the public may have full information and facts concerning the bill, we invite reporters from these newspapers to interview our officers or any stockman so that they may be apprised of the stockman's purpose in asking for the legislation.

NO. 13

Whereas, certain fundamental basic rights were granted the American people by the Constitution of the United States, insuring to the people among other things the right of appeal to the courts, and

Whereas, the livestock industry of the West being dependent on Federal lands for its existence, yet having neither basic law governing its governmental land contracts nor the right of appeal from any arbitrary bureaucratic rulings, and

Whereas, House No. 4023* and Senate No. 1491 do forthwith grant these basic rights to the livestock growers of the West,

Be It Resolved, that the Wyoming Stock Growers Association, believing in the basic principles, urges the passage of this legislation and that its members individually and as a group support to the utmost those representatives of the people who agree with the basic concepts of this legislation and who are working for its passage, and that a copy of this resolution be forwarded to our Congressional delegation in Washington.

•

Over the 1953 convention at Jackson hung the shadow of a startling downward trend in cattle prices. The question "Where is it going to stop?" was in every cowman's mind. Nobody knew for sure.

*Replaced later in the year by H. 6787 and S. 2548.

CHAPTER TWENTY NINE

'NO TIME FOR FEAR'

Stock raising is the bone and sinew of Wyoming's industrial life. Oil fields may come and go; military establishments will vanish when wars cease; the exploration for and extraction of minerals from the bowels of the earth furnish fleeting and transitory sources of income; even the transportation industry undergoes radical changes. But ever since we drove the Indian and the buffalo from the range and firmly and effectively planted in their place the cowman and the sheepman and their herds, Wyoming has been primarily and essentially a stock-raising state. And it will be ever so, as long as a munificent sun continues to shine and the rains fall.

—Editorial, Lusk Herald, quoted in *Cow Country* Sept. 20, 1943.

Drought and depressed prices were the main worries in Wyoming cow country in 1953. The condition was not local. It affected most western range states.

In numbers of cattle, the industry—so government statisticians said—was in its sixth cycle since 1880. It was an upward swing, but it was believed to be nearing its end. Secretary of Agriculture Benson said in December that the expansion of cattle numbers was either completely halted or nearly so.

Secretary Benson also said that "few events in the history of the live stock industry have precipitated as sharp a price change as has the 1953 leveling out in cattle numbers. In a few short months, cattlemen have born the brunt of an adjustment in the cattle cycle that normally takes several years to complete."

By October 1953, cattle were bringing less than half the prices they brought two years previously.

217

The background to the situation was outlined by Secretary Benson, who said:

"Since 1949, we have been witness to the inflationary spending programs of the past administration, from which we have inherited much of our trouble today. These inflationary programs—plus the price controls which came later—complicated the marketing processes and created multiple problems. It is apparent now that they created more problems than they solved.

"One of these problems was the oversupply of cattle from which the live stock industry is reacting today. Increased marketings from this oversupply caused the market to break sharply. But on top of this a severe drought brought on untimely marketing of the cattle in dry areas. The total effect on the market was devastating. And it wasn't only the speculator and the johnny-come-lately who had to take the rap, but the legitimate long-time producer and the young men embarking on their careers as well.

"In short, the drought last summer aggravated an already bad marketing situation which confronted us when we took office in January. We moved quickly to wipe out some of the bad legacies such as price controls and compulsory grading, but the damage had already been done."

An advisory committee of leaders of the industry was established. This committee opposed any price and wage control legislation and supported the move to eliminate price controls and compulsory grading. It urged an informational program to promote consumer use of beef, particularly the lower grade of cows, in order to divert them from normal marketing channels. By December 1, 1953, the government had purchased more than 241 million pounds of beef products in the western states and nearly 845 thousand head of lower grade cattle had been diverted from the market. Further relief in the form of reduced feed prices to help legitimate cattle producers keep their foundation herds was also put in operation, and by December 1 more than 777 thousand tons of feed had been made available in 681 counties throughout the drought area. Railroads provided reduced rates for shipment of feed into drought areas and the shipment of cattle out. Additional credit facilities were made available; by December 1, loans totaling 19 million dollars had been made to 1,887 live stock producers to help them meet normal operating expenses, so as to avoid the liquidation of foundation herds and enable producers to stay in business.

Sam Hyatt, past president of the Wyoming Stock Growers Association and president of the American National Cattlemen's Association 1952-1954, was chairman of the Cattle and Beef Industry Committee, a widely representative group of producers, feeders, packers and retailers which helped formulate drought relief plans and worked on other industry problems. Reporting in the *American Cattle Producer* in August 1953, Hyatt said:

"The cattle situation has been bad for some time. Ranchers in the drought areas have asked for help but no overall government relief has been requested by cattlemen generally and I do not think one is contemplated. Everything that has been done to date has been in the nature of self-help. Aid for the drought area is not a general relief program for those who have lost money in their business but rather like relief granted to those visited by a disaster. It is similar to a situation where an area is wiped out by a tornado or a city is destroyed by an earthquake. Government has helped in such situations for many years . . .

"We must try to the best of our ability not to let the pendulum of supply and demand swing too far to the left and then to the right. Someone always gets hurt at the extreme end of the swing. It has now swung in the direction of overproduction. The next swing will be toward scarcity. It is to the interest of all of us that the supply be as normal as possible.

"If we believe in the principles that this country was founded upon, then this is no time for fear for the future of the live stock industry."

•

In Wyoming, the 1953 drought was worst in the southwest

part of the state. Here many ranchers, who were still feeling the financial effects of the disaster caused by the blizzards of 1949, were now threatened by the other extreme, lack of moisture. Range users in Sweetwater, Uinta and Lincoln counties reported rainfall there for the first eight months of 1953 had been 52.7 of normal, following a 25 per cent below normal summer and winter moisture in 1952. Range conditions in general averaged 20 to 30 per cent of normal. There were in this area 320,000 sheep and eight to ten thousand cattle to feed.

On September 8 and 15, 1953, the Wyoming State Agricultural Mobilization Committee, of which R. L. Henderson of Casper was chairman, after hearing requests by ranchers from Sweetwater, Uinta and Lincoln counties, recommended to the Secretary of Agriculture that the region be declared a drought disaster area, and on November 25 President Eisenhower telegraphed Governor C. J. Rogers at Cheyenne that this had been done. On November 30, R. L. Farrington, director of the Agricultural Credit Service at Washington, in a telegram to Governor Rogers defined the area as: "East of Rock Springs about forty miles to Table Rock, north to forest boundaries, west to Lyman to include Carter lease, south to Uinta mountains on Utah and Colorado line." The region thus eligible for federal assistance included parts of Sublette, Sweetwater, Fremont, Lincoln and Uinta counties. It took in most of the winter range lying south of the Bridger National Forest.

•

At the end of the year 1953, the Wyoming co-operative crop and live stock reporting service said that range and pasture conditions in the state were the worst since 1940, except for the heavy snow condition following the big storms of 1949. Except for counties along the eastern border, range grass was short, dry and dusty. Supplies of range feed and hay were plentiful in the northeast, but short and inadequate in the drought areas of central and southwestern Wyoming.

The state entomologist at the same time was saying that grasshoppers had caused $183,000 damage to crops in the state during the summer, in spite of the control program that had covered 44,000 acres of crop and range land in eight counties. A larger program would be needed in 1954.

The state board of equalization recognized the prevailing situation by ordering a reduction in 1954 assessed valuation for live stock—the first major reduction since before World War II. The decrease was to average 10 per cent for cattle and between 8 and 10 for sheep.

Were the people of Wyoming's cow country fearful of the future? Not so you could notice it. Said Joe Watt, of the T Triangle ranch, Moorcroft, in the Belle Fourche country of the northeastern part of the state:

"The stock men have never lost faith in their industry, regardless of dry summers, hard winters or depressions. The man who year in and year out makes money on his live stock is the operator who does not over graze his range, but keeps his cattle in good condition at all times.

"The rancher who keeps his feed and live stock in balance, with a generous reserve of feed, and who is more interested in the long term gain rather than squeezing the last cent of profit from his ranch every year, is the operator who is in a solid position today. This is as true as it was fifty years ago and as it will be fifty years hence.

"I firmly believe that the future holds as many opportunities, for the young man who is interested in live stock to build up a ranch of his own, as the pioneer had. He will be able to run more cattle on the same amount of land, due to new and better feeding practices, re-seeding of the range, removal of sagebrush, putting more land under irrigation and breeding a better and heavier class of beef cattle.

"It is in times of recession that a young man has a better opportunity to acquire his start in the ranching business. Never sell Wyoming short; it is still in its infancy so far as cattle production is concerned."

Oda Mason (Association president 1945-47) who raises registered and commercial Herefords at his ranch near Laramie, said in December of '53:

"I have been a cowpuncher and cowman for the past fifty-five years, and the only thing that remains the same over those years is that we still use cows.

"Even they are different critters, due to changes in breeding, feeding and methods of handling.

"When I was a boy working on the open range, stock roamed wherever they found conditions suited to their tastes as to grass, shade and water. Today we confine them in smaller enclosures and some of them are compelled to consume there the feed and water that they naturally would prefer to seek over distant hills in some other direction.

"Stock do better when they are not aware of someone watching them. Unnecessary handling does not make for good-doing cattle. When confined and brought together for feeding, the cattle are exposed to contagious and infectious diseases, so that to be successful in the business today one needs to be a good veterinarian. With the help of penicillin and the various 'wonder drugs' he can get along.

"I am satisfied that cattle in past years were more rugged, and therefore were stronger mentally, than is the case today; they had to be, in order to survive. Today they have learned to lean on man, and most cow help today do not stand much leaning on.

"Land, labor and all overhead have got so high that we are going to have to improve our breeding constantly, and carry on a stringent culling program even in high quality herds to eradicate the non-producing cattle. We must hold only the ones that maintain the highest degree of health, and the ability to reproduce their kind, and above all we must hold onto the ones that respond to feed to the point where they pay for the feed they eat. This is a big order but it will have to be done if one intends to stay in the business and prosper."

•

Time for fear? No, a time for continuance of the frontier fortitude that has made Wyoming great. A time for facing the future with the same sort of courage the earliest ranchers brought with them when they first rode into the short-grass country.

222

It is fitting to close this chapter with a statement by the current president of the Association, Clifford P. Hansen of Jackson, who was elected at the eighty-first meeting of the Association in June 1953. Mr. Hansen writes:

A history of the Wyoming Stock Growers Association is a record of man's successful attempts to overcome the natural obstacles of drought, pests, severe winters, predators, lawlessness, and ever changing economic conditions.

From a wide open expanse of free grazing in territorial days when few others were even interested in the range, Wyoming, responding to man's expanding numbers, today is grown to the full maturity of statehood with widely diversified economic interests evident everywhere.

When John B. Kendrick first trailed cattle from Texas to Wyoming for Otto Wulfjen, Wyoming's agricultural potential was barely a vision in the mind of any cowman. Still to come were irrigation ditches, storage dams and a test of the fertility of unbroken soils.

Undreamed of, too, were the mineral resources of this frontier land. Areas that apparently were good for nothing but grazing were later found to be underlain with oil. Today the splitting of the atom has opened an entirely new era of exploration for minerals only recently significant.

As our standard of living has raised, man has found himself with a greater amount of leisure time on his hands. Recreation assumes more and more prominence in the scheduling of his life. Quite naturally the out-of-doors becomes increasingly popular in man's pattern of relaxation. The stockman today finds that he is not alone in his interest in grazing lands, as hunting and fishing increase in popularity.

But not all of the stockman's problems have been domestic. We are constantly reminded, through actions of the federal government, that our place among nations is of great concern to the average citizen. Wars give bitter reality to the necessity of neighborly cooperation between nations as well as people. Here again our business must fit into the scheme of things for us as a nation.

Lessons and facts are discerned slowly on the horizon of time in this industry. However, drawing from our experience, certain conclusions seem self evident. Monopoly does not lend itself to the cow business. The average ranch is a family unit. Most members must work. When times are tough the family operation will pull through while the larger outfits, saddled with fixed labor costs and the inefficiency and carelessness of hired help, go broke. Concern, born of ownership and personal interest, cannot be duplicated on the labor market regardless of the stipend.

While the economics of the business discourage large outfits, by the same token cooperation between operators is a must. One of the early lessons of the range is that Biblical admonition, "love thy neighbor as thyself." Only by caring for a neighbor's stock whenever the opportunity presents itself can the livestock man hope to have his cared for. The reputation of being one who will go out of his way to do a good turn for a fellow rancher pays off.

The stock business, being one of the oldest in the state, might well be expected to have contributed its share of state leaders. It has done more than that.

Not only has an impressive number of governors, congressmen, and senators come from the ranks of the Association but it is generally conceded that the influence of representatives of the industry has been greater than their numbers.

Most things have changed in the four score years of Association activity. Some have not. Today, as eighty years ago, grass grows strong and lush on Wyoming's ranges. In all the centuries of progress and discovery, no other use has been found for grass but to grow and fatten livestock. It seems inevitable that this use will continue for centuries to come. No greater contribution can be made to man by Nature's generous gift of grass than to produce meat and fiber.

The cowman, fundamentally and necessarily self reliant, appreciates the need for cooperation. When adversity strikes, he either helps or is helped. Using public land in connection with private land, he knows that he is answerable for the care he gives this great resource. But he senses clearly his obligation to be a productive operator at the same time. His existence is justified, he believes, in his ability to satisfy basic human wants. He recognizes, always, that his interest must be dovetailed in with the public interest. Thus has been developed his civic consciousness.

'No Time for Fear'

Dealing directly with nature, the average cowman is a free enterpriser in his thinking. Panics, droughts, blizzards and depressions have taken their toll of livestock operators. Small and large ones alike have felt the pinch of hard times and known the bitter disappointment of losing their outfits. On this, however, they are agreed: Ranching in the rigorous climate of the West wouldn't be worth the effort if any less than the whole outfit were at stake. The mediocrity of accomplishment circumscribed by a supported, controlled economy fails to appeal to the average Wyoming cowman. The distance-imposed denial of telephones, electricity, regular mail, and many other commonly construed necessities most effectively insures that only strong characters stay in the business. Clear thinkers in this occupation, as in all others, perceive the fallacy of government dole in any form. History's oft-repeated lesson that control inevitably follows support has real meaning. Socialism never provided incentive for pioneering. It never fired man's ambition to put forth special effort or undergo hardship. It cannot today. Most cowmen recognize artificial price supports for just what they are. Their opposition, while obviously in the public interest, is motivated primarily by personal well being. Free markets make free men.

Wyoming cattlemen are steeped in the proven workable philosophy of free enterprise. They are living exponents of the conservationist's creed. Their concern for protection of the great gifts of Nature is as real as is their concern for their children. The undiminished productivity of the soil is their children's lifeblood.

With a neighborly concern for the other fellow's welfare, eager to contribute his share to society, willing to integrate his interests with others in the use of the public resources, shouldering his responsibilities in democracy with credit and distinction, the stockman of Wyoming has merited the esteem he is accorded generally.

In championing free enterprise, in rejecting aids which would lead to regimentation and socialism, in his insistence that personal freedom will best be preserved by living in the warm climate of a free economy, the cowman will make his most notable contribution to the prosperity and security of America. He has great faith in the future.

CHAPTER THIRTY

THAT WAS COW COUNTRY

Give me the plains
Where it seldom rains
And the wind forever blows;
It is there I would be
Though there's never a tree
And the farther you look
The less you see,
For there's where the beefsteak grows!

—Plains Song, in 'Cow Country,'
by Edward Everett Dale,
University of Oklahoma Press 1942.

Epitaph for a Cowboy: If there ever was such a thing as a "typical" Wyoming cowpuncher, perhaps it was Missou Hines, who died in 1943, at the age of 82. In reporting his death, *Cow Country* said: "He was a natural. He advanced through the range school, from wrangler and bronco buster to one of the best known wagon bosses on the Wyoming ranges." The late Judge Joseph M. Carey gave Missou his first job, on Carey's CY ranch. Missou was then 16, newly arrived from his native Missouri. The first time he got on a horse on the Carey ranch, Missou faced the rear. The foreman, watching him, said he never had but he supposed he could bridle that end of the horse. Missou explained it away by saying that back in Missouri he had never ridden anything but mules, and they always wanted to go the wrong way so he had got used to riding backward. He soon learned which way to face—and everything else there was to know about horses. He was, like most oldtime cowboys, a great practical joker. Put in charge of a big bunch of sheep, he sent to the ranch manager a request for three thousand pairs of green goggles—because the grass was dry and brown, but he thought the goggles might fool the sheep into eating it. On another occasion, turning in his time sheet, he showed that he had worked thirty days during February. Unperturbed, when asked about it, Missou said he didn't care what the calendar said, he had worked that many days that month. Missou is said by oldtimers to have been the cowboy who mixed up the babies at the ranchhouse dance, as related in Wister's *The Virginian*.

1885 Reform Wave: From By-Laws and Reports of the Wyoming Stock Growers Association and the Laws of Wyoming for the Protection of Stock Growers, as amended by the Eighth Assembly, 1885 (Page 32) : "Important Resolutions —XVII. Whereas, Much valuable time is lost and difficulties which terminate in the loss of valuable life are caused by the use of cards for gambling; and Whereas, The racing of horses while on general roundup is greatly to the detriment of the general good of this Association by injuring the stock and the morals of the camps: Resolved, That the members of the Association instruct their foremen to prohibit such practices in their camps and that the district foremen be instructed to prevent them, so far as they may be able."

Said the stranger to the rancher: "How do you manage to make enough on this place to run it?"

Said the rancher to the stranger: "See that feller over there (pointing to his hired man) ? Well, he works for me and I can't pay him. In two more years, he gits the ranch. Then I'm goin' to work for him until I git it back."—*Cow Country*, December 1943.

Reps: In range language, a rep was a cowboy sent out from his own ranch to represent his owner's interests in a general roundup, or in working cattle on distant ranges. W. P. Ricketts, a member of the Wyoming Stock Growers Association for more than sixty years, in *Cow Country* for October 12, 1942, wrote: "In the days of no fences, cattle drifted a hundred miles or more from their home range. I would start reps out the middle of April and they'd be gone until Thanksgiving. I had one man who married a week before he started, and when he returned his wife had a divorce action pending, on a charge of desertion. One came home in time for Christmas dinner and found a new-born baby boy. At that time, Hereford cattle were just coming into favor. A neighbor asked this man about his new baby, and he said, 'He's fine, first class,—but not a whiteface or anything like that.' " Ricketts died in 1944, "almost the last survivor of the colorful oldtimers who helped lay the foundations of Wyoming," as *Cow Country* said. Born in Lexington, Ky., in 1859, he reached Cheyenne in 1876, and first worked for the Searights near Chugwater. Later he entered business for himself, near Gillette, and at one time he ran 20,000 cattle. He retired in 1930 to Sheridan, met financial reverses and physical misfortune. Blind, bedfast and alone after his wife's death, and no longer wealthy, but still cheerful, Ricketts wrote his memoirs, *Fifty Years in the Saddle*. In a letter to *Cow Country*, issue of December 6, 1943, Ricketts wrote that he had "no eyes and only one leg, but very fortunately good general health."

Style in Deadwood: Item from the Carbon County (Wyoming) *Journal*, December 2, 1882, reprinted in *Cow Country* September 1, 1943—"One of the Deadwood girls is having a dress made and embroidered with the cattle brands of the various cattlemen she counts among her admirers. It is evident that she is in cahoots with the coroner and surgeons and is taking this way to promote domestic discords. The Black Hills *Pioneer* says the above is correct and adds: 'The dress is not only receiving the brands of many of our thoughtless young stock men but their initials as well . . . The brands and initials of her particular favorites cover the side of her neck and bosom, and the brands of those occupying but an indifferent corner in her affections are attached to the bottom of her skirt. Some are located so as to be frequently sat down upon'."

"In excerpts from the Buffalo *Bulletin* of December 24, 1896, I note the name 'George M————.' This old fellow made me my first pair of buckskin gloves, when I was about six years old. He once killed a boy, buried him under his bed and slept on him all winter." J. Elmer Brock in *Cow Country,* May 15, 1947.

Historical Mavericks: "Ten herds of cattle, approximating 28,000 head, have passed near Lusk on their way to the northern ranges, in the past ten days. Among the better known brands represented were the N Bar N, XIT, Long X and Horseshoe Bar. There were five separate XIT herds." —From the Lusk (Wyo.) *Herald,* June 30, 1893.

"There is quite a roar being made since the barbers raised their prices. Several men have gone to work and ground up their old razors, butcher knives and jack knives and are doing their own hair cutting. Personally, the *Herald* editor feels that ten cents is enough for a shave. If a barber can't make a living on ten-cent shaves he ought to starve; fifteen cents is too much."—Lusk *Herald* June 30, 1893.

"Johnny Williams, a well-known cowboy who had busted many a bad bronc and roped many a steer in this region, has finally passed in his checks as a result of being too free with his six-shooter. He went into Signor's saloon on the Sweetwater a week ago Wednesday, picked a quarrel with the bartender, and then emptied his six-shooter at the man behind the bar without hitting him. The bartender walked to the adjoining room, took down his 30-30 rifle, drew a bead on Williams. The ball passed through his forehead, killing him instantly. The bartender was not arrested, but a plan is on foot to award him a medal."—Lusk *Herald,* October 28, 1887.

In Cow Language: When Brand Inspector Murphy of Sioux City married, he sent his friends this invitation to the wedding: "Come and see our Gary-Cooper cowboy brand-inspector Murphy do his part in slapping that famous three-letter brand MRS on this white-face, black-haired slick yearling critter. Have your own roll with you Wednesday night so you can camp at close quarters as this ringing brand work will take place in the corrals at St. Boniface's church at 6 a.m. Thursday, May 15."—From *Cow Country*, June 28, 1941.

He Liked It Better Here: From *Cow Country*, March 8, 1943—"In Memoriam: Sir Oliver Wallop, Earl of Portsmouth, 82, who died at Colorado Springs February 9, 1943. Oliver Henry Wallop, who came to America in 1883 from England, became the Earl of Portsmouth on the death of his brother. He had become a naturalized citizen at Sheridan, Wyo., however, and refused to relinquish his citizenship to take over the ninth ranking seat in the British House of Lords. He established his ranch near Sheridan in the early '80s and operated it continuously until his death. He was a member of the Wyoming Stock Growers Association for many years."

How To Spot a Cowboy: Russell Thorp says Charles M. Russell, the cowboy artist, once told this on himself: While he was still young, Russell made a trip back east by train. He was anxious not to be taken for a cowboy, so he outfitted himself with a bald-faced shirt and a hard hat. He was amazed, the morning after his first night on the sleeper rolling eastward, to have a neighbor across the aisle casually ask, "Where do you punch cows?" Russell told him, and added, "How did you know I was a cowpuncher?" The man answered: "Why, because the first thing you did when you rolled out of bed this morning was to put on your hat."

Who Wasn't Happy Then?: Walter Palmer of Pasadena, California, in *Cow Country*, October 9, 1943: "I spent not only my best but the happiest days of my career in Wyoming, but who wasn't happy in Wyoming 55 years ago? I can even backtrack to 1884, in November, when we were on the No Wood roundup, and we heard our cow boss say, 'It's election day and 40 miles to the Em Bar ranch to vote.' It was many weeks later before we learned the results of our trip to the

Em Bar ranch that day from No Wood creek. Roe Avant, then wagon boss for George W. Baxter of Cheyenne and the LV brand, was the only one of twelve cow hands who knew who was up for president. It was Cleveland, and we learned months later that he had been elected. I remember the judge of the election held a cocked six-shooter in his hand and told me how to vote . . . I knew Nate Champion, and Nick Ray, and Harry Leroy, in those days—and Tom Horn. Tell me some time whatever became of Harry Leroy; I know what became of the others. Tom Horn had no bed with him, and I split with him on the November roundup on No Wood."

'How Does the Old Ranch Look?' Ashley Gleason was foreman of the oldtime PO Arbuckle horse ranch (later he worked for the Fiddleback outfit) and when he was 70 he wrote to the PO Arbuckle owner, Fred Boice, a letter that read in part as follows: "Fred, tell me how the old ranch looks! Are the big corrals intact that I helped work thousands of horses in? Are the bunkhouse, stud barns and sheds there yet? . . I remember when I was running the Butterfly wagon we corralled hundreds of horses in your pens. Took us three and a half hours to corral them and they were strung out from the head of the breaks on Horse creek along your east line fence. Tore down many of the cross fences coming in; 37 riders did the job, and we had reps from the PO, CY, 7XL, Two Bar, Necktie, McCarthys, VT, Rithenberg and other big outfits. Each rider had ten head of saddle horses, and so our cavvy was too big for one rider to trail. Fellow named Dray, a PO man, was the nighthawk and he never lost a horse. I forget the day jingler's name. Old Scoon was the cook and the best dutch oven wrestler I ever saw. His bread was so light you had to put a weight on it to keep it from ballooning away, and his poison pup was a dessert the punchers laid to. Many a bellyache resulted from fast riding too soon after eating."

Friend of the Cowboy: Moreton Frewen, "of Leicestershire, England, and Wyoming territory," as a New York paper referred to him in 1881, was one of many Englishmen who built up big ranching interests on the Plains in the days of the cattle boom. Moreton Frewen founded the Powder River Cattle Company, with the 76 brand. Here is a sidelight of the man, from a letter in *Cow Country*, in recent years, from Ed F. Williams of Blythe, California, who was eighty years old when he wrote: "Who among the cowmen of today ever heard of Moreton Frewen? Well, I can remember when a 76 cow would drop a calf a thousand miles from the home range, and that calf would be branded 76 by the first passing cowpuncher simply because Moreton Frewen was known by every puncher from the Hashknife to the XIT as being the best friend an old illiterate cowpuncher ever had."

Bob Fudge: Here is a thumbnail sketch of the man whose experiences trailing cattle and horses through Wyoming are related in Chapters Four and Six; this is from *The XIT Ranch of Texas* by J. Evetts Haley, who quotes Tex Willis: "Bob Fudge was the most typical cowboy the Xs (XIT) ever had. He weighed 235 pounds, was a fine roper, and could ride a small pony farther and easier than any other man I ever saw."

A Few Figures: As of January 1, 1954, there were in Wyoming 1,178,000 cattle and calves with a total value of $108,376,000.00, according to Lester J. Hofmann, agricultural statistician in charge, USDA Agricultural Marketing Service, Cheyenne. The number of cattle and calves was exactly the same as on January 1, 1953, but their value had dropped $30,628,000.00. Mr. Hofmann's figures for the last three years:

Number and Value of Cattle and Calves
in Wyoming January 1:

Year	Number	Value per Head (Dollars)	Total Value (Dollars)
1952	1,144,000	193.00	220,792,000.00
1953	1,178,000	118.00	139,004,000.00
1954	1,178,000	92.00	108,376,000.00

Wyoming, incidentally, stood 31st among the states, as of January 1, 1954, in numbers of cattle and calves. The ten leading cattle-producing states, by Mr. Hofmann's figures, were: Texas, 8,587,000; Iowa, 5,746,000; Nebraska, 4,752,-000; Kansas, 4,298,000; Wisconsin, 4,275,000; Missouri, 3,950,000; Illinois, 3,946,000; Minnesota, 3,900,000; California, 3,349,000; and Oklahoma, 3,315,000.

During 1953, Wyoming inspectors checked brands on 353,503 animals, of which 288,662 were Wyoming critters, *Cow Country* reported in its February 15, 1954, issue. The largest number of total animals inspected at any one shipping center was 111,661 at Denver. Omaha led in numbers of Wyoming cattle inspected, with 89,582 as compared with 75,965 at Denver.

Mister President: The 1953 president of the Wyoming Stock Growers Association, Clifford Hansen, of Jackson, is a graduate of the University of Wyoming with a BS degree, and is on the board of trustees of the University. He served as a compact commissioner for Wyoming on the Snake River at the time a compact was negotiated between Idaho and Wyoming. He is a member of the Columbia River Compact Commission for Wyoming. The 2,000-acre Hansen ranch is just west of the city of Jackson and just south of Yellowstone National Park. Associated with him are his mother and a younger brother, Robert. The Clifford Hansens have a teen-age son and daughter.

He Rode for the Two Bar: Asked for a bit of personal data about himself, the 1953 chairman of the executive committee of the Wyoming Stock Growers Association, Hugh Stemler of Elkhorn ranch, Douglas, Wyoming, submitted this: "Born at Lagrange, Wyo., son of Ed and Esther Stemler, pioneers of Goshen county. Attended school at Lagrange, Weiser, Idaho, and business college at Cheyenne. Rode roundup with Shotgun and Two Bar wagons in Goshen Hole for many years. Rode with C. B. Irwin shows two years. Won steer roping at Cheyenne in 1913, fourth in

1916. Managed Hills Land and Cattle Company in Colorado from 1922 to 1933. Was executive member of North Park Stock Growers Association. Operated own ranch in Goshen county and in present location three years. Married in 1915 to an Omaha girl who is now a Cow-Belle."

How To Be a Ranch Hand: On Sept. 20, 1943, *Cow Country* printed a letter to a "Mr. John Doe, Richlandtown, Pa.," answering Mr. Doe's inquiry as to his chances of getting a job on a ranch if he came to Wyoming. The letter to Doe said in part:

". . . Nowadays a capable ranch hand is pretty much of a jack-of-all-trades. He is kept busy at odd times building and repairing fences, corrals, sheds and implements. Usually little farming is undertaken except under irrigation. Most years on most ranches there is an extended season when haying is the main work. To be valuable, one should be able to get along with horses. If, during a summer on a ranch, a man shows that he may become valuable with further experience, he may be offered a winter job. This is the time when he might come most in contact with live stock. Ordinarily, and particularly during the present critical meat shortage, a good ranch hand is the servant of the cattle. . . . The first requisite in this or any other business is a deep and abiding interest in the job. You will need patience. You will need tact. To be an invaluable ranch hand one need not be of more than average strength and stamina. What you are from the ears up is more important. If, instead of ranching, your interest is in cowboys, I suggest you come no farther than some western pool hall. There the boot heels are the highest, the hats the widest, the shirts the most striking, and the talk most garrulous in all the West. Stay with the pool hall cowboys and you won't get cold or dirty or tired as you might if you work with me but neither will you get much else."

In a note attached to the little classic, *Cow Country* said "Dan Hanson made us promise not to tell who wrote the letter."

The 'Banditti' Book: In 1894, A. S. Mercer of Cheyenne wrote and published a paperbound book which he called *The Banditti of the Plains, or the Cattlemen's Invasion of Wyoming in 1892 (The Crowning Infamy of the Ages)*. The book has been reprinted at various times, in various forms. Its first edition is a rarity, and a collector's item. The Wyoming Stock Growers Association in its files at Laramie has an interesting copy of the original edition. It is re-bound in the covers of a South Omaha telephone directory dated October, 1920. The book was originally given to Dan Adamson by Herman Oswald, an Omaha commission man. Adamson was an old-time CY cowboy, later retired wealthy cattle man of the Nebraska sandhills. When he died, the book was returned to Oswald, who in 1938 gave it to the Association.

They Dug the First Ditches: "The first steps toward the reclamation of this State were not taken by farmers but by stock men. The earlier ditches were not built by men who made the production of crops their principal business, but (by men who) constructed ditches as an incident in the management of range stock in order to provide winter feed. Not only were the first ditches built under these conditions, but also more than half of all the ditches in the State. The managers and owners of herds of cattle recognized the future value and importance of the irrigable lands."—From Page 10, First Biennial Report of the State Engineer to the Governor of Wyoming, 1891-92.

Another Enemy: "Wolves in the past two years have killed fully one third of the calf crop in eastern and northern Wyoming. Bounties in Nebraska, Dakota and Montana have resulted in wolves being driven into Wyoming in large numbers."—From Board of Live Stock Commissioners Report 1892.

Charring Cross to Rawlins: The Sand Creek Land and Cattle Co., Ltd., some of whose "boys" are shown in the picture section following Page 48, was a British outfit whose office address in 1884 was 20 Spring Gardens, Charring Cross, London S.W. Its range address was Rawlins, Wyo., and its foreman for many years was Boney Earnest. Russell Thorp says Earnest, who died at his ranch in Bates Hole about 1933 at the age of ninety, to his last days retained the dress and appearance of the trapper, mountain man and early cowman type.

Beer Mug Ranch: The old photograph reproduced on the dust jacket of this book shows a roundup crew of the Beer Mug ranch in the 1880s. The Beer Mug is three miles from the mouth of Difficulty creek, seventeen miles northwest of Medicine Bow, in Carbon county, on the Medicine Bow-Seminoe road. It is owned by John Ellis. The original owners, Jim Ross and John Massingale (known as Missouri John) came in about 1879. They headquartered in Carbon, and Jim Mills handled the ranch. Jim Ross was sheriff 1884-88. Missouri John sold to McManus and Mills, who sold to Bill Davis, who sold to Richard Brothers, who sold to George Sturgeon—and Ellis bought it in 1946. In open range days, the Beer Mug was a regular stopping place for roundup crews and for outfits trailing cattle to the Rock River shipping point.

This IS Cow Country: Yes, it was—and is—a land of lifting hills, of fragrant sagebrush flats and white peaks shining in the sun—of little rivers and great grasslands— rich in the earthy lore of the range, in historic tradition—a land of fulfillment for the old and promise for the young—a country of everlasting opportunity for all with courage in their hearts to match their love of freedom.

The good old days are gone.

But the new day is here—and it is a good day, too.

APPENDIX

Officers and Brand Inspectors, 1953.

The 1953 officers of the Wyoming Stock Growers Association:

President, Clifford P. Hansen, Jackson; vice president, Norman Barlow, Cora; chairman executive committee, Hugh Stemler, Glendo; secretary-treasurer-chief inspector, Robert D. Hanesworth, Cheyenne; assistant secretary-treasurer, Myrna F. Agee, Cheyenne.

Honorary vice presidents: J. Elmer Brock, Kaycee; Sam C. Hyatt, Hyattville; George A. Cross, Dubois; Oda Mason, Laramie; Clarence H. Gardner, Thermopolis; Manville Kendrick, Sheridan; Lloyd Taggart, Cody.

Honorary life members: Charles Berry, Gillette; Henry Swan, Denver; Dr. A. F. Vass, Laramie; Russell Thorp, Cheyenne; T. D. O'Neil, Big Piney.

Executive committeemen:

Albany county: John Stevenson, Oliver Wallis, Holly Hunt, Laramie; Jack Dinwiddie, Centennial.

Big Horn county: P. Milton Hyatt, Hyattville; Howard Flitner, Greybull.

Campbell county: John Christensen, Gillette; Frank Greenough, Recluse.

Carbon county: Carl Dolling, Elk Mountain; Robert W. Taylor, Saratoga; Leeland U. Grieve, Savery.

Converse county: George H. Cross, Jr., Joe Reynolds and J. A. Horr, all of Douglas.

Crook county: L. H. Robinson, Moorcroft; Maurice Williams and Ed. B. Chatfield, Sundance.

Fremont county: Ted Graham and Sandford Mills, Lander; Frank Mockler, Dubois.

Goshen county: Joe Waggoner, Jay Em; Bryan Patrick, Torrington; Ed. W. Johnson, Lagrange.

Hot Springs county: Lester L. Kellogg, Grass Creek; Durward Jones, Robert McKone, Thermopolis.

Johnson county: J. Elmer Brock, Leon Keith, Kaycee; Alfred L. Smith, Buffalo.

Laramie county: Bert McGee, Fred Boice, Jr., Cheyenne; R. O. Whitaker, Horse Creek.

Lincoln county: Joe E. Linford, Sidney Bagley, Afton; Aaron McGinnis, Kemmerer.

Natrona county: Archie Sanford, Alcova; William Clark, Natrona; George Snodgrass, Fulton C. Jameson, Casper.

Niobrara county: Dan Hanson and George S. Mill, Hat Creek; Andrew McMaster, Van Tassell.

Park county: Mac Taggart, Cody; E. R. May, Jr., Sunshine; James M. Woodhouse, Jr., Pitchfork.

Platte county: W. E. Dover, Wheatland; Hugh Stemler, Glendo; Fred Prewitt, Slater.

Sheridan county: A. G. Yonkee, Parkman; Lawrence S. Fuller, Wyola, Mont.; Charles Kane, Wolf; Alonzo Shreve, Sheridan.

Sublette county: Joe L. Budd, Donald W. Jewett, Robert O'Neil, Big Piney.

Sweetwater county: John Clifton Anderson, McKinnon; Leonard W. Hay, Rock Springs; L. W. Grandy, Farson.

Teton county: William A. Wilson, Carroll James, Jackson; Lloyd Van Deburg, Wilson.

Uinta county: John W. Myers, Evanston; Joe Micheli, Fort Bridger; Frank Wadsworth, Lonetree.

Washakie county: R. W. Spratt, Lost Cabin; Ted Rice, Tensleep; Ray Brown, Worland.

Weston county: Verne F. Barton, Upton; Joe H. Watt, Moorcroft; Ed. C. Dixon, Newcastle.

Brand inspectors (with markets, and year of beginning employment with Association):

Denver, Colorado: Earl W. Carpenter, inspector-in-charge, 1918; C. E. Maddox, 1950.

Omaha, Nebraska: W. W. McVicker, inspector-in-charge, 1924; J. Lee Sackett, 1947; Frank Pitzer, 1943.

Idaho Falls, Idaho: Lee F. Dull, inspector-in-charge, 1941.

Ogden, Utah: Warren Burgess, inspector-in-charge, 1946.

Special investigator: John J. Smith, 1937.

SOURCES

Primary sources for the information that has gone into this book are, of course, the records of the Wyoming Stock Growers Association. These records fill a room on the third floor of the Library of the University of Wyoming, in Laramie, where they are under supervision of the university archivist, Dean F. Krakel. By vote of the Association in annual convention at Gillette in 1942, the records were transferred to the university June 7, 1944.

Miss Lola M. Homsher, director of the Wyoming State Archives and Historical Department, has said: "The Wyoming Stock Growers Association records are probably the most complete and valuable collection of papers covering the range industry to be found anywhere."

Miss Alice Smith, secretary of the Association for 26 years, was instrumental in assembling and preserving these records. Russell Thorp, who succeeded Miss Smith as secretary, recognizing their historical value, suggested having them placed in the hands of the university so that they might be available to students of the cattle industry.

Archivist Krakel has compiled this list of the collection:

Sixty-nine letter file boxes of correspondence received, sixty-three letter press books of correspondence mailed, twenty-six dues and assessment books, fourteen cash books, three estray receipt books, thirteen membership and assessment books, one application for membership book, one volume of reports on cattle killed, banking records, two expense account ledgers, thirteen volumes of official brands, records of inspectors, sets of fall and spring roundup maverick books, reports of estrays and shipments, sixteen volumes containing inspector's reports, reports of members and agreements, the complete files of the proceedings of annual meetings and conventions, forty bound volumes of the Weekly Livestock Reports, thirty-three volumes pertaining to the American National Cattlemen's Association, fifty-six volumes of the American Hereford Herd and record books, two complete files of *Cow Country* (one set is bound), one bound file of the Northwest Livestock Journal, complete set of brand books, a complete photograph collection of officials and dignitaries, a large companion library of authentic and evaluated Western Americana, paintings, a number of excellent museum display items, and five legal size filing drawers containing a tremendous assortment of indexed original and authentic secondary W.S.G.A. materials.

At its annual convention in 1914, at Cheyenne, the Association adopted a resolution calling for an Historical Committee of three members "to gather data for a history of the Association and development of the cattle business in Wyoming." Harry E. Crain was named chairman of the committee, by John B. Kendrick, then president; the other members were N. K. Boswell and B. J. Erwin. On June 5, 1923, this committee published a 55-page paperbound pamphlet containing letters from twelve old members of the Association, recalling some of their early experiences on the Wyoming ranges. This pamphlet is now a collector's item; its title was *Letters From Old Friends and Members of the Wyoming Stock Growers Association.*

In 1932, when the Association observed its sixtieth anniversary, another historical committee published another paperbound brochure, of 74 pages, which was written by Dan W. Greenburg of Casper, for many years editor of the Midwest Review. In charge of this publication was a committee appointed by J. Elmer Brock, then president; the committee consisted of George H. Cross, Eugene B. Willson and John Clay. Title of the brochure—whose cover picture was drawn by Will James—was *Sixty Years: A Brief Review of Wyoming Cattle Days.*

A. L. Brock, Bert McGee and Bryan Patrick were the members of the historical committee that engaged Agnes Wright Spring to pick up the threads of the story ten years later. Her book, *Seventy Years Cow Country,* was published in 1942, when Charles A. Myers was president of the Association. This was a 276-page book, bound in paper except for a hundred cloth-covered copies. The work of a careful historian, *Seventy Years* is a treasured piece of Western Americana and an indispensable source book.

The files of the official *Bulletin* of the Association have also been heavily used in preparation of *Cow Country Cavalcade.* The *Bulletin* began its career in 1930 as a mimeographed sheet, and three years later was renamed *Cow Country.* It has been published since 1950 as a slick-paper monthly magazine.

Annals of Wyoming, historical magazine published biannually by the Wyoming State Historical Department at Cheyenne, has been of much help.   M.F.

INDEX

Murphy, Mat, 17, 19.
Myers, Chas. A., 158, 173, 206.

Natural Resource Bd., 205.
Nebraska: Counties join WSGA, 47-8.

Operation Snowbound, 195-8.
Oregon, cattle from 12, 13.
Osgood, Ernest Staples, 52, 134.
Owen, John, 28.

Palmer, Walter, 230.
Pape, Mrs. Paul C., 169.
Penrose, Chas. B., 133, 143.
Public lands: Assoc. stand on, 173-190.

Quealy, Mrs. P. J., 166.

Reel, Alexander H., 63.
Reps, 170, 227.
Richardson, Warren, ix, 40.
Ricketts, W. P., 13, 227.
Roosevelt, Pres. F. D., 173, 177.
Roundups, early cow hunts, 38; organized, 43; 64; chapter on, 77-84.
Russell, Charles M., 230.
Rustlers, 85, 134, 208.
Rustling, ease of in early days, 38, 85. (See also Johnson County War.)

Saddles, 32, 33, 34.
Sartoris, Lionel, 13.
Senate Bill 2548, p. 183.
Shaw, James C., pres. WSGA, 156.
Sheep, 119, 123.
Shonsey, Mike, 143.
Smith, Capt. John R., 23, 136.
Snodgrass, John, 1874 roundup, 79.
Spaugh, A. A., 80, 122.
Stemler, Hugh, 233.
Stock Bill of 1871, 40; 54, 55.
Stevick, Harry H., 195.
Story, Nelson, 8, 9, 23.
Sturgis, Thomas, sec. WSGA, 26, 45, 46, 51.
Sun, Tom, 14.
Swan, Alexander H., 45, 50.
Swan, Henry and Will F., 13, 50.

TA ranch, 144, 151.
Taggart, Lloyd, pres. WSGA, 205; 210-11.

Talbot, Claud L., insp., 96.
Taylor grazing act and Taylor, Edward T.: 177-182.
Texas fever, 124-126.
Texas Trail, 9.
Thom, W. J., 148.
Thomas, John B., 51, 52.
Thorp, Russell: 92-3; insp., 100; field sec. WSGA, 157; cow country relics to museum, 185; spearheads blizzard relief 1949, p. 192.
Tisdale, John A., killed 138-9.

Underwood, J. C., pres. WSGA, 156.
U. S. Chamber of Commerce, 174.

Van Tassel, R. S., 40.
Virginian, The, 227.

Waggoner, Tom, lynched, 137.
Walcott, Frank, 39, 142.
Wallop, Oliver Henry, 230.
Warren, Fred E., on '49 blizzard, 197-8.
Warren, F. E., ranch, 29; 1887 storm loss, f.n. 60.
Watt, Joe H., 160-1.
Webb, Walter P., 109.
Wellman, George, killed, 146.
Whitaker, Dugald R., pres. WSGA, 162.
Whitten, Mrs. Fred, 168.
Wyoming, name, f.n. 6; early history, 7.
Wyoming Stock Graziers Assoc., 39, 40.
Wyoming Stock & Wool Growers Society, 39.
Wyoming Stock Growers Association: Birth in Cheyenne, 41; early meetings, 42 on; name adopted, 45; purposes stated, 47; early convention color, 52; unchallenged sovereign of Wyo. Terr., 53; power in legislature, 53, 54, 208; at low point, 63-5; in Johnson County War, 140; turning point of 1930, p. 156-7; rescue operations in 1949, p. 192 on; resolutions 1953, p. 212-16.